The EVERYTHING
Pizza Cookbook

Dear Reader,

Several years ago, my husband and I traveled to China to adopt our daughter Sophie. The two-week trip was exciting, the country fascinating and mystical, and our anxieties palpable. One night, exhausted and overwhelmed by it all, we went in search of comfort food. And in Guangzhou, amidst all the noodle emporiums and open markets and banquet restaurants, we found exactly what we needed: a pizza parlor. Better still, a pizza parlor that offered take-out pies.

We sat in our hotel room watching our beautiful sleeping daughter and happily munching on a "supreme" pizza. Never mind that in addition to sausage, pepperoni, mushrooms, and extra cheese the pizza also boasted a handful of corn kernels. It was still pizza and it was just the balm our psyches needed.

That memory, and the feeling of diving into that soul-satisfying pie, came flooding back when I was offered the opportunity to write a pizza cookbook. Pizza, I believe, is part of a universal culinary language. It's a simple, primal dish with infinite variations.

Pizza also is a dish that begs to be shared. Whether you're serving a gaggle of first graders or a coterie of unacquainted adults, pizza platters on the table invariably lead to convivial conversation and good times. It's impossible to stand on ceremony when grabbing wedges from a communal pie.

I personally have never met a pizza I didn't like. But I do think the best pizzas are homemade, either strategically dotted with a few perfect toppings or piled high with a custom blend of meats, cheeses, and veggies. Writing this book gave me a chance to try out all my favorite pizza combinations and add a few dozen more to the repertoire. It also gave Sophie—now school-age and a fledgling cook—a chance to test her palate (and sometimes palette). I hope the recipes here will inspire you to create your own signature pizzas.

Belinda Hulin

The EVERYTHING® Series

Editorial

Publisher	Gary M. Krebs
Managing Editor	Laura M. Daly
Executive Editor, Series Books	Brielle K. Matson
Associate Copy Chief	Sheila Zwiebel
Acquisitions Editor	Kerry Smith
Development Editor	Katie McDonough
Production Editor	Casey Ebert

Production

Director of Manufacturing	Susan Beale
Production Project Manager	Michelle Roy Kelly
Prepress	Erick DaCosta
	Matt LeBlanc
Interior Layout	Heather Barrett
	Brewster Brownville
	Colleen Cunningham
	Jennifer Oliveira
Series Cover Artist	Barry Littmann

Cover photographs ©Foodicon 06 Pizza & Pasta.

Visit the entire Everything® Series at *www.everything.com*

THE

EVERYTHING®

PIZZA
COOKBOOK

300 crowd-pleasing slices of heaven

Belinda Hulin

Adams Media
Avon, Massachusetts

To my husband and tablemate Jim Crissman, with thanks for both the sugar and spice.

An Everything® Series Book.
Everything® and everything.com® are registered trademarks of F+W Publications, Inc.

Published by Adams Media, an F+W Publications Company
57 Littlefield Street, Avon, MA 02322 U.S.A.
www.adamsmedia.com

ISBN 10: 1-59869-259-3

ISBN 13: 978-1-59869-259-4

Printed in the United States of America.

J I H G F E D C B A

Library of Congress Cataloging-in-Publication Data
Hulin, Belinda.
The everything pizza cookbook / Belinda Hulin.
p. cm. – (An everything series book)
ISBN-13: 978-1-59869-259-4 (pbk.)
ISBN-10: 1-59869-259-3 (pbk.)
1. Pizza. I. Title.

TX770.P58H85 2007
641.8'248–dc22
2007002720

This book is available at quantity discounts for bulk purchases.
For information, please call 1-800-289-0963.

Contents

Acknowledgments

Many thanks to the patient, creative minds at Adams Media for their guidance and support. In particular, I'd like to thank project editor Kerry Smith, development editor Katie McDonough, and managing editor Laura M. Daly.

My husband Jim Crissman and children Dylan and Sophie experienced the feast-and-famine of cookbook writing. They ate pizza every night for a month while recipes were being developed, then had to fend for themselves while the book was being written. They didn't complain—even while dining on some of my rejected formulas—and for that I am supremely grateful. I'm also grateful for my mother, Audrey Hulin, and her encyclopedic memory of recipes and cooking techniques. Even as she reclaimed her home from the flooding of Hurricane Katrina, she was able to put her hands on the exact information I needed whenever I called.

Finally, thanks to the friends who sampled and supported my efforts, and who graciously accepted "writing recipes" as an excuse for ducking social gatherings and leisurely conversations.

Introduction

It's an ancient seduction: good bread, aromatic and dense, topped with pure oils and the best fruits of earth and sea. Although modern pizza devotees consume $32 billion worth of the crusty delight each year, the tradition is as old as recorded history. And it is truly an international dish.

Early Greeks baked a flat bread on heated stones, topped it with oils and herbs, and called it *plankuntos*, which loosely translates as "edible plate." The dish moved to Italy, where the first history of Rome from the third century B.C. speaks of "flat round dough dressed with olive oil, herbs and honey, baked on stones." Tomatoes—an ingredient some consider essential to a well-rounded pie—were added after Columbus introduced the native American fruit to Europe.

Modern pizza history begins with a Neapolitan baker who prepared a pie in the colors of the Italian flag in honor of a visit from the queen. A few years later, Italian immigrants brought the dish to New York, and from there it flourished in Italian neighborhoods along the East Coast from Philadelphia to Boston. Years later, after United States servicemen came home from Europe with a taste for pizza and other ethnic fare, an era of all-American innovation began, and pizzas of all shapes and sizes, with all manner of toppings, began turning up in cities across the land.

Today, pizza restaurants exist on every continent and in hundreds of big and small countries around the globe. In the United States alone, there are more than 62,000 pizzerias, with pizza shops accounting for 17 percent of all restaurants in the country. Industry statistics show that Americans eat 100 acres' worth of pizza a day, or sixty-three slices a year for every man, woman, and child in the country. America's favorite topping? Pepperoni, with a whopping 250 million pounds consumed annually.

Of course, that only covers commercially prepared pizzas. What about pizzas made at home? There are no statistics to chart the rise of homemade pizzas—only anecdotal evidence. Consider, for instance, that ready-to-use pizza components like frozen and shelf-stable crusts and jarred pizza sauce represented a nearly $3 billion industry in 2005, and industry analysts expect the figure to rise. Virtually every discount store carries some form of pizza pan, including once hard-to-find pizza screens and pizza stones, as well as pizza cutters and other tools. Countertop appliances for baking pizzas can be found in housewares departments everywhere, although far more telling is the proliferation of gas and wood-fired pizza ovens. These authentic Italian stone pizza domes cost from $2,000 to more than $10,000, and builders say they're the new must-have appliance in upscale homes.

Whether your household budget leans toward the pizza stone or the stone pizza oven, it is absolutely possible to make fresh, fabulous pizza at home. The trickiest part of making homemade pizza is working with yeast-risen dough; but with a little practice, that can be mastered. In the meantime, if you want to start your home pizza tradition using store-bought dough or ready-to-top bread crusts, we promise no one will complain. The scent of warm bread and bubbling cheese from the kitchen will seduce even the toughest pizza snobs.

Using *The Everything® Pizza Cookbook* as your guide, explore the vast world of pizzas and pizza-inspired dishes. Try out a few pies on close friends and family, then work your way up to a full-fledged pizza party. The oohs and aahs from guests as you pull a fragrant, cheesy pizza from the oven will warm your heart . . . and make you wonder why you ever called for delivery.

CHAPTER 1

Pizza Basics

Pizza has come full circle. The dish originated as peasant food, a simple life-sustaining recipe meant to fill stomachs without emptying purses. It evolved into a world-recognized ethnic treat, then graduated to a gourmet wonder topped with luxury ingredients like duck confit and caviar. Now—although fancy pizzas and purist Italian pizzerias still exist—the dish has returned to its origins. Pizza is an everyday family favorite, sometimes ordered in, sometimes meticulously crafted from scratch, and sometimes thrown together from leftovers. However it arrives at the table, it's always a hunger-abating, soul-satisfying pleasure.

The Origins of Pizza

The first bread baked was a pizza crust. The Neolithic-era cooks who prepared grain paste and baked it into flat rounds over burning coals probably didn't call it that, but a hot, crispy, chewy pizza crust by any other name is still a pizza crust. Leavened flatbreads—made lighter by the introduction of wild yeast spores—appeared in Egypt around 4000 B.C. It's a good bet that condiments of the day—honey, onion, garlic, goose fat, herbs, and plant extracts—found their way onto and into doughs made from wheat, barley, and other grains. After that, it was just a matter of time, improved culinary technology, and the discovery of new ingredients before the now-classic pizza was born.

European Traditions

Ancient Greeks can claim credit for the first pizza-like dishes, which included flat breads—some no doubt similar to modern pita—topped with herbs and spices. But similar thrifty meals were being eaten by workers and their families in countries around the Mediterranean. Food historians say that in the sixth century B.C., Persian soldiers baked flatbread on their shields and topped it with dates and cheeses. In his third-century B.C. history of Rome, Cato the Elder speaks of flat rounds of dough baked on hot stones and dressed with olive oil, herbs, and honey. Meanwhile, Etruscans in Central Italy baked focaccia-like bread with toppings.

The first Italian cookbook author, Marcus Gavius Apicius, included in his first-century A.D. book a recipe for a hearth-baked bread topped with chicken, pine nuts, cheeses, herbs, peppers, and oil—a precursor to chicken pesto pizza. And, in the ruins of Pompeii, which was frozen at A.D. 79 by the eruption of Mount Vesuvius, archaeologists found evidence of shops bearing a striking resemblance to modern pizzerias.

A step toward the familiar bread-tomato-cheese pie formula came in the sixteenth century when Columbus's voyages brought Peruvian tomatoes to Europe. Most Europeans eschewed the fruit, fearing them poisonous. The poor men and women of Naples, however, decided to risk a little in order to add variety to their monotonous diets. They added tomatoes to their hearth-baked dough rounds. By the seventeenth century, diners from all over Italy were venturing into Neapolitan bakeries and trattorias in search of the country's best pizzas.

Naples, the Italian birthplace of the modern pizza, was once a Greek settlement known as Neopolis, further cementing the connection between pizza and ancient Greek culinary arts.

Pizza as most people know it first appeared in 1889 with baker Raffaele Esposito of Naples. In honor of a visit by Queen Margherita of Savoy, he prepared a patriotic pizza in the colors of the Italian flag: green basil, white mozzarella cheese made from water buffalo milk, and red tomatoes. He named it Pizza Margherita, a variety of pie still served today. In fact, the descendants of Esposito and his wife Maria Brandi still operate Brandi Pizzeria in Naples.

Pizza in America

In 1897, Gennaro Lombardi, an Italian immigrant in New York, opened a store in Little Italy where one of his employees made pizza. It became so popular that by 1905 Lombardi had opened New York's first pizzeria. Lombardi's on Spring Street in Little Italy eventually spawned more "Lombardi's" pizza outlets in the city. By 1924, Lombardi's original *pizzaiolo* (the Italian word for pizzamaker), Antonio Totonno Pero, opened his own shop on Coney Island. Descendants of Pero and other Lombardi employees eventually launched pizza enterprises up the East Coast in Connecticut, Rhode Island, and, eventually, Boston. In 1929, Italian immigrants in South Philadelphia opened Marra's on Passyunk Avenue, which served thin-crust pizzas baked in brick ovens built with stone bricks imported from Italy. It remains the oldest surviving restaurant in the neighborhood.

Until World War II, pizza in the United States was largely an ethnic affair, served by Italians to Italians. During the war, soldiers and sailors—sick of rations—sought out local dishes and discovered the Italian food of the masses, pizza. They came home with a taste for the stuff and began making pilgrimages to Italian restaurants in their own cities. By the 1950s, a boom in pizza consumption had begun that has not abated to this day.

FACT

Roman Pizza Mix, a pizza kit in a box, was introduced in 1948 as the first home pizza convenience product. The first frozen pizza was marketed in 1957 by the Celentano Brothers. Eventually, pizza became the top-selling frozen entrée in the United States.

The first truly American pizza was born in 1943 when Chicagoan Ike Sewell introduced deep-dish pizza to the Windy City. Pizzeria Uno offered pies worthy of oversized appetites, with a thin crust lining a cake pan filled with many layers of cheese, meats, veggies, and sauce. Shortly thereafter, the development of gas-fired pizza ovens made pizza entrepreneurship easier and more affordable, resulting in mom-and-pop pizza shops springing up around the U.S.

The next major change in American pizza-dom was the advent of fast-food and delivery-focused pizza chains. Shakey's Pizza opened in California in 1954, Pizza Hut opened in Kansas in 1958, Little Caesar's launched in Michigan in 1959, and Domino's began in Michigan in 1960. The major chains have served billions of pizzas around the world since that time, making pizza more accessible but less of an artisan product. Perhaps as a backlash, "gourmet," or California-style, pizzas emerged in the 1980s. Spago founder Wolfgang Puck created a small, thin-crust pie with toppings as varied as caviar, artichokes, crème fraiche, and Gorgonzola cheese. In 1985, Larry Flax and Rick Rosenfield, two Beverly Hills attorneys, traded the courtroom for the dining room. They founded the California Pizza Kitchen chain, most notably the creator of the Barbecue Chicken Pizza.

Global Pizza

During the late nineteenth and early twentieth centuries, Italians migrated to countries throughout South America, Australia, Central Europe, and Northern Africa, as well as North America. Those families brought their pizza recipes with them, and eventually pizza vendors raised their shingles, attracting neighborhood folk as well as adventurous visitors.

Those Italian neighborhood shops got a boost after World War II. American GIs weren't the only world citizens who acquired a taste for pizza during their time abroad. Many Australians, Canadians, and Northern Europeans sampled pizza for the first time as well. When they returned home, they sought out their own countries' pizzerias. Their appetites fueled pizza booms and reinforced the pizza traditions of Italian immigrant families in far corners.

Pizza-loving soldiers and their families also created a market that attracted global food purveyors. American corporate pizza giants like Pizza Hut and Domino's spread across North America and onto other continents, which in turn helped build an even wider interest in pizza. As pizza became more entrenched in local cultures, the toppings and styles became more varied.

Today, one can order pizza topped with kimchee (fermented vegetables) in Korea, with potatoes and mayonnaise in Japan, with Russian or Thousand Island dressing in Hong Kong, with bananas and nuts in Brazil, with tandoori chicken in India, with corn in China, and with Gouda cheese in the Netherlands. In Canada, "Punjabi-style" pizza refers to pies topped with hot peppers, with Ranch dressing as a popular dip. In Ireland, some pizza toppings are piled onto soda bread, and in Scotland, deep-fried pizzas are served with fries, while in Iran pizzas come with a side of ketchup.

Classic Pizza Styles

Although pizza toppings can range from pickled cabbage in Asia to crab and crème fraiche in California, there are some commonly accepted pizza styles with regional variations. Some of these include Neapolitan, Sicilian, Chicago style, and California style.

Neapolitan

Many pizzas are variations on the original pie of Naples—a flat, hearth-baked, chewy crust topped with tomatoes or tomato sauce and mild cheese. A few of the most common variations are New York–style pizza, which is bigger and flatter than the original pizza of Napoli, designed to be cut into large, flexible wedges that can be folded and eaten while walking or working. New Haven–style pizza often refers to white pizza with clams. Philadelphia pizzas can be classic Neapolitan or a variation with slightly sweet canned peppers and onions as a topping. There's also the eastern Pennsylvania "tomato pie," which is square; it's topped with thick tomato sauce and eaten cold.

FACT

Long Island, New York claims to be the home of the "pizza bagel," an individual-size pizza that substitutes a bagel half for the pizza crust. Beyond that, the toppings can include any of the usual meats, veggies, and cheeses.

Sicilian

True Sicilian pizza is a rectangular slab of bread with toppings—which typically do not include cheese—pushed into the dough before baking. The American version is radically different, usually with a thick layer of cheese encasing all the toppings. Sicilian pizza can be found in major metro areas with large Italian-American populations, and homogenized versions occasionally turn up on the menu of pizza chain restaurants. Scranton-style pizza, served at pubs and bakeries in Northeastern Pennsylvania, is a thick, pillowy rectangular crust with a crisp bottom, topped with thick tomato sauce and a thin layer of grated hard cheeses. One can argue that pizza variations like French-bread crust pizza and focaccia pizza pay homage to the original Sicilian pizzas.

Chicago Style

Around the world, Chicago-style pizza usually refers to the deep-dish, multilayered pizzas first created by Ike Sewell in the mid-twentieth century. That pie, almost a casserole, offers a unique pizza experience. It has also spawned some lesser pizzas, generally called pan pizzas. Pan pizzas are round with a thick, well-oiled crust—somewhat similar to a Sicilian crust—with an indentation to hold more toppings.

There is also a Chicago-style thin crust pizza. The crust tends to be flat and crisp, topped with a sweet, oregano-heavy tomato sauce and plenty of meats and cheese. Although it's a round pie, this Chicago-style pizza is cut into squares, not wedges, making it easy to munch without the toppings sliding off. St. Louis–style pizza is similar to Chicago thin crust, with the addition of Provel cheese—a processed cheese flavored with Cheddar, Swiss, and provolone cheeses.

Chicago is known for its meat industry and love of thick steaks and chops. But the most popular topping for Chicago-style pizza? Spinach and lots of cheese. It seems Midwesterners love their veggie pies.

California Style

Although San Franciscans have long adored their hearty sourdough-crust pizzas topped with the freshest ingredients, those Neapolitan-style pies aren't what most of the world knows as "California style." Instead California-style pizza is characterized by a plate-sized, very thin crust and a range of unusual toppings. Barbecue, pineapple, Thai shrimp, curry chicken, fiddlehead ferns, roast duck, and all manner of herbs and cheeses turn up on California-style pizzas. Some gourmet pizza devotees assume Californians invented the grilled pizza, but that distinction actually goes to chefs in Rhode Island.

Ingredients

Pizza purists may argue, but in the twenty-first century there's wide latitude regarding acceptable ingredients for pizza. The only thing everybody agrees upon is quality. To make good pizza, you must start with fresh, good-quality ingredients. Beyond that, the choice is yours.

Crust

Bread flour, which is an unbleached, hard wheat flour with a high protein content, generally makes the best pizza crust. It rises easily and bakes up crusty and chewy. Whole-wheat flour and flours with a variety of whole grains mixed in also make a substantial crust, and have the added benefit of being "good," high-fiber carbohydrates. Semolina flour, the granular flour that gives the best dried pasta its bite, makes a firming addition to pizza crust. Rye flour adds substance and flavor, making it a great addition to crust being prepared for the grill.

A special Italian flour known as OO or Caputo flour is often used to make a soft dough for authentic Neapolitan crust. It can sometimes be found in specialty stores and from mail-order sources.

Wild yeast spores exist on the surface of plants and often travel in the wind, causing organic compounds to ferment. Long before packaged yeast existed, bakers maintained a supply of live yeast by keeping a crock of fermenting dough "starter." Adding the starter to fresh dough allows the yeast to multiply.

Sauce

Anything that can add moisture and flavor to your pizza crust can be used as a sauce. Thick tomato sauce or olive oil with garlic are the two classic toppings, but substitutions can range from chopped tomatoes or herb pesto to ground olive or pepper pastes to barbecue sauce or teriyaki glaze. Creamy salad dressings, nut butters, cream sauces, and vegetable purèes can work as well. Experiment with your own sauce combinations. The important thing to remember is proportion. Too much of a good thing can make your pizza a soggy mess.

Cheese

Water-buffalo milk mozzarella cheese—a fresh, dense, creamy-tasting mozzarella—is the preferred topping for Neapolitan-style pizza. Cow's milk mozzarella is the most common substitute. Provolone is a smoke-flavored version. But most modern pizzamakers use a combination of cheeses. Try pairing strong-flavored cheeses like sharp Cheddar, aged Romano and Parmesan, Asiago, or aged Manchego with a mild buttery cheese like mozzarella, Butterkase, Gouda, or Monterey jack. Intensely flavored blue or green-veined cheeses should be used as accents, rather than full layers.

Depending on the effect you want, cheeses can be added in dollops, cubes, slices, or shreds. Just remember that thinly shredded cheeses melt, and sometimes burn, more quickly than larger shreds or cubes.

Toppings

The sky's the limit on pizza toppings. Virtually any meat, cheese, vegetable, fruit, herb, nut, or seed can become the star of your homemade pizza. However, it's important to remember that raw ingredients release moisture and possibly fats during cooking, which can turn your pizza and your oven into a nightmare. Always fully cook raw sausage, meats, fish, and seafood before adding to pizzas. Spinach and other greens should be well-drained, and oily ingredients used in moderation.

Equipment

You don't need a $10,000 brick oven to make great pizza at home. A regular oven and a few baking sheets will suffice. But if you really want to make great pizza, there are a few pieces of equipment that will make your pies better and the pizzamaking experience easier.

Bread Machines and Mixers

Some people love the tactile experience of mixing and kneading dough, punching it down and kneading it again before rolling it into a flat crust. For others it's a necessary evil. If you love making pizza but hate making yeast-risen dough, invest in a bread machine. Bread machines with pizza dough cycles make short work of pizza crust. Just spoon or pour ingredients into the bread machine pan, set the cycle, and hit the start button. The machine will mix the ingredients, knead the dough, and hold it at the right temperature for rising, while you peruse the fridge for toppings. Within an hour or so, you'll be ready to stretch or roll your dough into a crust.

Even if you don't have a bread machine, you can use a mixer fitted with a dough hook to do a lot of the ingredient mixing and kneading. Then just throw a clean towel or plate over the bowl and set it in a draft-free place to rise.

Pizza Stones, Tiles, and Peels

Pizza stones are porous slabs—either circles or squares—that mimic the surface and floor of a brick or stone pizza oven. The stones absorb heat, then release it evenly, resulting in a crisp-bottomed pizza. Ovens equipped with pizza stones can produce crusts with an amazing hearth-baked taste and texture. Tiles work similarly, with small squares that can be lined up inside a baking sheet for convenience.

Stones should be allowed to heat up and cool down with the oven to keep from cracking. And both stones and tiles should be cleaned with a damp cloth or brush, never detergent. The porous surface can absorb soaps and cleansers, resulting in off-flavored crusts. Pizza peels—giant wooden paddles—are the best way to transfer pizzas to and from hot stones or tiles. Just coat the peel with coarse corn meal to keep the dough from sticking, then build your pizza. Slide the uncooked pie onto the hot stone using the peel. Once the pizza is cooked, the pie can be removed using the peel as a giant spatula.

Pizza Screens and Pans

Every household should have a pizza screen. These perforated metal pans allow heat to get to the bottom of crusts, resulting in a crispy, chewy pizza. Whether you're baking a from-scratch Neapolitan or California-style pizza or just reheating a ready-made crust, a pizza screen can give a much better result than a solid pan.

That said, Chicago-style and generously topped Sicilian pizzas require a solid, deep-sided pan to keep oils and wet ingredients contained. The best deep-dish pizza pans are heavy metal pans with a nonstick surface. Just remember that dark pans hold more heat, so pizzas should be baked at a lower temperature or watched carefully while baking.

Pizza wheels allow you to cut through cheesy pizzas without dragging toppings off the pie. Invest in a heavy, stable pizza wheel or use a long sharp knife with a rocking motion to cut slices.

Keep a good supply of nonstick foil for baking dessert pizza crusts and small cocktail pizzas. Just line a baking sheet or flat round baking pan with foil and bake away.

Pizza Safety

Anyone who's ever bitten into a delicious-looking hot pizza—only to get her mouth seared with hot cheese—knows it's important to be careful when dealing with pizza. Keep heavy-duty oven mitts at the ready for pulling pizza in and out of the oven. When baking, always keep a place on the stove or a portion of counter space cleared and ready to accept a hot pizza pan as it is removed from the oven. Allow pizzas to settle and cool slightly before cutting, and never try to remove a hot pizza stone from the oven.

ALERT!

Never leave perishable foods at room temperature for more than two hours. That's the point at which ingredients become vulnerable to bacteria that can cause food poisoning. Remember that most bacterial infestations cannot be seen or smelled, so a quick sniff won't tell you if something's gone bad.

To reduce the chance of contaminating your pizzas with bacteria, make sure countertops and work surfaces have been cleaned with antibacterial soap. Never handle raw animal products without washing your hands thoroughly, and never allow raw ingredients to come in contact with cooked ingredients. Leftover pizza should be wrapped and refrigerated promptly after meals.

Tips for Entertaining

Pizza is comfort food, and even if you're topping yours with filet mignon and lobster, the sight of pizza on the table will make guests feel at home. Pizza makes a great entrée to pair with simple salads and soups because it's a hardy dish that can be prepared with a range of complementary toppings.

Armchair tailgating is always a good excuse for a pizza party, but other televised events—the Academy Awards, the Grammys, even the season finale of your favorite TV series—can offer great opportunities for making and sharing a homemade pie.

Consider inviting guests over for a before-theatre pizza tart and champagne party, or a pizza holiday brunch, or a book-club pizza dessert party. Grilled pizza makes a great alternative to burgers and hot dogs at a backyard barbecue. And anyone who has children knows that pizza is at the top of the food chain for kids 3 to 11. You can't go wrong offering pizza at any birthday party or after-school event.

Just remember to allow for two slices of pizza per child and at least three for each adult invited. Unless you know your guests' preferences very well, always offer at least one cheese-only pizza for those with an aversion to particular toppings. If you're having a large party, one cheese-only and one pizza featuring a single meat—beef or chicken preferably—is a good idea. Then go wild with the remaining pies on your buffet.

FACT

Pizza Hut and Domino's combined deliver more than 3 million pizzas during the Super Bowl, with most orders coming in just before and in the first hour after kick-off. Pepperoni is the most requested topping.

Most home ovens can accommodate two pizzas at the most. Don't worry. Once the crust is rolled out and the toppings chopped or sliced, a pizza takes very little time to prepare. By the time your first pie is out of the oven, slightly cooled, and sliced, your next round of pizzas will be ready to pull from the fire. And do prepare to bake several pies. Once your guests learn you're making homemade pizza, you won't have many regrets.

CHAPTER 2
Good Foundations: Pizza Crusts

Classic Crust

*Makes crust for four
12-inch pizzas*

2 packages active dry yeast
1¹/₂ cups warm water,
    about 100°
1 teaspoon sugar
1¹/₂ teaspoons salt
6¹/₂ cups bread flour
2 tablespoons olive oil

This recipe makes dough that's moist, but still manageable. For dough that's not as sticky, add a little more flour to the mix, or work in more flour during kneading.

✳   ✳   ✳

1. In a large measuring cup, dissolve yeast in water. Let stand 5 minutes or until bubbly. Combine sugar, salt, and bread flour in the bowl of a mixer with a dough hook. Or, to mix by hand, place in a large bowl. Make a well in the flour mixture and pour in the water, followed by 1 tablespoon of oil.

2. Turn the mixer on low to blend, or begin stirring the flour into the liquid with a wooden spoon, a little at a time. When ingredients are well combined, turn the mixer on medium-low to knead for 5 minutes. If working dough by hand, turn the dough onto a well-floured work surface. Use a pressing motion with the heels of your hands. Work dough until the mixture is slightly shiny and not too sticky to the touch.

3. The kneaded dough should be divided into four equal pieces. Store any dough not being used in a resealable bag in the refrigerator. Oil remaining dough and place in a bowl, covered, to rise for 1 hour. Punch the dough down, shape into 2 disks, and let rest for 30 minutes.

4. Grab dough by the edges, turning the disk a few inches at a time, allowing gravity to stretch the dough without tearing. Roll the dough into a crust shape or press into a pizza pan. Top as directed in recipe.

Dough for Tomorrow
Pizza dough will rise, albeit slowly, in the refrigerator. To use dough that's been refrigerated overnight, place in a covered bowl on the counter. Punch dough down, then let stand until dough reaches room temperature. Use as directed.

Bread Machine Crust

*Makes crust for four
12-inch pizzas*

*Be sure to read your bread machine instruction manual before making
pizza dough. Feel free to experiment with flavors, but never
put in more ingredients in than your machine can hold.*

❅   ❅   ❅

1. Place ingredients in bread machine pan in the order listed. Turn machine on pizza dough cycle. Dough should be ready in slightly more than an hour, depending on your machine.

2. Remove dough from machine and place on a lightly floured work surface. Divide dough in half, placing half in a resealable plastic bag if you won't be using all the dough at once. Refrigerate plastic bag. Divide remaining dough in half, pat into two thick disks, and let rest for a few minutes.

3. Shape dough into free-form crusts or press into pizza pans as desired.

Great Gadgets
Bread machines with pizza dough cycles can be the pizza lover's best friend. The machines mix and knead crust ingredients and provide a temperature-controlled environment for rising. Since pizzas aren't actually baked in bread machines, you'll have to handle the dough a bit, but the convenience is still significant.

*1²/₃ cups warm water,
about 100°
2 tablespoons olive oil
2 tablespoons sugar
2 teaspoons salt
2 tablespoons powdered milk
4¹/₂ cups bread flour
1 package active dry yeast*

Sicilian Crust

Makes crust for two
11 x 16-inch pizzas

2 packages active dry yeast
2 cups warm water,
    about 100°
7 cups bread flour
2 teaspoons salt
$^1/_3$ cup plus 1 tablespoon
    olive oil

*Warm bread topped with oil, meats, vegetables, and cheese
can be found all over southern Italy, particularly in bakery shops.
This popular snack is probably the origin of what we
now call "Sicilian" pizza.*

*   *   *

1. Dissolve yeast in warm water. In a large bowl, or in the bowl of a mixer with a dough hook, combine flour and salt. Add yeast mixture and ½ cup oil to flour. Stir by hand or with mixer on low until combined.

2. Knead dough for 5 minutes in a mixer with dough hook on medium-low speed. To knead by hand, place dough on a well-floured surface. Work dough back and forth with the heels of your hands until dough is slightly shiny and elastic.

3. Place dough on a nonstick surface or in a large bowl. Oil well with remaining olive oil. Cover and let rise for 2 hours. Punch dough down and divide in half. Press dough halves into two well-oiled 11" × 16" pans. Let rise an additional 30 minutes. Follow recipe instructions for topping and baking.

Chicago Deep-Dish Crust

This is the crust for the original American Pie, a pizza invented in Chicago by a non-Italian restaurateur to satisfy hearty appetites. Don't bother rolling this dough—just press it into a well-oiled deep-dish pan.

❈   ❈   ❈

1. Combine yeast, ½ cup water, sugar, and 1 cup flour in a large bowl. Stir, then cover and set aside for 15 to 20 minutes. Uncover and add remaining water, flour, cornmeal, salt, and ½ cup oil.

2. With a wooden spoon, stir ingredients until just blended. Turn mixture onto a well-floured nonstick surface and knead until shiny and elastic, about 10 minutes. Oil dough with olive oil, cover, and place in a warm spot to rise until doubled in size, about 2 hours.

3. Punch dough down and knead briefly. Divide into four equal portions. Press each portion into a well-oiled deep-dish pan. Let stand 10 to 20 minutes or until dough rises again. Press dough up sides of the pan and to a uniform thickness at the center. Fill and bake according to recipe instructions.

Makes crust for four 12-inch pizzas

---

2 packages active dry yeast
2½ cups warm water, about 100°
1 tablespoon sugar
7 cups all-purpose flour
1 cup cornmeal
2 teaspoons salt
½ cup plus 2 tablespoons olive oil

Makes crust for four
12-inch pizzas

2 cups reduced-fat milk
2 packages active dry yeast
6 cups all-purpose flour
4 tablespoons sugar
1 teaspoon salt
5 tablespoons olive oil

Pan Pizza Crust

Pan pizza crust is extremely rich. To achieve the flaky exterior crust many pizza lovers prize, use a generous amount of olive oil to coat the pan when making your pan pizza.

✳ ✳ ✳

1. Warm milk in the microwave to about 100°, or just warm, not hot, to the touch.

2. In the bowl of a mixer with a dough hook, combine yeast, flour, sugar, and salt. Stir to combine. With dough hook running on low speed, slowly add the warm milk followed by 4 tablespoons olive oil.

3. Turn mixer to medium-low or proper speed for kneading. Allow mixer to knead the dough for 5 minutes or until mixture is slightly glossy and springy to the touch. If the dough seems too wet, add a small amount of flour and knead a little longer.

4. Remove dough to a lightly floured work surface. A pastry board or silicone baking sheet is good. Waxed paper or nonstick foil on the counter will do. Divide the pizza dough in half and shape into two even balls. Grease two metal or glass bowls with the remaining olive oil and place the dough balls in the bowls, turning to lightly oil the dough.

5. Cover the bowls with plastic wrap and place in a warm spot. Allow dough to rise 30 minutes or until doubled in size. Punch down. If making two pizzas, place one dough ball in a resealable plastic bag, press out the air, and refrigerate for later use. Take remaining ball and divide in half. Lightly pat each half into a flattened circle, cover, and let stand 20 to 30 minutes before placing in plans. Refrigerated dough should be allowed to come to room temperature before using.

California Thin Crust

Thin-crust pizza dough requires flour with a high protein content in order to develop the characteristic crispness pizza lovers enjoy. It also benefits from a longer rising period.

✳   ✳   ✳

Makes crust for four 12-inch pizzas

1 packet active dry yeast
1 cup warm water, about 100°
2 tablespoons vegetable oil
2 teaspoons sugar
6¹/₂ cups high-protein flour
1¹/₂ teaspoons salt

1. In a large mixer bowl, combine water, yeast, oil, and sugar. Using a mixer with a dough hook, stir on low speed until the yeast dissolves and the mixture is well combined. Slowly add flour and salt. Continue stirring until a stiff ball of dough forms.

2. Place dough in a large (2-gallon) resealable plastic bag or place in a bowl and cover with plastic wrap. Refrigerate the dough for 24 hours. Remove from refrigerator and allow to come to cool room temperature.

3. Turn pizza onto a well-floured surface. Divide into four sections. (Return any sections that aren't being used to the refrigerator.) Roll sections into very thin circles, dusting liberally with flour as you go. Prick pizza crust several times with a fork and top according to recipe directions.

Ultra-Thin Pizza Crust
To get your pizza super-thin, use the California Thin Crust recipe and a pasta roller. Run strips of dough through the rollers and line them up, overlapping slightly on a well-oiled pizza pan. Smooth out the seams, prick the crust with a fork, then use as directed in your recipe.

*Makes crust for four
12-inch pizzas*

2 packages active dry yeast
*1¹/₂ cups warm water,
    about 100°*
2 teaspoons sugar
1¹/₂ teaspoons salt
*6¹/₂ cups stone-ground whole-
    wheat flour*
2 tablespoons olive oil

Whole-Wheat Crust

*Whole-wheat lovers and those embracing the healthy-carb
lifestyle should love this pizza crust. Use it in place of classic or
flavored crust in any recipe to add a hearty, rustic flavor.*

❊   ❊   ❊

1. In a large measuring cup, dissolve yeast in water. Let stand
    5 minutes or until bubbly. Combine sugar, salt, and bread
    flour in the bowl of a mixer with a dough hook. Or, to mix by
    hand, place in a large bowl. Make a well in the flour mixture
    and pour in the water, followed by 1 tablespoon of oil.

2. Turn the mixer on low to blend, or begin stirring the flour
    into the liquid with a wooden spoon, a little at a time. When
    ingredients are well combined, turn the mixer on medium-
    low to knead for 5 minutes. If working dough by hand, turn
    the dough onto a well-floured work surface. Use a pressing
    motion with the heels of your hands to push and stretch the
    dough. Work dough until mixture is slightly shiny and not
    too sticky to the touch.

3. The kneaded dough should be divided into four equal
    pieces. Store any dough not being used in a resealable bag
    in the refrigerator. Oil remaining dough and place in a bowl,
    covered, to rise for 1 hour. Punch the dough down, shape
    into two disks, and let rest for 30 minutes.

4. Grab dough by the edges, turning the disk a few inches at a
    time, allowing gravity to stretch the dough without tearing.
    Roll the dough into a crust shape or press into a pizza pan.
    Top as directed in recipe.

Honey-Wheat Crust

Use this crust for a hint of hearty whole-wheat flavor. It's a great option for those transitioning to healthy carbs and pizza lovers who want variety without a too-heavy dose of coarse grains.

❋ ❋ ❋

Makes crust for four 12-inch pizzas

2 packages active dry yeast
1½ cups warm water, about 100°
2 tablespoons honey
1 teaspoon sugar
1½ teaspoons salt
3½ cups bread flour
3 cups whole-wheat flour
2 tablespoons olive oil

1. In a large measuring cup, dissolve yeast in water. Let stand 5 minutes or until bubbly. Add honey to liquid. Combine sugar, salt, and both flours in the bowl of a mixer with a dough hook. Or, to mix by hand, place in a large bowl. Make a well in the flour mixture and pour in the water, followed by 1 tablespoon of oil.

2. Turn the mixer on low to blend, or begin stirring the flour into the liquid with a wooden spoon, a little at a time. When ingredients are well combined, turn the mixer on medium-low to knead for 5 minutes. If working dough by hand, turn the dough onto a well-floured work surface. Use a pressing motion with the heels of your hands to push and stretch the dough. Work dough until mixture is slightly shiny and not too sticky to the touch.

3. The kneaded dough should be divided into four equal pieces. Store any dough not being used in a resealable bag in the refrigerator. Oil remaining dough and place in a bowl, covered, to rise for 1 hour. Punch the dough down, shape into two disks, and let rest for 30 minutes.

4. Grab dough by the edges, turning slowly, allowing gravity to stretch the dough without tearing. Roll the dough into a crust shape or press into a pizza pan. Top as directed in recipe.

A Yeasty Blend
Yeast is a single-celled organism that comes in myriad varieties and lives in our atmosphere. The version that comes in "active dry yeast" packets is dormant, and comes alive in warm liquid. It feeds on sugars and starch (as in flour) and expels carbon dioxide; the gluten in the flour traps those bubbles, causing the dough to rise.

Multigrain Crust

Makes crust for four
12-inch pizzas

2 packages active dry yeast
1 1/2 cups warm water,
    about 100°
2 tablespoons honey
1 teaspoon sugar
1 1/2 teaspoons salt
3 1/2 cups bread flour
3 cups multigrain flour mix
2 tablespoons olive oil

Multigrain flours add complex flavors and extra crunch to your pizza crust. Bits of fat-rich seeds and nuts in many of these blends make the flours perishable. Store unused portions in your refrigerator.

✳   ✳   ✳

1. In a large measuring cup, dissolve yeast in water. Let stand 5 minutes or until bubbly. Add honey to liquid. Combine sugar, salt, and both flours in the bowl of a mixer with a dough hook. Or, to mix by hand, place in a large bowl. Make a well in the flour mixture and pour in the water, followed by 1 tablespoon of oil.

2. Turn the mixer on low to blend, or begin stirring the flour into the liquid with a wooden spoon, a little at a time. When ingredients are well combined, turn the mixer on medium-low to knead for 5 minutes. If working dough by hand, turn the dough onto a well-floured work surface. Use a pressing motion with the heels of your hands to push and stretch the dough. Work dough until mixture is slightly shiny and not too sticky to the touch.

3. The kneaded dough should be divided into four equal pieces. Store any dough not being used in a resealable bag in the refrigerator. Oil remaining dough and place in a bowl, covered, to rise for 1 hour. Punch the dough down, shape into two disks, and let rest for 30 minutes.

4. Grab dough by the edges, turning the disk a few inches at a time, allowing gravity to stretch the dough without tearing. Roll the dough into a crust shape or press into a pizza pan. Top as directed in recipe.

Cornmeal Crust

Crunchy cornmeal gives this pizza crust a uniquely American regional flavor, making it perfect for toppings that pay homage to Old South or Southwest classics.

✳ ✳ ✳

1. In a large measuring cup, dissolve yeast in water. Let stand 5 minutes or until bubbly. Combine sugar, salt, flour, and cornmeal in the bowl of a mixer with a dough hook. Or, to mix by hand, place in a large bowl. Make a well in the flour mixture and pour in the water, followed by 1 tablespoon of oil and the egg.

2. Turn the mixer on low to blend, or begin stirring the flour into the liquid with a wooden spoon, a little at a time. When ingredients are well combined, turn the mixer on medium-low to knead for 5 minutes. If working dough by hand, turn the dough onto a well-floured work surface. Use a pressing motion with the heels of your hands to push and stretch the dough. Work dough until mixture is slightly shiny and not too sticky to the touch.

3. The kneaded dough should be divided into four equal pieces. Store any dough not being used in a resealable bag in the refrigerator. Oil remaining dough and place in a bowl, covered, to rise for 1 hour. Punch the dough down, shape into two disks, and let rest for 30 minutes.

4. Grab dough by the edges, turning the disk a few inches at a time, allowing gravity to stretch the dough without tearing. Roll the dough into a crust shape or press into a pizza pan. Top as directed in recipe.

Makes crust for four
12-inch pizzas

2 packages active dry yeast
1¹/₂ cups warm water,
    about 100°
1 tablespoon sugar
1¹/₂ teaspoons salt
4¹/₂ cups bread flour
2 cups cornmeal
2 tablespoons olive oil
1 egg, beaten

2 packages active dry yeast
1½ cups warm water,
    about 100°
2 tablespoons honey
1 teaspoon sugar
1½ teaspoons salt
5 cups bread flour
1½ cups granola or old-
    fashioned oatmeal
2 tablespoons olive oil

Oatmeal Crust

Baked solo, this crust makes a great edible plate for cheese-topped scrambled eggs and sausage. Add extra sugar and cinnamon to the mix for a cookie-like dessert crust.

✳   ✳   ✳

1. In a large measuring cup, dissolve yeast in water. Let stand 5 minutes or until bubbly. Add honey to liquid. Combine sugar, salt, flour, and oatmeal in the bowl of a mixer with a dough hook. Or, to mix by hand, place in a large bowl. Make a well in the flour mixture and pour in the water, followed by 1 tablespoon of oil.

2. Turn the mixer on low to blend, or begin stirring the flour into the liquid with a wooden spoon, a little at a time. When ingredients are well combined, turn the mixer on medium-low to knead for 5 minutes. If working dough by hand, turn the dough onto a well-floured work surface. Use a pressing motion with the heels of your hands to push and stretch the dough. Work dough until mixture is slightly shiny and not too sticky to the touch.

3. The kneaded dough should be divided into four equal pieces. Store any dough not being used in a resealable bag in the refrigerator. Oil remaining dough and place in a bowl, covered, to rise for 1 hour. Punch the dough down, shape into two disks, and let rest for 30 minutes.

4. Grab dough by the edges, turning the disk a few inches at a time, allowing gravity to stretch the dough without tearing. Roll the dough into a crust shape or press into a pizza pan. Top as directed in recipe.

No-Yeast Crust

Solid vegetable shortening works just fine for this super-quick crust.
But if you're willing to go old-school, you can always substitute
lard for all or part of the shortening.

✻   ✻   ✻

1. In a large bowl, pour flour and whisk to break up any lumps. Add shortening and salt to the bowl and work ingredients together with two knives or a pastry blender. Continue cutting and blending until mixture resembles pea-sized granules.

2. Add cold water and egg to the mixture and stir. Work with hands until mixture is well blended and holds together in a ball. Divide ball into four equal portions.

3. On a well-floured surface, roll each portion into a circle large enough to cover the bottom and sides of a 12" pizza or tart pan. (If you aren't making four pizzas, place any extra dough in resealable plastic bags and refrigerate for later use.) Use pizza crust as directed in recipe.

Makes crust for four 12-inch pizzas

5 cups all-purpose flour
1 cup vegetable shortening
1¹/₂ teaspoons salt
¹/₂ cup ice-cold water
1 egg, beaten

Herb-Laced Crust

*Makes crust for four
12-inch pizzas*

2 packages active dry yeast
1½ cups warm water,
     about 100°
1 teaspoon sugar
1½ teaspoons salt
6½ cups bread flour
2 tablespoons olive oil
1 cup tightly packed fresh
     basil, parsley, oregano,
     and thyme leaves
1 tablespoon Italian-blend
     mixed dried herbs
     (optional)

*Use any mix of fresh herbs that suits your taste buds.
Just remember that aromatics like rosemary, thyme, and
sage can be overpowering in large quantities.*

✳   ✳   ✳

1. In a large measuring cup, dissolve yeast in water. Let stand 5 minutes or until bubbly. Combine sugar, salt, and bread flour in the bowl of a mixer with a dough hook. Or, to mix by hand, place in a large bowl. Make a well in the flour mixture and pour in the water, followed by 1 tablespoon of oil.

2. Finely chop fresh herbs by hand or in a food processor. Do not purée.

3. Turn the mixer on low to blend, or begin stirring the flour into the liquid with a wooden spoon, a little at a time. When ingredients are almost combined, add the chopped herbs and continue mixing until herbs are well distributed.

4. Turn the mixer on medium-low to knead for 5 minutes. If working dough by hand, turn the dough onto a well-floured work surface. Use a pressing motion with the heels of your hands to push and stretch the dough. Work dough until mixture is slightly shiny and not too sticky to the touch.

5. The kneaded dough should be divided into four equal pieces. Store any dough not being used in a resealable bag in the refrigerator. Oil remaining dough and place in a bowl, covered, to rise for 1 hour. Punch the dough down, shape into two disks, and let rest for 30 minutes.

6. Grab dough by the edges, turning the disk a few inches at a time, allowing gravity to stretch the dough without tearing. Roll the dough into a crust shape or press into a pizza pan. If desired, sprinkle dried herbs around the edges of the crust. Top as directed in recipe.

Spinach Crust

Spinach flour can be found in markets that sell ingredients for pasta or tortilla making. If desired, substitute up to a cup of bread flour in this recipe with spinach flour.

❈   ❈   ❈

1. In a large measuring cup, dissolve yeast in water. Let stand 5 minutes or until bubbly. Combine sugar, salt, and bread flour in the bowl of a mixer with a dough hook. Or, to mix by hand, place in a large bowl. Make a well in the flour mixture and pour in the water, followed by 1 tablespoon of oil.

2. Squeeze as much liquid as possible from the spinach. Finely chop spinach by hand or with a food processor. Mix chopped spinach with lemon zest and nutmeg.

3. Turn the mixer on low to blend, or begin stirring the flour into the liquid with a wooden spoon, a little at a time. When ingredients are almost completely combined, add the spinach mixture and continue mixing.

4. When the spinach has been incorporated, turn the mixer on medium-low to knead for 5 minutes. If working dough by hand, turn the dough onto a well-floured work surface. Use a pressing motion with the heels of your hands to push and stretch the dough. Work dough until mixture is slightly shiny and not too sticky to the touch.

5. The kneaded dough should be divided into four equal pieces. Store any dough not being used in a resealable bag in the refrigerator. Oil remaining dough and place in a bowl, covered, to rise for 1 hour. Punch the dough down, shape into two disks, and let rest for 30 minutes.

6. Grab dough by the edges, turning slowly, allowing gravity to stretch the dough without tearing. Roll the dough into a crust shape or press into a pizza pan. Top as directed in recipe.

*Makes crust for four
12-inch pizzas*

2 packages active dry yeast
1½ cups warm water,
    about 100°
1 teaspoon sugar
1½ teaspoons salt
7 cups bread flour
1 pound fresh spinach, lightly
    steamed
1 teaspoon lemon zest
⅛ teaspoon ground nutmeg
2 tablespoons olive oil

Pepper Crust

*To make this crust more elegant, crack a multicolored mix of
peppercorns, including green, pink, white, and black. If you don't
have a coarse grinder, just put the peppercorns in
a clean towel and strike with a hammer.*

❋   ❋   ❋

1. In a large measuring cup, dissolve yeast in water. Let stand
   5 minutes or until bubbly. Combine sugar, salt, and bread
   flour in the bowl of a mixer with a dough hook. Or, to mix by
   hand, place in a large bowl. Make a well in the flour mixture
   and pour in the water, followed by 1 tablespoon of oil.

2. Turn the mixer on low to blend, or begin stirring the flour
   into the liquid with a wooden spoon, a little at a time. When
   ingredients are well combined, turn the mixer on medium-
   low to knead for 5 minutes. If working dough by hand, turn
   the dough onto a well-floured work surface. Use a pressing
   motion with the heels of your hands to push and stretch the
   dough. Work dough until mixture is slightly shiny and not
   too sticky to the touch.

3. The kneaded dough should be divided into four equal
   pieces. Store any dough not being used in a resealable bag
   in the refrigerator. Oil remaining dough and place in a bowl,
   covered, to rise for 1 hour. Punch the dough down, shape
   into two disks, and let rest for 30 minutes.

4. Grab dough by the edges, turning the disk a few inches at a
   time, allowing gravity to stretch the dough without tearing.
   Roll the dough into a crust shape or press into a pizza pan.
   Top as directed in recipe.

Stuffed Crust

Like pan pizza, this crust is soft and benefits from the aid of a mixer with a dough hook. If you must work the dough by hand, keep your fingers well-floured.

❋ ❋ ❋

*Makes crust for four
12-inch pizzas*

2 cups reduced-fat milk
2 packages active dry yeast
7 cups all-purpose flour
2 teaspoons sugar
1 teaspoon salt
4 tablespoons olive oil
1 pound well-chilled
    mozzarella or Cheddar
    cheese, cubed

1. Warm milk in the microwave to about 100°, or just warm, not hot, to the touch.

2. In the bowl of a mixer with a dough hook, combine yeast, flour, sugar, and salt. Stir to combine. With dough hook running on low speed, slowly add warm milk, followed by 3 tablespoons olive oil.

3. Turn mixer to medium-low or proper speed for kneading. Allow mixer to knead the dough for 5 minutes or until mixture is slightly glossy and springy to the touch. If the dough seems too wet, add a small amount of flour and knead a little longer.

4. Remove dough to a lightly floured work surface. A pastry board or silicone baking sheet is good. Divide the pizza dough in half and shape into two even balls. Grease two metal or glass bowls with the remaining olive oil and place the dough balls in the bowls, turning to lightly oil the dough.

5. Cover the bowls with plastic wrap and place in a warm spot. Allow dough to rise 30 minutes or until doubled in size. Punch down. If making two pizzas, place one dough ball in a resealable plastic bag, press out the air, and refrigerate for later use. Take remaining ball and divide in half. Lightly pat each half into a flattened circle, cover, and let stand 20 to 30 minutes.

6. Roll or press pizza crust into 14-inch circles. About 1 inch from the edge of the crust, make a ring of cold cheese cubes. Carefully turn the edges of the pizza over the cheese cubes and press the dough together, completely encasing the cheese. Cover center of crusts with sauce and toppings as desired and bake on a screen or pizza stone for 20 minutes.

Focaccia Crust

Makes crust for four
12-inch pizzas

2 packages active dry yeast

1¹/₂ cups warm water, about 100°

7 cups bread flour

1 teaspoon sugar

2 teaspoons salt

²/₃ cup olive oil

2 tablespoons extra virgin olive oil

1 teaspoon dried Italian herb blend

For pizza, focaccia loaves should be split in half horizontally, with each round serving as a pizza crust. Whole loaves can be topped with oil, herbs, and hard cheese—but saucy toppings will slide off.

❋ ❋ ❋

1. Dissolve the yeast in water and let stand for 5 minutes. In a large bowl, combine flour, sugar, and salt. Slowly add the yeast, water, and ⅔ cup olive oil. Stir until ingredients are well blended. Sprinkle on dried herbs.

2. Turn focaccia dough onto a well-floured surface and knead with the heels of your hands for 10 minutes. Place dough on a dry surface and cover with a large bowl. Let stand in a warm place for at least 1 hour.

3. Punch the dough down and divide in half. Smooth dough into two well-oiled pizza pans. Brush tops with extra virgin olive oil and let stand for 1 hour. Bake focaccias in a 400° preheated oven for 15 to 20 minutes. Remove from oven and let cool.

4. To use as pizza crust, split focaccias and top each half as directed in recipe. Return to oven if necessary to heat toppings.

Asiago Cheese Crust

Any firm shredded cheese can be substituted for the Asiago in this recipe. Work Cheddar or Monterey jack into your crust for a hearty meat pie. Try Gruyère or Manchego for veggies.

✳   ✳   ✳

Makes crust for four 12-inch pizzas

---

2 packages active dry yeast
1½ cups warm water, about 100°
1 teaspoon sugar
1½ teaspoons salt
6½ cups bread flour
2 tablespoons olive oil
1½ cups shredded Asiago cheese

1. In a large measuring cup, dissolve yeast in water. Let stand 5 minutes or until bubbly. Combine sugar, salt, and bread flour in the bowl of a mixer with a dough hook. Or, to mix by hand, place in a large bowl. Make a well in the flour mixture and pour in the water, followed by 1 tablespoon of oil.

2. Turn the mixer on low to blend, or begin stirring the flour into the liquid with a wooden spoon, a little at a time. When ingredients are well combined, turn the mixer on medium-low to knead for 5 minutes. If working dough by hand, turn the dough onto a well-floured work surface. Use a pressing motion with the heels of your hands to push and stretch the dough. Work dough until mixture is slightly shiny and not too sticky to the touch. In the last few minutes of kneading, add cheese and work into dough until well blended.

3. The kneaded dough should be divided into four equal pieces. Store any dough not being used in a resealable bag in the refrigerator. Oil remaining dough and place in a bowl, covered, to rise for 1 hour. Punch the dough down, shape into two disks, and let rest for 30 minutes.

4. Grab dough by the edges, turning the disk a few inches at a time, allowing gravity to stretch the dough without tearing. Roll the dough into a crust shape or press into a pizza pan. Top as directed in recipe.

Makes crust for four 12-inch pizzas

2 (1-pound) loaves frozen bread dough, white or wheat
2 tablespoons olive oil

Speed-Scratch Crust

Get the fresh-baked smell of dough in the oven without all the from-scratch effort. Be sure to buy raw frozen bread dough and not partially baked frozen bread.

❊ ❊ ❊

1. Place bread dough on a work surface and cover with a damp, clean towel. Allow dough to thaw, then cut loaves in half with a sharp bread knife. Coat each dough section with olive oil, cover, and let stand until dough doubles in size and comes to room temperature, about 1 hour.
2. Punch dough down. Let rest 10 minutes, then roll into a round crust or press into a pizza pan. Follow recipe as directed.

Good to Go

Packaged pizza crusts can be found in the supermarket refrigerator case next to the biscuits and dinner rolls. While these products are fine for some purposes, actual bread dough is more likely to result in a thick, chewy crust. Except for the longer rising time, frozen bread dough isn't much harder to use than a roll-out crust.

Pizza Crust for the Grill

The mix of flours in this recipe gives the crust added texture and helps it stand up to the heat and smoke flavors of the grill.

* * *

Makes crust for four 12-inch pizzas

2 packages active dry yeast
1½ cups warm water, about 100°
1 teaspoon sugar
1½ teaspoons salt
5 cups bread flour
1 cup semolina flour
½ cup whole-wheat or rye flour
2 tablespoons olive oil

1. In a large measuring cup, dissolve yeast in water. Let stand 5 minutes or until bubbly. Combine sugar, salt, and all flours in the bowl of a mixer with a dough hook. Or, to mix by hand, place in a large bowl. Make a well in the flour mixture and pour in the water, followed by 1 tablespoon of oil.

2. Turn the mixer on low to blend, or begin stirring the flour into the liquid with a wooden spoon, a little at a time. When ingredients are well combined, turn the mixer on medium-low to knead for 5 minutes. If working dough by hand, turn the dough onto a well-floured work surface. Use a pressing motion with the heels of your hands to push and stretch the dough. Work dough until mixture is slightly shiny and not too sticky to the touch.

3. The kneaded dough should be divided into four equal pieces. Store any dough not being used in a resealable bag in the refrigerator. Oil remaining dough and place in a bowl, covered, to rise for 1 hour. Punch the dough down, shape into two disks, and let rest for 30 minutes.

4. Grab dough by the edges, turning the disk a few inches at a time, allowing gravity to stretch the dough without tearing. Roll the dough into a crust shape or press into a pizza pan. Top as directed in recipe.

Practice, Practice
While it may seem like "everybody" is making grilled pizza, the truth is that the technique requires a bit of practice. If you'd like to start slowly, try grilling your pie indoors on an electric breakfast griddle or heavy stovetop grill pan. Cook the crust on both sides, turning once, then top and slide into the oven to finish.

2 packages active dry yeast
1¹/₂ cups warm water,
    about 100°
¹/₃ cup sugar
1¹/₂ teaspoons salt
7 cups bread flour
2 tablespoons softened butter
1 egg, beaten
2 teaspoons vanilla

Sweet Crust

Depending on how you plan to top this dessert pizza crust, you might want to add a few shakes of cinnamon to the flour before mixing.

✳   ✳   ✳

1. In a large measuring cup, dissolve yeast in water. Let stand 5 minutes or until bubbly. Combine sugar, salt, and bread flour in the bowl of a mixer with a dough hook. Or, to mix by hand, place in a large bowl. Make a well in the flour mixture and pour in the water, followed by the butter, egg, and vanilla.

2. Turn the mixer on low to blend, or begin stirring the flour into the liquid with a wooden spoon, a little at a time. When ingredients are well combined, turn the mixer on medium-low to knead for 5 minutes. If working dough by hand, turn the dough onto a well-floured work surface. Use a pressing motion with the heels of your hands to push and stretch the dough. Work dough until mixture is slightly shiny and not too sticky to the touch.

3. The kneaded dough should be divided into four equal pieces. Store any dough not being used in a resealable bag in the refrigerator. Place remaining dough in a bowl, covered, to rise for 1 hour. Punch the dough down, shape into two disks, and let rest for 30 minutes.

4. Roll the dough into a crust shape or press into a pizza pan. Top as directed in recipe.

Sweet Treats
Dessert pizzas are a fairly new phenomenon, but the concept is as old as Danish pastries. Essentially, you're pairing a pastry or sweet roll crust with such toppings as fruit, cream, chocolate, dessert cheese, nuts, and custard. Come up with your own signature dessert pizza and wow your guests.

Chocolate Crust

Small chocolate chips or slivered almonds can be kneaded into this dough for an extra treat. In a pinch, this dough can be baked, cooled, and frosted for a quick tea-time treat.

✻　✻　✻

1. In a large measuring cup, dissolve yeast in water. Let stand 5 minutes or until bubbly. Combine sugar, salt, bread flour, and cocoa in the bowl of a mixer with a dough hook. Or, to mix by hand, place in a large bowl. Make a well in the flour mixture and pour in the water, followed by the butter, egg, and espresso.

2. Turn the mixer on low to blend, or begin stirring the flour into the liquid with a wooden spoon, a little at a time. When ingredients are well combined, turn the mixer on medium-low to knead for 5 minutes. If working dough by hand, turn the dough onto a well-floured work surface. Use a pressing motion with the heels of your hands to push and stretch the dough. Work dough until mixture is slightly shiny and not too sticky to the touch.

3. The kneaded dough should be divided into four equal pieces. Store any dough not being used in a resealable bag in the refrigerator. Place remaining dough in a bowl, covered, to rise for 1 hour. Punch the dough down, shape into two disks, and let rest for 30 minutes.

4. Roll the dough into a crust shape or press into a pizza pan. Top as directed in recipe.

Makes crust for four 12-inch pizzas

2 packages active dry yeast
1½ cups warm water, about 100°
½ cup sugar
1½ teaspoons salt
6⅓ cups bread flour
⅔ cup dark cocoa
2 tablespoons softened butter
1 egg, beaten
1 tablespoon brewed espresso

*Makes crust for one
12-inch pizza*

1 cup butter, softened
³/₄ cup white sugar
³/₄ cup brown sugar
1 teaspoon vanilla extract
2 eggs
2¹/₄ cups all-purpose flour
1 teaspoon salt
1 teaspoon baking soda
1 cup each dark, milk, and
     white chocolate chips

Cookie Pizza Crust

*This recipe makes only one thick dessert pizza cookie. If you
need more, make a separate batch for each pizza.
Doubling the recipe produces uneven results.*

✲   ✲   ✲

1. In a large bowl, cream butter with a mixer on medium speed. Add sugars and vanilla and beat until fluffy. Beat in eggs, one at a time, until well blended.

2. Combine flour, salt, and baking soda and stir with a whisk to break up any lumps. Slowly add to butter mixture and beat until well blended. Lightly stir in chocolate chips.

3. Press dough into a 12" pizza pan and bake at 375° for 30 minutes. Remove from oven and let cool in pan. Top as desired.

Dessert in a Hurry

If you're in a rush, do what mothers have been doing for decades: buy refrigerated cookie dough at the supermarket. Pick sugar cookie or chocolate chip dough, spread it into a pizza pan, and bake until just done. You'll get that great cookie-crust smell and minimal mess.

CHAPTER 3
Pizza Sauces and Spreads

Slow-Simmered Tomato Sauce

Makes 3 cups

---

1 tablespoon olive oil
6 ounces tomato paste
1 (29-ounce) can tomato sauce
4 cloves garlic, pressed
1 small onion, finely chopped
1 teaspoon sugar
1 teaspoon dried oregano
1/2 teaspoon dried basil
Pinch thyme
1 teaspoon red pepper flakes
Salt to taste
2 cups water

This basic, all-purpose pizza sauce can be prepared in large batches and frozen for later use.

* * *

1. In a large kettle over medium-high heat, combine olive oil and tomato paste. Cook, stirring with a wooden spoon, for 2 minutes. Add tomato sauce and stir to dissolve paste in the sauce.

2. Add remaining ingredients. Bring to boil, then reduce heat to medium and simmer for 2 to 3 hours, stirring often. Cooked sauce should be reduced and thick.

Speed-Scratch Tomato Sauce

Makes 4 cups

---

2 tablespoons olive oil
2 cloves garlic, minced
3 cups jarred pasta sauce
1 (15-ounce) can tomatoes with oregano and garlic
1/2 teaspoon red pepper flakes

Diced canned tomatoes come with a variety of seasoning options. Oregano and garlic is a classic mix for pizza, but other flavors might appeal to your tastes as well.

* * *

1. In a large saucepan, combine olive oil and garlic. Cook over medium heat, stirring, for 2 minutes. Add pasta sauce.

2. Place canned tomatoes with liquid in a blender and pulse until puréed. Add tomatoes to saucepan along with red pepper flakes. Bring mixture to a boil, then reduce heat and simmer for 20 minutes. Sauce should be reduced and thickened. Cool slightly before using in recipes.

Chunky Tomato Sauce

This sauce calls for a substantial crust to keep the coarsely chopped tomatoes contained and to soak up the herb-laced tomato juices.

✳   ✳   ✳

1. Place well-drained tomatoes in a food processor and pulse to chop. Tomatoes should be chunky, not puréed.

2. Pour tomatoes into a saucepan. Add tomato paste and remaining ingredients. Cook over medium heat for 10 minutes. Remove from heat and cool before using in recipes.

Cans on Hand

A ready supply of canned tomatoes—plain and seasoned—plus canned beans, canned broths, nut butters, and dried fruits make it easy to whip up an almost-from-scratch supper. Purée beans with a little broth and cumin and serve with a swirl of chopped tomatoes or sour cream for a simple soup. Or poach fish or chicken breasts in chunky tomato sauce.

Makes 4 cups

2 (28-ounce) cans plum
    tomatoes, drained
2 tablespoons tomato paste
4 cloves garlic, pressed
1 green onion, minced
1/4 cup minced fresh basil
1/4 cup minced fresh parsley
1 teaspoon sugar
Salt and pepper to taste

6 cups ripe tomatoes,
    small-diced
1 teaspoon salt
2 tablespoons extra virgin
    olive oil
1/3 cup fresh basil ribbons
Freshly ground black pepper

Fresh Tomato Sauce

*Never underestimate the power of salt and time. The salt
draws some of the water from the tomatoes, leaving
less volume but more flavor.*

✳   ✳   ✳

1. Place diced tomatoes in a colander and sprinkle with salt.
    Toss to mix well. Place colander over a bowl, cover loosely,
    and place in the refrigerator overnight.

2. Remove tomatoes from the refrigerator and lightly press
    the top with the back of a spoon to release more liquid.
    Spoon tomatoes from the colander to a bowl. Discard liquid.
    Drizzle olive oil over tomatoes and add basil ribbons. Add
    freshly ground black pepper and toss to combine.

Hours over a Hot Stove?

*Long cooking times can meld and condense flavors, making
the resulting sauce more substantial than the sum of its parts.
However, if you don't have time to watch a hot pot, try
cooking sauce in a slow-cooker. Just omit added water.*

Pesto Sauce

A little pesto sauce packs a lot of flavor. Experiment with a variety of herbs, nuts, and cheeses to create your own signature pesto.

❋ ❋ ❋

1. Combine basil, garlic, pine nuts, and cheeses in a food processor fitted with a metal blade. Pulse to finely chop ingredients.

2. With processor running, add olive oil to ingredients in a steady stream. Continue processing just until mixture is completely puréed and blended.

Makes 2 cups

2¹/₂ cups fresh basil leaves
6 cloves garlic, chopped
²/₃ cup pine nuts
²/₃ cup grated Parmesan
    cheese
¹/₄ cup grated Romano cheese
²/₃ cup extra virgin olive oil

Cilantro Pesto

Cilantro pesto is a great way to add the distinctive flavor of cilantro to Asian and Southwest-inspired recipes.

❋ ❋ ❋

1. Combine cilantro, parsley, garlic, lime zest, pecans, and cheeses in a food processor fitted with a metal blade. Pulse to finely chop ingredients.

2. With processor running, add olive oil to ingredients in a steady stream. Continue processing just until mixture is completely puréed and blended.

Makes 2 cups

2¹/₄ cups fresh cilantro leaves
¹/₄ cup fresh parsley leaves
6 cloves garlic, chopped
¹/₂ teaspoon grated lime zest
²/₃ cup pecans
²/₃ cup grated aged
    Manchego cheese
¹/₄ cup grated Parmesan
    cheese
²/₃ cup extra virgin olive oil

Garlic and Oil Sauce

Makes 2 cups

2 cups extra virgin olive oil
20 cloves garlic, minced
1 tablespoon minced fresh
    parsley
1/2 teaspoon red pepper flakes

Although this sauce is super-simple, care must be taken not to burn the garlic. Burnt garlic will make the sauce bitter.

❋　❋　❋

1. In a saucepan or skillet, warm the olive oil over medium-low heat. Add garlic, parsley, and red pepper flakes. Cook, stirring often, for 4 to 5 minutes or until garlic has softened.

2. Remove from heat and cool slightly before using in recipes. Excess sauce can be tossed with pasta and Parmesan or refrigerated for later use.

Cheesy Cream Sauce

Makes 3 cups

1/3 cup butter
4 cloves garlic, pressed
1 tablespoon finely minced
    green onion
1 1/3 cups heavy cream
1 1/4 cups shredded Parmesan
    cheese
1/4 cup shredded Romano
    cheese
Salt and freshly ground black
    pepper to taste

This version of classic Alfredo sauce makes a rich backdrop for veggie and seafood pizzas. Refrigerate any leftover sauce. It can be thinned with a little light cream or broth and used on pasta.

❋　❋　❋

1. In a heavy saucepan, melt butter over medium heat. Whisk in garlic and green onion and cook, stirring constantly, for 2 minutes. Slowly whisk in heavy cream. Cook until cream is hot and just starting to bubble at the edges of the pan.

2. Add Parmesan and Romano cheeses, a small amount at a time, whisking until cheese has melted. Add salt and pepper to taste and remove from heat. Cool slightly, then use in pizza recipes.

Barbecue Sauce

This sweet-tart sauce may be a little more intense than your average sauce for the grill. It's designed to stand up to substantial crusts and a range of ingredients.

* * *

1. In a large saucepan over medium-high heat, combine oil, onion, bell pepper, and garlic. Sauté for 3 to 4 minutes until vegetables begin to soften. Spoon into a blender. Add remaining ingredients and pulse to purée.

2. Return sauce mixture to the saucepan. Bring to a boil over medium-high heat, stirring constantly. Reduce heat to medium-low and simmer for 1½ hours, stirring often. Cool before using in pizza recipes.

Makes 3 cups

2 tablespoons vegetable oil
1 large onion, finely chopped
1 small green bell pepper, cored and chopped
3 cloves garlic, minced
3 tablespoons balsamic vinegar
Juice of 1 large lemon
1 tablespoon country Dijon mustard
2 tablespoons Worcestershire sauce
½ cup brown sugar
4 strips bacon, cooked
2⅓ cups ketchup
½ cup water
Tabasco sauce to taste

Horseradish Sauce

Horseradish root starts losing pungency once it is grated and exposed to air. For peak flavor, grate horseradish just before adding to the sauce.

* * *

1. In a heavy saucepan over medium heat, melt butter and sauté garlic briefly. Add horseradish, cream, cream cheese, and Parmesan. Whisk until all ingredients are blended and cheese has melted.

2. Cook sauce a few minutes until thick and bubbly. Add salt and pepper to taste. Remove from heat and cool slightly before using in recipes.

Makes 3 cups

2 tablespoons butter
4 cloves garlic, minced
4 tablespoons finely grated fresh horseradish
1 cup heavy cream
1 cup softened cream cheese
1 cup shredded Parmesan cheese
Salt and freshly ground black pepper to taste

¼ cup butter
4 cloves garlic, pressed
1 tablespoon finely minced
    green onion
1 cup heavy cream
1¼ cups shredded Parmesan
    cheese
1½ cups steamed spinach,
    drained
Salt and freshly ground black
    pepper to taste
Pinch nutmeg

Spinach Sauce

*Other green veggies, such as finely chopped cooked broccoli,
watercress, or artichoke hearts, can be substituted
for spinach in this recipe.*

* * *

1. In a heavy saucepan over medium heat, melt butter. Add garlic and green onion and cook, stirring constantly, for 2 minutes. Whisk in heavy cream and cook until simmering.

2. Whisk in Parmesan cheese, a little at a time, whisking until melted. Squeeze spinach to remove as much moisture as possible. Finely chop and add to the sauce along with salt, pepper, and nutmeg. Remove from heat. Cool slightly before using in pizza recipes.

Popeye's Passion

Iron-rich spinach is a low-calorie, high-flavor food and a good source of disease-fighting carotenoids and folate. Raw spinach should be purchased when leaves are fully green and spongy. To cook, rinse spinach well to remove sand and grit, then simply place in a covered pot over medium heat for a few minutes. The high water content of the greens makes added water unnecessary. Cooking reduces spinach volume by as much as three-fourths.

Sesame-Soy Sauce

Thickening this sauce with cornstarch keeps more sauce on the pizza crust. To use this sauce in stovetop cooking, the cornstarch can be omitted.

1. Combine soy sauce, sesame tahini, sesame oil, garlic, green onion, ginger, and maple syrup in a blender. Process until smooth.

2. Pour sauce into a heavy saucepan and bring to a boil. Dissolve cornstarch in 2 tablespoons cold water. Add to boiling sauce and stir until mixture is glossy and thickened. Stir in sesame seeds. Remove from heat, cool, and use in recipes.

A Soy Sauce by Any Name

A great variety of sauces made from soybeans are available, and their flavors range from light and briny to dark and bitter. The soy sauce–making process is as complicated as winemaking, and different Asian cultures produce sauces with different flavor profiles. In general, products marketed as soy sauce contain a wheat byproduct, whereas those marketed as tamari do not. Some soy sauces are fully produced from fermentation, while others use chemical accelerants to quicken the process. Sample several brands to find your favorite.

Makes 2 cups

1¹/₃ cups soy sauce
¹/₄ cup toasted sesame tahini
¹/₄ cup Asian sesame oil
2 cloves garlic, minced
1 green onion, minced
1 tablespoon grated ginger
2 tablespoons maple syrup
1 tablespoon cornstarch
2 tablespoons cold water
2 tablespoons sesame seeds

1 tablespoon olive oil
1 medium onion, finely diced
1 green bell pepper, finely
    diced
3 cloves garlic, minced
2 small jalapeño peppers,
    minced
2 cups diced canned
    tomatoes, drained
1 cup tomato sauce
1 tablespoon red wine
    vinegar
1 tablespoon sugar
1 teaspoon cumin
1 teaspoon chile powder
Salt to taste

Picante Sauce

*This is a cooked picante sauce, not the fresh salsa some
might expect. For a fresh salsa-type pizza sauce, use the
Fresh Tomato Sauce recipe, substitute cilantro for
the basil, and add a spike of lime juice.*

❋   ❋   ❋

1. In a large saucepan, combine olive oil, onion, bell pepper,
   garlic, and jalapeños. Sauté for 2 to 3 minutes until vegetables begin to soften.

2. Add remaining ingredients. Cook over medium-low heat,
   stirring often, for 30 minutes or until mixture thickens.
   Remove from heat and cool slightly before using in recipes.

Vim and Vinegar

*Vinegar gives many sauces and condiments their character-
istic bite, and a few drops can brighten a bland gravy or
bowl of beans. Experiment with fruity cider and wine
vinegars, sweet balsamic vinegars, and herb-spiked vinegars
when preparing sauces. Also, acidic vinegar is an excellent
tenderizer and flavoring agent when used in marinades.*

Sauce Piquant

In South Louisiana, cooks often prepare fish fillets or shellfish in a Sauce Piquant (which means spicy sauce) to be served over rice. Cooked until thick, it makes a fine pizza sauce.

1. In a heavy saucepan, heat oil over medium-high heat. Add flour and cook, stirring constantly, until flour turns a rich brown color. Add half the chopped onion and stir until onions begin to soften and brown.

2. Whisk in tomato sauce, stirring until flour and oil roux is completely dissolved in the liquid. Add chopped tomatoes, followed by remaining onion and all other ingredients, and bring to a full boil.

3. Reduce heat to medium and allow sauce to simmer for 2 hours, stirring often, particularly at the end of the cooking time. Cooked sauce should be reduced and very thick. Taste for seasoning and add more pepper, if desired.

Makes 3 cups

$1/4$ cup vegetable oil
$1/4$ cup flour
1 medium onion, finely chopped
2 cups tomato sauce
1 cup finely chopped fresh tomatoes
1 small green bell pepper, cored and finely diced
1 stalk celery, finely chopped
3 cloves garlic, pressed
$1/2$ teaspoon thyme
$1/4$ teaspoon cayenne pepper
$1/4$ teaspoon black pepper
1 to 2 teaspoons Tabasco sauce
2 cups water
Salt to taste

2 (15-ounce) cans refried
    beans
½ cup chunky commercial
    salsa
Pinch cumin

Refried Bean Spread

Refried black or pinto beans can be used in this recipe. If you use homemade refried beans instead of canned, make sure to cook the beans down until very thick.

1. In a saucepan or microwave-safe bowl, warm the refried beans until softened and easy to stir.

2. Stir in salsa and cumin, mixing until well blended. Spread beans over pizza crust as directed in recipes.

A Bounty of Beans

Nutrient-packed, protein-rich legumes add healthful fiber and flavor to foods. But when puréed, well-cooked beans take on a creamy texture that seems downright indulgent. Thin puréed beans with broth or milk for an excellent sauce base. Swirl in pesto or chopped peppers for color and enjoy over grilled poultry or firm fish.

Mustard Cream Sauce

Although tarragon is a classic flavor to pair with mustard, feel free to substitute lemon thyme, parsley, or dill. Likewise, using a coarse-ground mustard or hot English mustard in place of Dijon will give your sauce a different color and taste.

* * *

1. In a heavy saucepan over medium heat, melt butter. Add garlic and tarragon and cook for 2 minutes. Whisk in mustard and cream, stirring until well blended. Cook just until cream begins to bubble around the edges of the pan.

2. Add Parmesan cheese in handfuls, stirring until sauce is smooth and cheese has melted. Add salt and pepper to taste and remove from heat. Allow to cool slightly before using in recipes.

¹/₄ cup butter
4 cloves garlic, pressed
1 tablespoon finely minced fresh tarragon
2 tablespoons Dijon mustard
2 cups heavy cream
1¹/₄ cups shredded Parmesan cheese
Salt and freshly ground black pepper to taste

Lemon Cream Sauce

Once the cream has been whisked into the sauce, do not allow the mixture to boil and do not attempt to reheat the sauce.

* * *

1. In a heavy saucepan over medium heat, melt butter. Add sauce flour and cook, stirring, for 2 minutes. Add wine and lemon juice and whisk until smooth. Bring to a boil. Whisk in lemon zest, garlic, and herbs and cook for 2 minutes.

2. Turn heat to low. Slowly whisk cream into the mixture and cook just until hot but not simmering. Add Parmesan cheese to the sauce and remove from heat. Stir occasionally. Once cheese has melted, use sauce in recipes.

¹/₄ cup butter
2 tablespoons sauce flour
¹/₃ cup white wine
2 tablespoons fresh-squeezed lemon juice
1 teaspoon grated lemon zest
4 cloves garlic, pressed
1 tablespoon finely minced fresh parsley or dill
2 cups heavy cream
1 cup shredded Parmesan cheese
Salt and freshly ground black pepper to taste

4 egg yolks
²⁄₃ cup sugar
2 cups mascarpone cheese,
    softened
1 teaspoon vanilla

Sweet Mascarpone Sauce

Tiramisu lovers will recognize this sauce as a version of the mascarpone cream layered into the famous Italian dessert.

❋   ❋   ❋

1. Combine egg yolks and sugar in a heatproof bowl. Set bowl over a pan of very hot, but not boiling, water. Make sure the water does not come in contact with the bottom of the bowl. With an electric mixer on medium speed, beat eggs and sugar together for 3 to 5 minutes or until mixture is thick and the beaters leave a trail in the egg yolks. Remove from heat and allow to cool completely.

2. In a large bowl, combine softened mascarpone and the vanilla. Add egg yolk mixture to the cheese and beat until smooth. Cover and refrigerate until ready to use in recipes.

Mad for Mascarpone

Mascarpone is a fresh, triple-cream cheese made from cow's milk. It is soft and shiny, with a pleasant fresh-cream scent and luscious flavor. It's also expensive and sometimes hard to find. If you need a quick substitute, combine equal parts good-quality cream cheese and sour cream in a food processor.

Cream Cheese Sauce

An alternative to this dessert sauce would be ready-to-serve cheesecake filling that's available in the dairy section of many supermarkets.

* * *

1. In a large bowl, combine cream cheese and sour cream. Beat with a mixer until blended and smooth. Beat in confectioners' sugar, cream, and vanilla.

2. Cover and refrigerate until ready to use.

Makes 3½ cups

2 (8-ounce) packages cream cheese, softened
1 cup sour cream
1 cup confectioners' sugar
¼ cup heavy cream
2 teaspoons vanilla

Caramel Sauce

Always use a heavy, tall pot that will allow your caramel mixture to bubble up without spilling over.

* * *

1. Place sugar in a large saucepan over high heat. Whisk constantly as sugar melts, stirring crystals until the sugar becomes a golden brown liquid.

2. Add butter, one piece at a time, to the sugar and stir until melted. Remove pan from heat and add heavy cream. Whisk until cream is incorporated and sauce is creamy-smooth. Pour sauce into a heatproof glass bowl and allow to cool until just warm before using in recipes.

Makes 3 cups

2 cups sugar
¾ cup butter, in 4 to 6 pieces
1 cup heavy cream

1 cup heavy cream
1 tablespoon butter
2¹/₃ cups finely chopped
    dark chocolate

Chocolate Ganache

*Use your favorite brand of chocolate candy bar to make this
sauce. If desired, a small amount of liqueur can be added
to the melted chocolate mixture.*

✳ ✳ ✳

1. Combine cream and butter in a heavy saucepan. Place
   chopped chocolate in a dry, heatproof bowl. Bring cream
   and butter to a boil, then immediately pour over the chocolate. Let stand for 3 to 5 minutes.

2. Whisk melted chocolate and cream until smooth. Use as
   directed in recipes.

Glorious Chocolate

*Ganache is essentially chocolate melted in cream. For a light,
free-flowing sauce, use equal parts chocolate and cream.
For a sauce that's more substantial or that can be used as
a coating for candy or cakes (or as a base for dessert pizza),
increase the percentage of chocolate. To get a glossy coating,
add a little butter or corn syrup to the mix. Use top-quality
eating chocolate, not baking chocolate or chocolate chips,
to make the best ganache.*

Almond Paste

Make simple syrup for this recipe by bringing equal parts sugar and water to a boil in a heavy saucepan. Stir until sugar is melted, then allow to cool.

❋   ❋   ❋

Makes 3 cups

2 cups blanched almonds
2 cups confectioners' sugar
1 teaspoon almond extract
1 cup simple syrup
¼ cup heavy cream

1. In a food processor fitted with a metal blade, grind almonds to a fine powder. Add confectioners' sugar and process to blend. Stir almond extract into the simple syrup. With food processor motor running, pour syrup into the almond mixture in a steady stream. Process until a soft paste forms.

2. Divide paste into 2 portions and cover until ready to use in recipes. Add heavy cream by tablespoons to soften paste as needed.

Marzipan Moments
Almond paste can be mixed with additional sugar and corn syrup to make marzipan, a popular filling for European pastries and bonbons. Mix 8 ounces of almond paste with 2 cups confectioners' sugar and 3 to 4 tablespoons of corn syrup. The mixture should be the consistency of dense cookie dough. Roll marzipan into logs and refrigerate for several days to ripen, then slice marzipan disks and dip into chocolate or caramel coatings for quick candy treats.

3 cups chopped or mashed
     fresh fruit
2 cups sugar
1 cup whole berries or finely
     diced tree fruit

Fruit Sauce

*Use whole berries, pitted cherries, or peeled and diced apples,
pears, peaches, or plums for this recipe.*

✳   ✳   ✳

1. In a heavy saucepan, combine chopped or mashed fruit
   and sugar. Cook over medium heat, stirring constantly, until
   sugar dissolves and mixture comes to a boil.

2. Boil fruit mixture for 5 minutes. Remove from heat and stir
   in whole berries or diced fruit. Allow to cool.

CHAPTER 4
From Classic to Creative: Cheese Pizzas

¹/₂ recipe Classic Crust dough (page 16) or Bread Machine Crust dough (page 17)
2 tablespoons cornmeal or 1 tablespoon olive oil
1¹/₂ cups Slow-Simmered Tomato Sauce (page 40)
1 cup shredded Parmesan cheese
3 cups shredded mozzarella cheese

Classic Cheese Pizza

Coarsely grate mozzarella and Parmesan cheese just before topping pizzas for best flavor.

✳   ✳   ✳

1. Roll or press pizza dough into two 12-inch circles, slightly thicker at the edges than in the center. If using pizza pans, sprinkle the bottom with cornmeal or coat with olive oil and place dough in pan. If using a pizza stone, sprinkle with cornmeal and place stone in oven. Preheat oven to 400°.

2. Spread ¾ cup sauce in the center of each pizza, leaving at least an inch around the edges bare.

3. Sprinkle ½ cup Parmesan over the sauce on each pizza. Distribute 1½ cups mozzarella evenly over each pizza, just covering the sauce.

4. If using a hot stone or tiles, use a well-floured pizza peel to carefully lift one pizza from preparation surface and place on stone. If using pizza pans, place first pizza in the center of the oven. Bake for 15 to 20 minutes or until the crust is lightly browned and cheese is melted.

5. Remove pizza from oven carefully (use peel if baking with a stone). Set aside to rest briefly before slicing. Repeat baking process with second pie.

Baking Basics

Commercial pizza ovens reach extraordinarily high temperatures and cook pizza quickly. However, most home ovens lack the even heat and air circulation of commercial ovens. More moderate heat can help avoid raw crust and burnt cheese. If you'd like to experiment with higher temperatures, or if you're lucky enough to have a brick oven, by all means crank up the heat. But watch your pie carefully!

Six-Cheese Pizza

Like a stronger Asiago flavor? More smoky provolone? Go ahead and change the proportions of these cheeses to suit your taste.

✳   ✳   ✳

1. Roll or press pizza dough into two 12-inch circles, slightly thicker at the edges than in the center. If using pizza pans, sprinkle the bottom with cornmeal or coat with olive oil and place dough in pan. If using a pizza stone, sprinkle with cornmeal and place stone in oven. Preheat oven to 400°.

2. Spread ¾ cup sauce in the center of each pizza, leaving the edges bare.

3. In a large bowl, combine all the cheeses and toss gently to mix. Sprinkle half the cheese blend over the sauce on each pizza, leaving edges bare.

4. If using a hot stone or tiles, use a well-floured pizza peel to carefully lift one pizza from preparation surface and place on stone. If using pizza pans, place first pizza in the center of the oven. Bake for 15 to 20 minutes or until the crust is lightly browned and cheese is melted.

5. Remove pizza from oven carefully (use peel if baking with a stone). Set aside to rest briefly before slicing. Repeat baking process with second pie.

Peel Me a Pizza
Using a pizza peel effectively takes a little practice. The peel must be well coated with flour or cornmeal to keep raw dough from sticking to the wood. A gentle back-and-forth motion of the paddle can tell you whether your pizza is sticking or not. Cooked pizzas are more easily loaded onto the peel, but do keep a heavy-duty oven mitt over your free hand in case the pizza needs a little coaxing off the stone.

Makes two 12-inch pizzas

½ recipe Classic Crust dough (page 16) or Bread Machine Crust dough (page 17)

2 tablespoons cornmeal or 1 tablespoon olive oil

1½ cups Slow-Simmered Tomato Sauce (page 40) or Speed-Scratch Tomato Sauce (page 40)

1½ cups shredded mozzarella cheese

½ cup shredded provolone cheese

½ cup shredded Asiago cheese

½ cup shredded Parmesan cheese

½ cup shredded Romano cheese

½ cup shredded white Cheddar cheese

*½ recipe Chicago Deep-Dish
  Crust dough (page 19)
2 pounds sliced mozzarella
  cheese
4 cups Chunky Tomato Sauce
  (page 41)
1 cup shredded Parmesan
  cheese*

Deep-Dish Cheese Pizza

*This recipe makes the most basic casserole-style pizza.
Be sure to serve with forks and plenty of napkins.*

✳   ✳   ✳

1. Coat two 12" deep-dish pizza or pie pans with olive oil.
   Divide dough and press into pans, making sure dough goes
   all the way up the sides of the pans. Preheat oven to 450°.

2. Lay mozzarella slices over the crust of each pizza, using
   about half the mozzarella.

3. Pour 1½ cups sauce in the center of each pizza and spread
   evenly over the mozzarella. Lay remaining mozzarella slices
   evenly over the sauce. Spread remaining sauce over the
   cheese layer, dividing evenly over the two pizzas.

4. Sprinkle ½ cup Parmesan over the top of each pizza.

5. Reduce heat to 400° and bake pizzas for 20 to 25 minutes
   or until crust is light brown and centers are browned and
   bubbly.

Variations on a Theme
*For a more complex flavor profile, substitute sliced provolone
and Gruyère for some of the mozzarella and use shredded
Asiago cheese in place of the Parmesan in your Deep-Dish
Cheese Pizza.*

White Pizza

This flavorful, simple pizza makes a great appetizer or cocktail snack when cut into thin slices. Be sure to use top-quality oil and cheeses for best flavor.

✳   ✳   ✳

Makes two 12-inch pizzas

¹/₂ recipe California Thin Crust
    dough (page 21)
2 tablespoons cornmeal or
    1 tablespoon oil
2 cloves garlic, pressed
¹/₂ cup extra virgin olive oil
¹/₄ teaspoon kosher salt
1 cup shredded mozzarella
    cheese
¹/₂ cup shredded Parmesan
    cheese
¹/₂ cup shredded Asiago
    cheese

1. Roll or press pizza dough into two very thin 12-inch circles, slightly thicker at the edges than in the center. If using pizza pans, sprinkle the bottom with cornmeal or coat with oil and place dough in pan. If using a pizza stone, sprinkle with cornmeal and place rolled dough directly on stone.

2. Whisk pressed garlic into olive oil. Spread olive oil evenly over each pizza. Sprinkle each with kosher salt.

3. In a large bowl, combine all the cheeses and toss gently to mix. Sprinkle half the cheese blend over the oil on each pizza.

4. Place one pizza in the oven at 425°. Bake 10 to 12 minutes or until crust is browned and cheese is melted. Repeat with remaining pizza.

5. Let pizzas rest briefly, then slice with a sharp knife or pizza wheel.

White Pizza by Any Name

All White Pizza is not created equal. Some folks insist it isn't White Pizza without a thick layer of ricotta cheese, while others just look for a sprinkle of Parmesan over olive oil. In parts of Italy, Pizza Bianca is just flat bread painted with olive oil and sprinkled with herbs—no tomatoes or cheese.

½ recipe Classic Crust dough
(page 16) or Bread
Machine Crust dough
(page 17)
2 tablespoons cornmeal or
1 tablespoon olive oil
2 tablespoons extra virgin
olive oil
1 clove garlic, minced
1½ cups whole-milk ricotta
cheese
2 teaspoons fresh chopped
basil or 1 teaspoon dried
oregano
3 cups shredded mozzarella
cheese

Ricotta Pizza

*For many pizza lovers, this is the true white pizza.
Instead of tomato sauce, the crust is covered
with a rich cushion of ricotta cheese.*

✳   ✳   ✳

1. Roll or press pizza dough into two 12-inch circles, slightly thicker at the edges than in the center. If using pizza pans, sprinkle the bottom with cornmeal or coat with olive oil and place dough in pan. If using a pizza stone, sprinkle with cornmeal and place stone in oven. Preheat oven to 400°.

2. Brush 1 tablespoon extra virgin olive oil over each pizza, leaving edges bare. Sprinkle minced garlic evenly over the oil.

3. Combine ricotta with basil or oregano. Spread ¾ cup ricotta over each pizza, leaving one inch around the edges bare. Sprinkle 1½ cups mozzarella over each pizza.

4. If using a hot stone or tiles, use a well-floured pizza peel to carefully lift one pizza from preparation surface and place on stone. If using pizza pans, place first pizza in the center of the oven. Bake for 15 to 20 minutes or until the crust is lightly browned and cheese is melted.

5. Remove pizza from oven carefully (use peel if baking with a stone). Set aside to rest briefly before slicing. Repeat baking process with second pie.

Herbed Cottage Cheese Pizza

The cottage cheese in this recipe retains its chunky texture. If you prefer a smoother topping, place drained cottage cheese in a food processor and pulse until it resembles ricotta.

Makes two 12-inch pizzas

1/2 recipe Classic Crust dough (page 16), Bread Machine Crust dough (page 17), or Whole-Wheat Crust dough (page 22)
2 tablespoons cornmeal or 1 tablespoon olive oil
2 tablespoons extra virgin olive oil
2 cloves garlic
1 green onion, chopped
1/4 cup parsley leaves
2 tablespoons fresh basil leaves
2 cups large-curd cottage cheese, drained
1/2 teaspoon coarsely ground black pepper
2 cups shredded mozzarella cheese

1. Roll or press pizza dough into two 12-inch circles, slightly thicker at the edges than in the center. If using pizza pans, sprinkle the bottom with cornmeal or coat with olive oil and place dough in pan. If using a pizza stone, sprinkle with cornmeal and place stone in oven. Preheat oven to 400°.

2. Brush 1 tablespoon extra virgin olive oil over each pizza, leaving edges bare. In a food processor or chopper, combine garlic, green onion, parsley, and basil. Pulse until minced.

3. Combine drained cottage cheese with herbs. Spread 1 cup cottage cheese over each pizza, leaving one inch around the edges bare. Sprinkle coarsely ground pepper over the cottage cheese. Sprinkle 1 cup mozzarella over each pizza.

4. If using a hot stone or tiles, use a well-floured pizza peel to carefully lift one pizza from preparation surface and place on stone. If using pizza pans, place first pizza in the center of the oven. Bake for 15 to 20 minutes or until the crust is lightly browned and cheese is melted.

5. Remove pizza from oven carefully (use peel if baking with a stone). Set aside to rest briefly before slicing. Repeat baking process with second pie.

Rustic Repasts
Instead of same-old chicken salad sandwiches, treat guests at your next luncheon event to a warm, crusty cheese pizza and a salad of greens tossed with balsamic vinaigrette. For dessert, try berries and a dollop of crème fraiche or whipped cream.

½ recipe Classic Crust dough
(page 16) or Bread
Machine Crust dough
(page 17)
2 tablespoons cornmeal or
1 tablespoon olive oil
1½ cups Slow-Simmered
Tomato Sauce (page 40)
1 cup shredded Colby cheese
1½ cups shredded Cheddar
cheese
1½ cups shredded mozzarella
cheese

Cheddarama Delight

Serve this pizza the next time your son or daughter has friends over for a meal. All kids love pizza, and this version offers comfortably familiar flavors. For a more adult pizza, use extra-sharp Cheddar.

❉   ❉   ❉

1. Roll or press pizza dough into two 12-inch circles, slightly thicker at the edges than in the center. If using pizza pans, sprinkle the bottom with cornmeal or coat with olive oil and place dough in pan. If using a pizza stone, sprinkle with cornmeal and place stone in oven. Preheat oven to 400°.

2. Spread ¾ cup sauce in the center of each pizza, leaving edges bare.

3. Sprinkle ½ cup Colby cheese over the sauce on each pizza. Combine mozzarella and Cheddar cheeses. Distribute 1½ cups mozzarella-Cheddar mixture evenly over each pizza, leaving edges bare.

4. If using a hot stone or tiles, use a well-floured pizza peel to carefully lift one pizza from preparation surface and place on stone. If using pizza pans, place first pizza in the center of the oven. Bake for 15 to 20 minutes or until the crust is lightly browned and cheese is melted.

5. Remove pizza from oven carefully (use peel if baking with a stone). Set aside to rest briefly before slicing. Repeat baking process with second pie.

Family Fun

Next time you serve pizza for supper, allow each family member to dress his or her own pie. Divide dough into 6-inch circles instead of 12-inch and place chopped meats and veggies and shredded cheeses in small bowls, ready to pile on.

Farmhouse Cheese Pizza

*This combination of mild and intense boutique cheeses makes
a wonderfully complex, yet simple to make, pizza.*

✳ ✳ ✳

Makes two 12-inch pizzas

$^1/_2$ *recipe Classic Crust dough
(page 16) or Bread
Machine Crust dough
(page 17)*
*2 tablespoons cornmeal or
1 tablespoon olive oil*
*1$^1/_2$ cups Slow-Simmered
Tomato Sauce (page 40)*
*1 cup diced Farmhouse
Cheddar cheese*
*2 cups diced Farmhouse
Gouda cheese*
*1 cup diced Farmhouse
Blue cheese*

1. Roll or press pizza dough into two 12-inch circles, slightly thicker at the edges than in the center. If using pizza pans, sprinkle the bottom with cornmeal or coat with olive oil and place dough in pan. If using a pizza stone, sprinkle with cornmeal and place stone in oven. Preheat oven to 400°.

2. Spread ¾ cup sauce in the center of each pizza, leaving the edges bare.

3. Sprinkle ½ cup Cheddar over the sauce on each pizza. Distribute 1 cup Gouda and ½ cup Blue cheese evenly over each pizza, leaving edges bare.

4. If using a hot stone or tiles, use a well-floured pizza peel to carefully lift one pizza from preparation surface and place on stone. If using pizza pans, place first pizza in the center of the oven. Bake for 15 to 20 minutes or until the crust is lightly browned and cheese is melted.

5. Remove pizza from oven carefully (use peel if baking with a stone). Set aside to rest briefly before slicing. Repeat baking process with second pie.

Straight from the Farm

The label Farmhouse or Farmstead on a cheese doesn't refer to a type of cheese. Instead, it means the cheese was made in small batches using only the milk from cows on a particular dairy farm or from a particular district. Boutique creameries in New England, California, Michigan, and several other states all have their own farmhouse varieties, with distinctive flavor characteristics.

½ recipe California Thin Crust dough (page 21)
3 tablespoons extra virgin olive oil
2 tablespoons cornmeal
2 cups prepared pimiento cheese
2 cups shredded mozzarella cheese
1 cup shredded Colby cheese

Southern Pimiento Cheese Pizza

Every Southern cook knows of at least one family pimiento cheese recipe. You can buy this kitschy regional favorite in jars, but it just isn't the same as homemade.

✳   ✳   ✳

1. Roll or press pizza dough into two very thin 12-inch circles, slightly thicker at the edges than in the center. Divide 1 tablespoon olive oil over the bottoms of two pizza pans or large quiche pans. Sprinkle cornmeal over the oil, 1 tablespoon on each pan.

2. Brush remaining olive oil evenly over each pizza.

3. Preheat oven to 400°. Place pizza pans in the oven and bake until crust is lightly browned, about 7 minutes. Remove pizza crust and let rest for 5 minutes.

4. Spread 1 cup of pimiento cheese over the top of each pizza crust, followed by 1 cup of shredded mozzarella and ½ cup of shredded Colby.

5. Return pizzas to the oven and bake just until shredded cheese has melted. Let pizzas rest briefly, then slice with a sharp knife or pizza wheel.

Favorite Pimiento Cheese

In a food processor, combine 3 cups shredded Cheddar cheese, 4 ounces softened cream cheese, 1 cup mayonnaise, 1 4-ounce jar drained diced pimiento, 1 tablespoon sugar, 1 teaspoon Worcestershire sauce, and a pinch of red pepper. Process until smooth and a uniform coral-pink color. Keep covered in the refrigerator until ready to use.

Brie Pizza

*This rich pizza tastes wonderful as is, or with the addition of
a few shrimp, blanched asparagus, or a cup of lightly
sautéed fresh spinach leaves.*

* * *

1. Roll out two circles of dough. Coat pans with olive oil and sprinkle with cornmeal. Place dough circles in the pans and press dough up the sides.

2. Divide Garlic and Oil Sauce over the two pizzas and spread over the bottom of the crust.

3. Spread 1½ cups of halved grape tomatoes over each crust, followed by ½ cup of pine nuts. Divide Brie between the two pizzas and distribute evenly over the crusts. Sprinkle fresh basil leaves and ½ cup of Gruyère cheese over each pizza.

4. Preheat oven to 400°. Bake pizzas until crust is light brown and cheese is melted and bubbly, about 15 to 20 minutes.

Makes two 12-inch pizzas

$^1/_2$ *recipe Pan Pizza Crust
    dough (page 20)*
2 tablespoons olive oil
2 tablespoons cornmeal
$^1/_3$ *cup Garlic and Oil Sauce
    (page 44)*
*3 cups grape tomatoes,
    halved lengthwise*
1 cup toasted pine nuts
*1 pound Brie, rind removed,
    diced*
$^1/_4$ *cup fresh basil leaves*
*1 cup shredded Gruyère
    cheese*

½ recipe Pepper Crust dough
    (page 30), Classic Crust
    dough (page 16), or
    Bread Machine Crust
    dough (page 17)
2 tablespoons cornmeal or
    1 tablespoon olive oil
1½ cups Slow-Simmered
    Tomato Sauce (page 40)
1 cup shredded Colby cheese
2 cups shredded smoked
    Gouda cheese
1 cup shredded provolone
    cheese

Smoked Gouda Pizza

Mixing Colby and provolone with the Gouda gives this pizza layers of flavor. If you prefer a more intense Gouda experience, use all smoked Gouda or a mix of smoked and regular Gouda.

❉   ❉   ❉

1. Roll or press pizza dough into two 12-inch circles, slightly thicker at the edges than in the center. If using pizza pans, sprinkle the bottom with cornmeal or coat with olive oil and place dough in pan. If using a pizza stone, sprinkle with cornmeal and place stone in oven. Preheat oven to 400°.

2. Spread ¾ cup sauce in the center of each pizza, leaving one inch around the edges bare.

3. Sprinkle ½ cup Colby cheese over the sauce on each pizza. Combine provolone and smoked Gouda cheeses. Distribute 1½ cups provolone-Gouda mixture evenly over each pizza, covering the sauce.

4. If using a hot stone or tiles, use a well-floured pizza peel to carefully lift one pizza from preparation surface and place on stone. If using pizza pans, place first pizza in the center of the oven. Bake for 15 to 20 minutes or until the crust is lightly browned and cheese is melted.

5. Remove pizza from oven carefully (use peel if baking with a stone). Set aside to rest briefly before slicing. Repeat baking process with second pie.

Smoke and Spice
Mellow, smoky flavors pair wonderfully with piquant, spicy ingredients. Experiment with smoked cheeses and meats combined with finely chopped hot peppers or sweet-tart tomato or barbecue sauces on your pizzas.

Gruyère and Emmentaler Pizza

This is the classic Swiss fondue combination. Both cheeses offer a nutty-sweet flavor, although the Gruyère is a bit fruitier. Experiment with adding a few dried cherries or chopped apricots to this pizza for a tea snack.

1. Roll or press pizza dough into two very thin 12-inch circles, slightly thicker at the edges than in the center. If using pizza pans, sprinkle the bottom with cornmeal or coat with oil and place dough in pan. If using a pizza stone, sprinkle with cornmeal and place rolled dough directly on stone.

2. Whisk pressed garlic into Lemon Cream Sauce. Spread ½ cup sauce evenly over each pizza. Sprinkle parsley over the sauce.

3. In a large bowl, combine the two cheeses and toss gently to mix. Sprinkle half the cheese blend over the sauce on each pizza.

4. Place one pizza in the oven at 425°. Bake 10 to 12 minutes or until crust is browned and cheese is melted. Repeat with remaining pizza.

5. Let pizzas rest briefly, then slice with a sharp knife or pizza wheel.

Makes two 12-inch pizzas

$^1/_2$ recipe California Thin Crust dough (page 21)
2 tablespoons cornmeal or 1 tablespoon oil
2 cloves garlic, pressed
1 cup Lemon Cream Sauce (page 51)
$^1/_4$ cup chopped fresh parsley
$1^1/_2$ cups shredded Gruyère cheese
$1^1/_2$ cups shredded Emmentaler cheese

*1/2 recipe Spinach Crust dough
    (page 29), Classic Crust
    dough (page 16), or
    Bread Machine Crust
    dough (page 17)
2 tablespoons cornmeal or
    1 tablespoon olive oil
1 1/2 cups Fresh Tomato Sauce
    (page 42)
1 1/2 cups shredded mozzarella
    cheese
2 cups crumbled bleu cheese
1/4 cup minced parsley
2 tablespoons minced
    green onion
Black pepper to taste*

Bleu Cheese Pizza

*Make this pizza a little richer, if you like, with the addition of
coarsely chopped, roasted walnuts. Sprinkle nuts over
the herbs just before baking.*

✳   ✳   ✳

1. Roll or press pizza dough into two 12-inch circles, slightly thicker at the edges than in the center. If using pizza pans, sprinkle the bottom with cornmeal or coat with olive oil and place dough in pan. If using a pizza stone, sprinkle with cornmeal and place stone in oven. Preheat oven to 400°.

2. Spread ¾ cup sauce in the center of each pizza, leaving one inch around the edges bare.

3. Sprinkle half the mozzarella cheese over the sauce on each pizza. Spread 1 cup crumbled bleu cheese evenly over each pizza, leaving edges bare. Sprinkle parsley and green onion over cheeses, along with black pepper to taste.

4. If using a hot stone or tiles, use a well-floured pizza peel to carefully lift one pizza from preparation surface and place on stone. If using pizza pans, place first pizza in the center of the oven. Bake for 15 to 20 minutes or until the crust is lightly browned and cheese is melted.

5. Remove pizza from oven carefully (use peel if baking with a stone). Set aside to rest briefly before slicing. Repeat baking process with second pie.

Gorgonzola Pizza Tarts

Makes 8 tarts

$^1/_2$ recipe No-Yeast Crust
    dough (page 27)
Oil for coating pans
2 cups Cheesy Cream Sauce
    (page 44)
$^1/_2$ cup chopped sun-dried
    tomatoes
Black pepper to taste
$2^2/_3$ cups crumbled
    Gorgonzola cheese
1 cup chopped toasted
    pecans
1 cup shredded mozzarella
    cheese

*Round or fluted tart pans can be used for this recipe. Individual quiche
or crème brûlèe dishes will work for these savory little pies as well.*

✳   ✳   ✳

1. Divide dough into eight portions. Press each portion into an oil-coated tart pan, pressing dough evenly up the sides of the pan.

2. Spoon ¼ cup sauce into each tart shell. Divide chopped sun-dried tomatoes evenly over sauce in each tart. Grind fresh black pepper to taste over each tart.

3. Place ⅓ cup Gorgonzola crumbles into each tart. Then sprinkle each tart with pecans and mozzarella cheese.

4. Place tart pans on baking sheets and bake at 350° for 10 to 15 minutes or until crusts have browned and centers are bubbly.

5. Cool slightly, then serve in individual tart pans.

Speaking Personally
Individual pizzas make perfect luncheon entrees when served with a simple salad and a glass of wine or fruity tea. If you stick to pan-type pizzas, which can be served in the baking dish, they're also incredibly easy to prepare.

1½ pound log of Chevre,
    very well chilled
2 eggs
¼ cup half-and-half
2 cups seasoned dry bread
    crumbs
Oil for frying
½ recipe California Thin Crust
    dough (page 21)
2 tablespoons olive oil
1½ cups Slow-Simmered
    Tomato Sauce (page 40)
3 cups shredded mozzarella
    cheese

Fried Cheese Pizza

This take off on the ever-popular fried goat cheese salad is both unusual and fun. To serve this dish to kids and teens, substitute fried mozzarella sticks for the more intensely flavored goat cheese.

✳   ✳   ✳

1. Slice Chevre into twelve even rounds. Whisk together eggs and half-and-half in a shallow bowl. Pour bread crumbs onto a plate. Dip cheese rounds into egg mixture, then coat with bread crumbs.

2. Pour about 2 inches of oil into a large, deep skillet and place over medium-high heat. When oil is hot, fry cheese quickly, a few slices at a time. Slices are done when coating turns a toasty brown. Set fried slices on paper towels to drain.

3. Coat two 12" pizza pans with olive oil. Roll out or press dough into pans to cover the bottoms. Spread ¾ cup pizza sauce over each pizza, then sprinkle each pizza with 1½ cups mozzarella.

4. Bake pizzas in a preheated 400° oven for 10 minutes. Add six fried cheese rounds to each pizza, allowing one round per slice. Continue baking pizzas for another 5 to 10 minutes or until crust is browned.

Feta and Black Olive Pizza

This pizza pays homage to Greece, the original home of meals prepared on an edible bread "plate."

* * *

1. Roll or press pizza dough into two 12-inch circles, slightly thicker at the edges than in the center. If using pizza pans, sprinkle the bottom with cornmeal or coat with olive oil and place dough in pan. If using a pizza stone, sprinkle with cornmeal and place stone in oven. Preheat oven to 400°.

2. Spread ¾ cup sauce in the center of each pizza, leaving one inch around the edges bare.

3. Sprinkle ¾ cup mozzarella cheese over the sauce on each pizza. Distribute 1 cup crumbled feta evenly over each pizza, leaving edges bare. Evenly distribute olives and oregano leaves, then grind black pepper to taste over each pizza.

4. If using a hot stone or tiles, use a well-floured pizza peel to carefully lift one pizza from preparation surface and place on stone. If using pizza pans, place first pizza in the center of the oven. Bake for 15 to 20 minutes or until the crust is lightly browned and cheese is melted.

5. Remove pizza from oven carefully (use peel if baking with a stone). Set aside to rest briefly before slicing. Repeat baking process with second pie.

More on Mozzarella

Adding mozzarella to specialty cheese pizzas like feta and Gorgonzola gives the pie more cheesy taste and texture without making the flavor overwhelming. If you're a hard-core pungent cheese fan, by all means up the proportion of your favorite variety.

Makes two 12-inch pizzas

½ recipe Spinach Crust dough
(page 29), Classic Crust
dough (page 16), or
Bread Machine Crust
dough (page 17)
2 tablespoons cornmeal or
1 tablespoon olive oil
1½ cups Slow-Simmered
Tomato Sauce (page 40)
1½ cups shredded mozzarella
cheese
2 cups crumbled feta cheese
1 cup chopped kalamata
olives
¼ cup fresh oregano leaves
Black pepper to taste

Makes two 12-inch pizzas

$^1/_2$ recipe Cornmeal Crust
  dough (page 25), Classic
  Crust dough (page 16),
  or Bread Machine Crust
  dough (page 17)
2 tablespoons cornmeal or
  1 tablespoon olive oil
$1^1/_2$ cups Slow-Simmered
  Tomato Sauce (page 40)
  or Picante Sauce (page 48)
2 cups shredded Colby cheese
2 cups shredded Monterey
  jack cheese
2 small jalapeño peppers,
  minced (optional)

Colby and Monterey Jack Pizza

This is a mild but satisfying pizza that's highly adaptable to other ingredients. Try it with a layer of leftover chili instead of pizza sauce, or top the cheese with a layer of ground beef and crumbled bacon for a cheeseburger flavor.

❋   ❋   ❋

1. Roll or press pizza dough into two 12-inch circles, slightly thicker at the edges than in the center. If using pizza pans, sprinkle the bottom with cornmeal or coat with olive oil and place dough in pan. If using a pizza stone, sprinkle with cornmeal and place stone in oven. Preheat oven to 400°.

2. Spread ¾ cup sauce in the center of each pizza, leaving one inch around the edges bare.

3. Combine Colby and Monterey jack cheeses. Distribute 2 cups cheese mixture evenly over each pizza, leaving edges bare. Sprinkle with minced pepper, if desired.

4. If using a hot stone or tiles, use a well-floured pizza peel to carefully lift one pizza from preparation surface and place on stone. If using pizza pans, place first pizza in the center of the oven. Bake for 15 to 20 minutes or until the crust is lightly browned and cheese is melted.

5. Remove pizza from oven carefully (use peel if baking with a stone). Set aside to rest briefly before slicing. Repeat baking process with second pie.

Hot Stuff

Fresh hot peppers contain oils that can seep into your skin and cause painful burns. Work quickly and rinse hands often when chopping peppers, or use thin latex gloves to cover your hands. Seeding peppers before adding them to food will make your dish less spicy.

Spicy Queso Pizza

This may not be the pizza you make for your ultra-sophisticated friends, but it has comfort-food familiarity for those of us who grew up eating Ro-Tel dip.

* * *

Makes two 12-inch pizzas

1/2 recipe Cornmeal Crust dough (page 25)
2 tablespoons cornmeal or 1 tablespoon olive oil
1/2 cup Slow-Simmered Tomato Sauce (page 40) or Speed-Scratch Tomato Sauce (page 40)
1 (10-ounce) can tomatoes with green chiles, drained
3 cups crumbled processed cheese
1 cup shredded mozzarella cheese

1. Roll or press pizza dough into two 12-inch circles, slightly thicker at the edges than in the center. If using pizza pans, sprinkle the bottom with cornmeal or coat with olive oil and place dough in pan. If using a pizza stone, sprinkle with cornmeal and place stone in oven. Preheat oven to 400°.

2. Combine sauce and drained tomatoes with green chiles. Divide sauce over the two pizzas and spread from the center, leaving one inch around the edges bare.

3. Distribute 1½ cups crumbled processed cheese evenly over each pizza, leaving edges bare. Sprinkle each pizza with mozzarella.

4. If using a hot stone or tiles, use a well-floured pizza peel to carefully lift one pizza from preparation surface and place on stone. If using pizza pans, place first pizza in the center of the oven. Bake for 15 to 20 minutes or until the crust is lightly browned and cheese is melted.

5. Remove pizza from oven carefully (use peel if baking with a stone). Set aside to rest briefly before slicing. Repeat baking process with second pie.

½ recipe Classic Crust dough
(page 16) or Herb-Laced
Crust dough (page 28)
2 tablespoons cornmeal or
1 tablespoon olive oil
1½ cups Slow-Simmered
Tomato Sauce (page 40)
or Picante Sauce (page 48)
1½ cups crumbled Manchego
cheese
1 cup shredded Monterey jack
cheese
1½ cups shredded mozzarella
cheese
½ cup chopped cilantro

Manchego Cheese Pizza

Manchego cheese originated in Spain and is widely produced in Mexico and the U.S. The longer it is aged, the more dry and sharp the cheese becomes. The firm, crumbly texture of aged Manchego makes it excellent for grating.

✳   ✳   ✳

1. Roll or press pizza dough into two 12-inch circles, slightly thicker at the edges than in the center. If using pizza pans, sprinkle the bottom with cornmeal or coat with olive oil and place dough in pan. If using a pizza stone, sprinkle with cornmeal and place stone in oven. Preheat oven to 400°.

2. Spread ¾ cup sauce in the center of each pizza, leaving edges bare.

3. Sprinkle ¾ cup crumbled Manchego cheese over the sauce on each pizza. Combine Monterey jack and mozzarella cheeses. Distribute 1¼ cups jack-mozzarella mixture evenly over each pizza, leaving edges bare. Top each with chopped cilantro.

4. If using a hot stone or tiles, use a well-floured pizza peel to carefully lift one pizza from preparation surface and place on stone. If using pizza pans, place first pizza in the center of the oven. Bake for 15 to 20 minutes or until the crust is lightly browned and cheese is melted.

5. Remove pizza from oven carefully (use peel if baking with a stone). Set aside to rest briefly before slicing. Repeat baking process with second pie.

Pizza Alfredo

This hearty, thick-crust pizza is a great dish to bring to potlucks. Cut it into 8 slices for an entrée portion or 16 for a cocktail buffet serving.

* * *

1. On a floured board, roll pizza dough into a rectangle. Coat a 9" × 16" metal baking dish with olive oil and sprinkle with cornmeal. Press dough into the pan, spreading it to the corners.

2. Spread Cheesy Cream Sauce over the top of the dough. Grind black pepper over sauce to taste.

3. Combine Parmesan, Asiago, Romano, and mozzarella cheeses. Spread evenly over the top of the sauce. Sprinkle with rosemary.

4. Preheat oven to 400°. Bake 20 to 25 minutes or until top is browned and bubbly.

Pizza Sicilian Style
Thick bread with simple toppings is sold in small shops all over central and southern Italy. In Sicily, the progenitor of the dish Americans call "Sicilian Pizza" is a dish called sfincione, *which is essentially a thick slab of bread dough topped with sausage, anchovies, olive oil, and oregano and baked.*

Makes one 9 x 16-inch pizza

½ recipe Sicilian Crust dough (page 18)
2 tablespoons olive oil
2 tablespoons cornmeal
2 cups Cheesy Cream Sauce (page 44)
Black pepper to taste
1 cup shredded Parmesan cheese
1 cup shredded Asiago cheese
1 cup shredded Romano cheese
2 cups shredded mozzarella cheese
2 tablespoons fresh rosemary

1 recipe No-Yeast Crust dough
    (page 27)
1 tablespoon olive oil
$1/2$ cup Pesto Sauce (page 43)
2 pounds cream cheese
6 ounces goat cheese
$1/2$ cup sour cream
6 eggs
1 cup shredded mozzarella
    cheese
Black pepper to taste

Savory Cheesecake Pizza

*This dish has its roots in ricotta-topped pizzas. Serve it in small
slices with a side of mixed greens or pear slices for
a small plate or appetizer course.*

❊   ❊   ❊

1. Divide dough into two portions and roll into 12-inch circles. Oil two 12" tart pans and press dough into the pans and up the sides. Put nonstick foil over center of crust and fill with dried beans or pie weights. Bake at 350° for 10 minutes. Remove from oven, remove foil, and let crusts cool slightly.

2. Brush insides of tart shells with Pesto Sauce.

3. In a large bowl, combine cream cheese, goat cheese, and sour cream. Beat with an electric mixer on medium speed until creamy. Add eggs one at a time, beating each until completely incorporated.

4. Pour cheesecake batter into tart pans and sprinkle shredded mozzarella over each. Grind black pepper to taste over each tart.

5. Bake pies for 30 minutes at 350° or until center is set. Serve at room temperature.

CHAPTER 5
Veggie Pizzas Even Carnivores Will Love

1/2 recipe California Thin Crust
   dough (page 21)
3 tablespoons olive oil
2 tablespoons cornmeal
2 cups Fresh Tomato Sauce
   (page 42)
2/3 cup finely diced carrots
1/3 cup finely diced celery
1/3 cup finely diced red onion
2/3 cup finely diced zucchini
2/3 cup finely chopped
   mushrooms
1/3 cup minced fresh herbs
4 cups mozzarella crumbles

Chopped Salad Pizza

*Choose any herbs you like to give this pizza a signature flavor.
A mix of parsley, green onion, and basil is a great place to start.*

✳ ✳ ✳

1. Roll or press pizza dough into two thin 12-inch circles, slightly thicker at the edges than in the center. Divide 1 tablespoon olive oil over the bottoms of two pizza pans or large quiche pans. Sprinkle cornmeal over the oil, 1 tablespoon on each pan.

2. Preheat oven to 400°. Place pizza pans in the oven and bake until crust is lightly browned, about 7 minutes. Remove from the oven and spoon 1 cup of tomato sauce over each pizza.

3. Combine carrots, celery, onion, zucchini, and mushrooms in a bowl. Toss with remaining olive oil until vegetables are coated. Divide vegetables evenly over each pizza.

4. Sprinkle fresh herbs evenly over the top of the vegetables. Top each pizza with 2 cups of mozzarella cheese.

5. Return pizzas to the oven and bake until cheese has melted and crusts darken slightly, about 5 to 7 minutes. Let pizzas rest briefly, then slice with a sharp knife or pizza wheel.

Lunch Crunch

Warmed but still crisp salad veggies give pizza a unique texture that's perfect for lunch or a hearty mid-afternoon tea offering. Serve with a cup of creamy squash or tomato bisque for a vegetarian feast.

Wild Mushroom Melt Pizza

A mix of different types of mushrooms gives this pizza layers of flavor and texture. For an artistic pie, distribute mushroom slices, flat mushrooms, and chopped mushrooms in an alternating pattern.

1. Roll or press pizza dough into two 12-inch circles, slightly thicker at the edges than in the center. If using pizza pans, sprinkle the bottom with cornmeal or coat with olive oil and place dough in pan. If using a pizza stone, sprinkle with cornmeal and place stone in oven. Preheat oven to 400°.

2. Spread ¾ cup sauce in the center of each pizza, leaving one inch around the edges bare.

3. In a large skillet, heat 2 tablespoons butter until bubbling. Add garlic and mushrooms and sauté until mushrooms are crisp-tender. Sprinkle with parsley.

4. With a slotted spoon, remove mushrooms from the skillet, draining as much liquid as possible. Distribute mushrooms evenly over pizza sauce.

5. Sprinkle ½ cup Asiago cheese over the mushrooms on each pizza. Then spread 1½ cups mozzarella evenly over each pizza, leaving edges bare.

6. If using a hot stone or tiles, use a well-floured pizza peel to carefully lift one pizza from preparation surface and place on stone. If using pizza pans, place first pizza in the center of the oven. Bake for 15 to 20 minutes or until the crust is lightly browned and cheese is melted.

7. Remove pizza from oven carefully (use peel if baking with a stone). Set aside to rest briefly before slicing. Repeat baking process with second pie.

Makes two 12-inch pizzas

---

¹/₂ recipe Classic Crust dough (page 16) or Bread Machine Crust dough (page 17)

2 tablespoons cornmeal or 1 tablespoon olive oil

1¹/₂ cups Slow-Simmered Tomato Sauce (page 40)

2 tablespoons unsalted butter

2 cloves garlic, minced

4 cups mixed wild mushrooms, coarsely chopped

¹/₄ cup minced fresh parsley

1 cup shredded Asiago cheese

3 cups shredded mozzarella cheese

½ recipe Focaccia Crust
   dough (page 32)
2 tablespoons olive oil
1 cup Pesto Sauce (page 43)
   or Garlic and Oil Sauce
   (page 44)
1 cup shredded Parmesan
   cheese
3 cups diced fresh mozzarella
   cheese
8 medium heirloom tomatoes,
   thinly sliced
¼ cup fresh basil ribbons
Freshly ground black pepper
   to taste

Heirloom Tomato Pizza

This pizza combines the classic flavors of creamy fresh mozzarella, sweet tomatoes, and basil with a substantial breadlike crust.

✳   ✳   ✳

1. Roll focaccia dough into two 12-inch circles. Grease deep-dish pizza pans with olive oil and press dough into the pans. Bake at 400° for 15 minutes, or until focaccias have just begun to brown.

2. Remove from oven and carefully spread Pesto Sauce or Garlic and Oil Sauce over each crust. Sprinkle with Parmesan cheese. Distribute 1 cup of the mozzarella evenly over the pizzas. Arrange tomato slices in overlapping concentric circles over the cheese, then sprinkle remaining diced mozzarella over tomatoes.

3. Sprinkle basil ribbons over each pizza and add freshly ground black pepper to taste.

4. Return pans to oven and bake for 10 minutes, or just long enough for mozzarella to melt and tomato slices to become warm and soft.

5. Remove from oven and let stand for a few minutes before slicing.

Vintage Beauties

Heirloom tomatoes come in a beautiful array of colors, ranging from pale green to orange to crimson, with plenty of mottled or striped varieties in between. Pick vine-ripened tomatoes in different shades for an eye-catching dish. Warmed heirloom tomatoes taste like summer on a plate.

Spinach-Artichoke Pie

If you have the time and energy to boil and clean fresh artichokes, by all means do so. Otherwise, frozen or canned artichoke bottoms will work just fine for this pizza.

1. Roll pizza dough into two circles large enough to cover bottom and sides of two 12" pizza or quiche pans. Spread a tablespoon of olive oil over the bottom of each pan, then press dough circles into the pans.

2. Ladle 1 cup of sauce into each pan and spread evenly over the crust.

3. In a large, flat-bottomed wok or Dutch oven, combine washed spinach leaves, garlic, and butter. Sauté just until spinach has wilted. Remove spinach to a fine sieve and press out as much liquid as possible.

4. Distribute cooked spinach evenly over each pizza crust, then sprinkle artichokes evenly over the spinach.

5. Spread Parmesan cheese over each pizza, then do the same with the mozzarella. Add freshly ground black pepper to taste. Bake pans in a preheated oven at 400° until crust has browned and cheese is bubbly, about 20 minutes.

$^1/_2$ recipe Pan Pizza Crust
   dough (page 20)
2 tablespoons olive oil
2 cups Cheesy Cream Sauce
   (page 44)
2 pounds spinach leaves,
   stemmed and washed
1 teaspoon minced garlic
1 tablespoon butter
3 cups coarsely chopped
   cooked artichoke
   bottoms
$1^1/_2$ cups Parmesan cheese
$2^1/_2$ cups mozzarella cheese
Freshly ground black pepper

Makes two 12-inch pizzas

2 large or 3 medium
    eggplants, sliced
    horizontally ¼-inch thick
1 to 2 teaspoons coarse salt
2 eggs
¼ cup milk
4 cups fine seasoned bread
    crumbs
Vegetable oil for frying
½ recipe Chicago Deep-Dish
    Crust dough (page 19)
2 tablespoons olive oil
4 cups Chunky Tomato Sauce
    (page 41)
2 cups shredded Parmesan
    cheese
4 cups shredded mozzarella
    cheese

Eggplant Parmesan Pizza

To make this pie with fewer calories, don't batter and fry the eggplant slices. Instead, spritz slices with cooking spray and bake at 400° until slightly softened. Then use as directed on pizza.

✳   ✳   ✳

1. Discard ends of eggplants. Sprinkle slices with coarse salt and set in a sieve or on paper towels to drain for 20 minutes. Rinse salt from eggplant slices and pat dry with paper towels.

2. Whisk together eggs and milk. Pour bread crumbs onto a large plate or pie pan. Dip each eggplant slice in egg mixture and coat lightly with seasoned bread crumbs.

3. In a large skillet, pour oil to a depth of about 2 inches. Heat over medium-high heat until a drop of water sizzles in the oil. Fry eggplant slices, a few at a time, until browned. Drain on paper towels.

4. Roll out two circles of pizza dough. Spread olive oil in two 12" deep-dish pizza or pie pans. Press dough circles into pans and prick bottoms a few times with a fork. Ladle 2 cups of tomato sauce into each pan, followed by ½ cup of Parmesan cheese and ½ cup of mozzarella cheese.

5. Arrange fried eggplant slices over the cheese, overlapping as necessary. Divide remaining 1 cup of Parmesan and 3 cups mozzarella over the eggplant slices. Bake at 400° until browned and bubbly, about 20 minutes.

Eggplant Savvy

Buy firm, unblemished eggplants that seem heavy for their size. Large eggplants with a lot of dark seeds inside will be more bitter tasting than those with white or pale brown seeds. Salting eggplants before preparing draws some of the bitter liquid from the vegetable and results in more compact, meatier slices.

Roasted Pepper and Caramelized Onion Pie

This pie pays homage to the French pissaladière, *a crust topped with olive oil, onions, and anchovies. It can easily go cheeseless for those who want a dairy-free dish.*

✳ ✳ ✳

Makes two 12-inch pizzas
_____

2 large Vidalia onions, sliced
3 tablespoons butter
$1/2$ teaspoon sugar
1 large green bell pepper
1 large red bell pepper
$1/2$ recipe California Thin Crust dough (page 21)
2 tablespoons olive oil or 2 tablespoons cornmeal
1 cup Slow-Simmered Tomato Sauce (page 40)
1 cup Asiago cheese (optional)
Freshly ground black pepper to taste

1. In a large skillet or Dutch oven, combine onions, butter, and sugar. Cook over medium heat, stirring often, until onions turn a rich brown.

2. To roast peppers, hold over a hot grill or open flame with a long-handled fork until skin is charred and blistered. (If it's more convenient, peppers can be cored and halved, then roasted on a rack in the oven until skin chars.) Place peppers in a paper or resealable plastic bag and close loosely. Allow to cool for 10 to 15 minutes, then peel off the charred skin. Core and seed peppers and cut into vertical strips.

3. Roll dough into two 12-inch circles, slightly thicker at the edges than in the center. If using pizza pans, sprinkle the bottom with cornmeal or coat with olive oil and place dough in pan. If using a pizza stone, sprinkle with cornmeal and place stone in oven. Preheat oven to 400°.

4. Spread a thin layer of pizza sauce over each crust, leaving one inch around the edges bare. Sprinkle pizzas with Asiago cheese, if desired. Spread a tangle of caramelized onions over the sauce. Arrange strips of roasted peppers in alternating colors in a spoke pattern over the pizzas.

5. Bake pizzas, one at a time if necessary, at 400° in the center of the oven for 15 minutes or until browned. Remove and let stand for 5 minutes, then slice and serve.

Makes two 12-inch pizzas

½ recipe California Thin Crust
    dough (page 21)
2 tablespoons cornmeal or
    1 tablespoon oil
1 cup Lemon Cream Sauce
    (page 51)
¼ cup chopped fresh parsley
1 pound thinly sliced
    Butterkase cheese
1 pound blanched asparagus
    spears, trimmed
Freshly ground black pepper
    to taste

Asparagus and Butterkase Cheese Pizza

Butterkase cheese is a mild, semisoft cheese that comes in both smoked and regular versions. To vary this pizza, use a combination of smoked and plain Butterkase slices.

❊ ❊ ❊

1. Roll or press pizza dough into two very thin 12-inch circles, slightly thicker at the edges than in the center. If using pizza pans, sprinkle the bottom with cornmeal or coat with oil and place dough in pan. If using a pizza stone, sprinkle with cornmeal and place rolled dough directly on stone.

2. Spread ½ cup Lemon Cream Sauce evenly over each pizza. Sprinkle parsley over the sauce.

3. Layer half the cheese slices, overlapping, over the sauce on each pizza. Arrange asparagus spears in a spoke pattern on top of each pizza. Sprinkle with freshly ground black pepper.

4. Place one pizza in the oven at 425°. Bake 10 to 12 minutes or until crust is browned and cheese is melted. Repeat with remaining pizza.

5. Let pizzas rest briefly, then slice with a sharp knife or pizza wheel.

Pick a Peck
Almost any vegetable can become the star attraction on a pizza, although some slow-cooking veggies should be blanched first. Try topping a white pizza with thinly sliced parboiled potatoes, drizzled with oil and garlic and topped with plenty of fresh herbs and a cheese blend.

Fried Green Tomato Pizza

Fried green tomatoes are made with tart, not-yet-ripe tomatoes.
Some cooks prefer to simply dredge seasoned tomato slices
in cornmeal and fry, skipping the egg-milk dip.

❉   ❉   ❉

Makes two 12-inch pizzas

6 firm green tomatoes,
   trimmed and sliced
Salt and pepper to taste
2 eggs
1/4 cup milk
4 cups corn flour
Vegetable oil for frying
1/2 recipe Classic Crust dough
   (page 16) or Bread
   Machine Crust dough
   (page 17)
2 tablespoons cornmeal or
   2 tablespoons olive oil
1 1/2 cups Slow-Simmered
   Tomato Sauce (page 40)
1 cup shredded Cheddar
   cheese
3 cups shredded mozzarella
   cheese

1. Sprinkle tomato slices with salt and pepper. Whisk together eggs and milk, and pour corn flour onto a platter or pie plate. Dip tomato slices in egg mixture, then dredge in corn flour.

2. In a large skillet, pour oil to a depth of about 2 inches. Heat over medium-high heat until a drop of water sizzles in the oil. Fry tomato slices, a few at a time, until lightly browned on the bottom. Gently turn slices and cook until light brown on both sides. Drain on paper towels.

3. Roll or press pizza dough into two 12-inch circles, slightly thicker at the edges than in the center. If using pizza pans, sprinkle the bottom with cornmeal or coat with oil and place dough in pan. If using a pizza stone, sprinkle with cornmeal and place in a 400° oven.

4. Spread ¾ cup of pizza sauce onto each crust, followed by ½ cup of Cheddar cheese and 1½ cups of mozzarella.

5. Arrange fried tomato slices over the cheese, overlapping as necessary. If using a pizza stone, carefully place the first pizza onto the stone using a pizza peel. If using pans, place the first pizza in the center of the oven. Bake at 400° until browned and bubbly, about 15 to 20 minutes. Remove from the oven and repeat with the remaining pizza. Let pizzas stand for 5 minutes before cutting with a sharp knife or pizza wheel.

1/2 recipe Pan Pizza Crust
    dough (page 20)
2 tablespoons olive oil
1 cup Garlic and Oil Sauce
    (page 44)
1 cup diced zucchini
1 cup diced yellow squash
1 cup coarsely chopped white
    mushrooms
1 cup diced Japanese
    eggplant
2 cups diced fresh plum
    tomatoes
2 tablespoons fresh oregano
    leaves
Salt and pepper to taste
1 cup shredded Asiago cheese
1 cup shredded Parmesan
    cheese
2 cups shredded mozzarella
    cheese

Ratatouille Pizza

*This is a quick-cooked take on the classic Provençal vegetable
stew. If you have leftover ratatouille from another meal, that can
be used in place of the sauce and vegetables listed here.
The precooked veggies will be a little less crisp but still tasty.*

✳   ✳   ✳

1. Roll pizza dough into two circles large enough to cover
    bottom and sides of two 12" pizza or quiche pans. Spread
    a tablespoon of olive oil over the bottom of each pan, then
    press dough circles into the pans.

2. Spread ½ cup sauce over the bottom of each pie crust. In
    a bowl, combine zucchini, squash, mushrooms, eggplant,
    and tomatoes. Distribute vegetables evenly over each crust.
    Sprinkle with oregano leaves, salt, and pepper.

3. Combine Asiago, Parmesan, and mozzarella cheeses. Dis-
    tribute evenly over the top of each pizza.

4. Bake pies at 400° for 20 minutes or until browned and bub-
    bly. Let stand for 5 minutes before serving.

Broccoli and Fontina Cheese Pizza

*For non-vegetarian meals, add crumbled bacon or finely
diced ham to this pizza for a salty, smoky accent.*

❅   ❅   ❅

1. Roll or press pizza dough into two 12-inch circles, slightly thicker at the edges than in the center. If using pizza pans, sprinkle the bottom with cornmeal or coat with olive oil and place dough in pan. If using a pizza stone, sprinkle with cornmeal and place stone in oven. Preheat oven to 400°.

2. Spread ¾ cup sauce in the center of each pizza, leaving one inch around the edges bare.

3. Combine Parmesan and mozzarella cheeses. Sprinkle 1 cup over the sauce on each pizza. Distribute 2 cups broccoli florets evenly over each pizza, leaving edges bare. Top with 1 cup diced fontina sprinkled over each pizza. Add pepper to taste.

4. If using a hot stone or tiles, use a well-floured pizza peel to carefully lift one pizza from preparation surface and place on stone. If using pizza pans, place first pizza in the center of the oven. Bake for 15 to 20 minutes or until the crust is lightly browned and cheese is melted.

5. Remove pizza from oven carefully (use peel if baking with a stone). Set aside to rest briefly before slicing. Repeat baking process with second pie.

Makes two 12-inch pizzas

---

¹/₂ recipe Pepper Crust dough
(page 30) or Herb-Laced
Crust dough (page 28)
2 tablespoons cornmeal or
1 tablespoon olive oil
1¹/₂ cups Slow-Simmered
Tomato Sauce (page 40)
1 cup shredded Parmesan
cheese
1 cup shredded mozzarella
cheese
4 cups small broccoli florets,
blanched
2 cups finely diced fontina
cheese
Freshly ground black pepper
to taste

Makes two 12-inch pizzas

½ recipe Honey-Wheat Crust
    dough (page 23)
2 tablespoons cornmeal or
    1 tablespoon olive oil
2 tablespoons extra virgin
    olive oil
2 cloves garlic, minced
3 cups whole-milk ricotta
    cheese
1 cup finely chopped sun-
    dried tomatoes
2 tablespoons fresh basil
    ribbons
Black pepper to taste
3 cups shredded mozzarella
    cheese

Sun-dried Tomato and Ricotta Pizza

For this recipe, use oil-packed dried tomatoes. Buy a commercial brand or make your own by marinating dry-packed tomatoes in olive oil and your favorite herbs. Cover and refrigerate for a few days before using.

✳   ✳   ✳

1. Roll or press pizza dough into two 12-inch circles, slightly thicker at the edges than in the center. If using pizza pans, sprinkle the bottom with cornmeal or coat with olive oil and place dough in pan. If using a pizza stone, sprinkle with cornmeal and place stone in oven. Preheat oven to 400°.

2. Brush 1 tablespoon extra virgin olive oil over each pizza, leaving edges bare. Sprinkle minced garlic evenly over the oil.

3. Combine ricotta with sun-dried tomatoes, basil, and black pepper. Spread half the ricotta mixture over each pizza, leaving edges bare. Sprinkle 1½ cups mozzarella over each pizza.

4. If using a hot stone or tiles, use a well-floured pizza peel to carefully lift one pizza from preparation surface and place on stone. If using pizza pans, place first pizza in the center of the oven. Bake for 15 to 20 minutes or until the crust is lightly browned and cheese is melted.

5. Remove pizza from oven carefully (use peel if baking with a stone). Set aside to rest briefly before slicing. Repeat baking process with second pie.

Fresh Salsa Pie

This pizza calls for homemade fresh salsa. Jarred salsa can be used, but the end result will be a very different pizza.

❋ ❋ ❋

Makes two 12-inch pizzas

6 large plum tomatoes, small-diced
2 minced jalapeño peppers
$1/3$ cup minced cilantro
1 small onion, minced
Juice of 2 large limes
Salt to taste
$1/2$ recipe Cornmeal Crust dough (page 25)
2 tablespoons olive oil
1 cup shredded Cheddar cheese
3 cups shredded Monterey jack cheese

1. In a large bowl, combine diced tomatoes, minced jalapeños, cilantro, minced onion, and lime juice. Mix well and add salt to taste. Cover and let stand in a cool place for 1 hour.

2. Drain excess liquid from salsa.

3. Roll dough into two circles, slightly larger than 12 inches. Oil two pizza pans with olive oil and press dough into the pans, covering the bottom and sides. Prick dough with a fork and bake at 400° for 10 minutes.

4. Spread half the drained salsa over the bottom of each pizza. Sprinkle Cheddar cheese over salsa, followed by Monterey jack.

5. Return pizzas to the oven and bake an additional 5 to 10 minutes or until cheese is melted and bubbly. Let stand 5 minutes before slicing with a sharp knife or pizza wheel.

Saucy Pies

Don't be afraid to make pizzas with saucy centers. Drain excess watery liquid from tomatoes or other vegetables to keep crusts from getting too soggy. Then just bake well filled pies in a sided pizza or quiche pan and serve wedges with forks and plenty of napkins.

½ recipe Sicilian Crust dough
    (page 18)
2 tablespoons olive oil
2 tablespoons cornmeal
2 cups Slow-Simmered
    Tomato Sauce (page 40)
¼ cup extra virgin olive oil
1 green bell pepper, cored
    and thinly sliced
1 red bell pepper, cored and
    thinly sliced
1 yellow bell pepper, cored
    and thinly sliced
1 large fennel bulb, trimmed
    and thinly sliced
1 large red onion, diced
Black pepper to taste
1 cup shredded Parmesan
    cheese
1 cup shredded Asiago cheese
1 cup shredded Romano
    cheese
2 cups shredded mozzarella
    cheese

Fennel and Peppers Pizza

Fresh fennel looks a bit like celery when sliced, but it adds an aromatic hint of licorice flavor to this dish.

✳   ✳   ✳

1. On a floured board, roll pizza dough into a rectangle. Coat an oblong metal baking dish with olive oil and sprinkle with cornmeal. Press dough into the pan, spreading it to the corners.

2. Spread tomato sauce over the top of the dough.

3. In a large skillet or Dutch oven, heat extra virgin olive oil over medium-high heat. Add peppers, fennel, and onion and sauté until crisp-tender. Add black pepper to taste.

4. Combine Parmesan, Asiago, Romano, and mozzarella cheeses. Spread evenly over the top of the sauce. Remove pepper-fennel mixture with a slotted spoon and distribute vegetables over the top of the pizza.

5. Preheat oven to 400°. Bake 20 to 25 minutes or until top is browned and bubbly. Cut into square slices with a sharp knife.

Roasted Cauliflower Pizza

Roasted cauliflower can be made ahead of time and stored in the refrigerator for a few hours or overnight until you're ready to make the pizzas.

❄   ❄   ❄

Makes two 12-inch pizzas

4 cups cauliflower florets
3 tablespoons extra virgin
   olive oil
2 cloves garlic, pressed
1 teaspoon white balsamic
   vinegar
Salt and pepper to taste
2 tablespoons olive oil
1/2 recipe California Thin Crust
   dough (page 21)
1 1/2 cups Cheesy Cream Sauce
   (page 44)
2 cups shredded Parmesan
   cheese

1. Preheat oven to 425°. Toss cauliflower florets with extra virgin olive oil, garlic, vinegar, salt, and pepper. Roast for 12 to 15 minutes, stirring occasionally. Remove from oven. When cool, break into smaller florets.

2. Coat two 12" pizza pans with olive oil. Roll out or press dough into pans to cover the bottoms. Spread ¾ cup sauce over each pizza, then distribute roasted cauliflower over pizzas.

3. Sprinkle Parmesan over cauliflower. Bake pizzas in a 400° oven for 15 minutes or until crust is browned. Let stand 5 minutes, then slice with a sharp knife or pizza cutter.

Roasted 'n' Ready
Roasting gives vegetables a sweet, caramelized coating and helps concentrate flavor. Summer squash, onions, parsnips, carrots, asparagus, and baby beets are all good candidates for roasting. Make up a big batch for a side dish, then save the leftovers for pizza toppings.

1/2 recipe Asiago Cheese Crust
   dough (page 33)
2 tablespoons cornmeal or
   1 tablespoon olive oil
1 cup Garlic and Oil Sauce
   (page 44)
2 medium Vidalia onions,
   thinly sliced
1/2 cup golden raisins
1/2 cup dark raisins
1 cup toasted pine nuts
Freshly ground black pepper
   to taste

Pine Nut, Raisin, and Vidalia Onion Pizza

Dried cranberries make a great substitute for raisins in this savory-sweet pizza.

✳   ✳   ✳

1. Roll or press pizza dough into two 12-inch circles, slightly thicker at the edges than in the center. If using pizza pans, sprinkle the bottom with cornmeal or coat with olive oil and place dough in pan. If using a pizza stone, sprinkle with cornmeal and place stone in oven. Preheat oven to 400°.

2. Spread 1/2 cup sauce over each pizza, leaving edges bare.

3. Separate onion slices and spread over each pizza, overlapping as necessary. Sprinkle dark and golden raisins over onions, followed by toasted pine nuts. Add black pepper to taste.

4. If using a pizza stone or tiles, use a well-floured pizza peel to carefully lift one pizza from preparation surface and place on stone. If using pizza pans, place first pizza in the center of the oven. Bake for 15 to 20 minutes or until the crust is lightly browned.

5. Remove pizza from oven carefully (use peel if baking with a stone). Set aside to rest briefly before slicing. Repeat baking process with second pie. Let stand 5 minutes before slicing with a sharp knife or pizza wheel.

Hot or Cold

As any college student will tell you, pizza served at room temperature can be quite satisfying. Some pies, especially those with minimalist sauces, taste excellent after cooling, particularly when served with a glass of wine or dry sherry.

Chopped Herb and Roasted Plum Tomato Pizza

This pizza is a tomato lover's dream. It's as fragrant as it is delicious!

Makes two 12-inch pizzas

✳ ✳ ✳

1. Coat halved tomatoes with ¼ cup olive oil. Place on a sheet of nonstick foil on a baking pan and roast tomatoes at 400° for 25 minutes. Set aside and allow tomatoes to cool slightly.

2. Place garlic, green onions, parsley, basil, oregano, sage, and thyme in a food processor. Pulse until herbs are all finely chopped. Spoon into a large bowl. Place roasted tomatoes in food processor and pulse until coarsely chopped. Add to bowl with herbs and toss until well blended. Add salt and pepper to taste.

3. Coat two 12" deep-dish pizza or pie pans with remaining olive oil. Divide dough and press into pans, making sure dough goes all the way up the sides of the pans.

4. Lay mozzarella slices over the crust of each pizza, using about half the mozzarella for both crusts. Spoon tomato-herb mixture into each crust, spreading to cover the cheese. Sprinkle with shredded Parmesan.

5. Lay remaining mozzarella slices evenly over the pies. Bake pizzas for 20 to 25 minutes or until crust is light brown and centers are browned and bubbly. Let stand for 5 minutes before cutting into wedges.

Plum Perfect

Plum tomatoes are meatier than other tomato varieties. When roasted, plums give off less liquid and yield more usable, sweet-tasting pulp. Grape tomatoes, which are essentially miniature plums, can be roasted as well.

16 plum tomatoes, halved vertically
¼ cup plus 2 tablespoons olive oil
2 cloves garlic
2 green onions, trimmed
⅓ cup fresh parsley leaves
¼ cup fresh basil leaves
2 tablespoons fresh oregano leaves
1 tablespoon fresh sage leaves
2 teaspoons fresh thyme leaves
Salt and pepper to taste
½ recipe Chicago Deep-Dish Crust dough (page 19)
2 pounds sliced mozzarella cheese
1 cup shredded Parmesan cheese

½ recipe Classic Crust dough
(page 16) or Cornmeal
Crust dough (page 25)
2 tablespoons cornmeal or
1 tablespoon olive oil
1½ cups Picante Sauce
(page 48)
½ cup shredded Manchego
cheese
1 cup shredded Cheddar
cheese
2 cups shredded Monterey
jack cheese
½ cup shredded mozzarella
cheese
2 cups cooked black beans,
drained
2 cups roasted corn kernels
1 bell pepper, cored and diced
1 small red onion, finely
chopped
¼ cup minced cilantro

Roasted Corn and Black Bean Pizza

*Canned black beans and frozen roasted corn kernels work just
fine for this pizza, making it an easy, economical supper.*

❋   ❋   ❋

1. Roll or press pizza dough into two 12-inch circles, slightly
    thicker at the edges than in the center. If using pizza pans,
    sprinkle the bottom with cornmeal or coat with olive oil
    and place dough in pan. If using a pizza stone, sprinkle with
    cornmeal and place stone in oven. Preheat oven to 400°.

2. Spread ¾ cup sauce in the center of each pizza, leaving
    edges bare.

3. In a large bowl, combine all the cheeses and toss gently to
    mix. Sprinkle half the cheese blend over the sauce on each
    pizza, leaving edges bare.

4. Divide black beans, corn, bell pepper, and onion evenly
    over each pizza. Sprinkle with minced cilantro.

5. If using a hot stone or tiles, use a well-floured pizza peel to
    carefully lift one pizza from preparation surface and place
    on stone. If using pizza pans, place first pizza in the center
    of the oven. Bake for 15 to 20 minutes or until the crust is
    lightly browned and cheese is melted.

6. Remove pizza from oven carefully (use peel if baking with a
    stone). Set aside to rest briefly before slicing. Repeat baking
    process with second pie.

Triple-Olive Pizza

Ricotta cheese forms a mild, creamy foil for the intense flavor of olives in this olive-lovers' delight.

Makes two 12-inch pizzas

$^1/_2$ *recipe Classic Crust dough (page 16) or Bread Machine Crust dough (page 17)*
2 tablespoons cornmeal or 1 tablespoon olive oil
2 tablespoons extra virgin olive oil
1 clove garlic, minced
1$^1/_2$ cups whole-milk ricotta cheese
3 cups shredded mozzarella cheese
1 cup sliced black olives
1 cup seeded and chopped kalamata olives
1 cup sliced pepper-laced green olives

1. Roll or press pizza dough into two 12-inch circles, slightly thicker at the edges than in the center. If using pizza pans, sprinkle the bottom with cornmeal or coat with olive oil and place dough in pan. If using a pizza stone, sprinkle with cornmeal and place stone in oven. Preheat oven to 400°.

2. Brush 1 tablespoon extra virgin olive oil over each pizza, leaving edges bare. Sprinkle minced garlic evenly over the oil.

3. Spread ¾ cup ricotta over each pizza, leaving edges bare. Sprinkle 1½ cups mozzarella over each pizza. Evenly distribute black olives, kalamata olives, and green olives over cheese on each pizza.

4. If using a hot stone or tiles, use a well-floured pizza peel to carefully lift one pizza from preparation surface and place on stone. If using pizza pans, place first pizza in the center of the oven. Bake for 15 to 20 minutes or until the crust is lightly browned and cheese is melted.

5. Remove pizza from oven carefully (use peel if baking with a stone). Set aside to rest briefly before slicing. Repeat baking process with second pie.

Pluck an Olive

There are dozens of varieties of olives now available in supermarkets, including brine- and oil-cured, green and ripe, marinated and flavored. Aside from being rich in heart-healthy monosaturated fats, olives are so intensely flavored that a little goes a long way. Experiment with different types to find your favorite combination.

1 tablespoon butter
1 clove garlic, minced
6 to 8 vegetable-based
    sausage patties, chopped
1 pound sliced white
    mushrooms
1 green bell pepper, cored
    and diced
$^1/_3$ cup minced parsley
$^1/_2$ recipe Classic Crust dough
    (page 16) or Bread
    Machine Crust dough
    (page 17)
2 tablespoons cornmeal or
    1 tablespoon olive oil
$1^1/_2$ cups Slow-Simmered
    Tomato Sauce (page 40)
1 cup shredded Parmesan
    cheese
3 cups shredded mozzarella
    cheese

Veggie-Sausage, Pepper, and Mushroom Pizza

Who says vegetarians can't enjoy a nice meaty pizza? The sausage may not be real, but it will give your pizza a hearty flavor.

✳   ✳   ✳

1. In a large skillet over medium-high heat, melt butter. Add garlic and vegetable-based sausage and cook until sausage pieces become browned. Combine sausage with mushrooms, peppers, and parsley.

2. Roll or press pizza dough into two 12-inch circles, slightly thicker at the edges than in the center. If using pizza pans, sprinkle the bottom with cornmeal or coat with olive oil and place dough in pan. If using a pizza stone, sprinkle with cornmeal and place stone in oven. Preheat oven to 400°.

3. Spread ¾ cup sauce in the center of each pizza, leaving edges bare.

4. Sprinkle ½ cup Parmesan over the sauce on each pizza. Distribute 1½ cups mozzarella evenly over each pizza, leaving edges bare. Spread sausage mixture evenly over cheese on each pizza.

5. If using a hot stone or tiles, use a well-floured pizza peel to carefully lift one pizza from preparation surface and place on stone. If using pizza pans, place first pizza in the center of the oven. Bake for 15 to 20 minutes or until the crust is lightly browned and cheese is melted.

6. Remove pizza from oven carefully (use peel if baking with a stone). Set aside to rest briefly before slicing. Repeat baking process with second pie.

Hash Brown Pizza

Serve slices of this pizza topped with poached eggs for a different brunch dish. To save time, use packaged hash browns from the supermarket refrigerator case.

✻ ✻ ✻

1. Roll or press pizza dough into two 12-inch circles, slightly thicker at the edges than in the center. If using pizza pans, sprinkle the bottom with cornmeal or coat with olive oil and place dough in pan. If using a pizza stone, sprinkle with cornmeal and place stone in oven. Preheat oven to 400°.

2. Spread ¾ cup sauce in the center of each pizza, leaving the edges bare.

3. In a large bowl, combine mozzarella and Monterey jack cheeses and toss gently to mix. Sprinkle half the cheese blend over the sauce on each pizza, leaving edges bare.

4. Spread hash browns evenly over each crust, then top with the Cheddar. Sprinkle with salt and pepper to taste.

5. If using a hot stone or tiles, use a well-floured pizza peel to carefully lift one pizza from preparation surface and place on stone. If using pizza pans, place first pizza in the center of the oven. Bake for 15 to 20 minutes or until the crust is lightly browned and cheese is melted.

6. Remove pizza from oven carefully (use peel if baking with a stone). Set aside to rest briefly before slicing. Repeat baking process with second pie.

Makes two 12-inch pizzas

¹/₂ recipe Classic Crust dough (page 16) or Cornmeal Crust dough (page 25)
2 tablespoons cornmeal or 1 tablespoon olive oil
1¹/₂ cups Slow-Simmered Tomato Sauce (page 40) or Picante Sauce (page 48)
1¹/₂ cups shredded mozzarella cheese
2 cups shredded Monterey jack cheese
6 cups prepared hash brown potatoes
1¹/₂ cups shredded Cheddar cheese
Salt and pepper to taste

2 tablespoons dark
   sesame oil
1 tablespoon vegetable oil
2 cloves garlic, minced
1 teaspoon minced fresh
   ginger
1 cup fine julienne carrots
1 cup fine julienne celery
1 cup matchstick-sliced
   mushrooms
$^1/_2$ cup fine julienne bamboo
   shoots
2 green onions, minced
1 cup chopped bok choy
2 cups crumbled firm tofu
$^1/_2$ cup soy sauce
Red pepper flakes to taste
$^1/_2$ recipe California Thin Crust
   dough (page 21)
2 tablespoons cornmeal or
   1 tablespoon oil

Moo-Shu Tofu Pizza

*This meat-free, cheese-free pizza takes the classic Moo-Shu
pancake and turns it into a thin, crisp pizza crust.*

❄   ❄   ❄

1. In a large, flat-bottomed wok over high heat, combine ses-
    ame and vegetable oils, garlic, and ginger. Stir-fry for 10 sec-
    onds before adding carrots, celery, mushrooms, bamboo
    shoots, green onions, and bok choy. Stir-fry until vegetables
    are crisp-tender, about 5 minutes. Reduce heat and add tofu,
    soy sauce, and red pepper flakes. Simmer just until tofu is
    heated through and has absorbed some of the sauce.

2. Roll or press pizza dough into two very thin 12-inch circles,
    slightly thicker at the edges than in the center. If using pizza
    pans, sprinkle the bottom with cornmeal or coat with oil
    and place dough in pan. If using a pizza stone, sprinkle with
    cornmeal and place rolled dough directly on stone.

3. Divide tofu mixture evenly over each crust. Place one pizza
    in the oven at 425°. Bake 10 to 12 minutes or until crust
    is browned. Repeat with remaining pizza. Let pizzas rest
    briefly, then slice with a sharp knife or pizza wheel.

CHAPTER 6
Chicken Pizzas

$^1/_2$ *recipe Classic Crust dough*
  (page 16) or Bread
  Machine Crust dough
  (page 17)
2 tablespoons cornmeal or
  1 tablespoon olive oil
2 cups Barbecue Sauce
  (page 45)
2 cups shredded Cheddar or
  Colby cheese
2 cups shredded Monterey
  jack cheese
3 cups shredded roasted or
  poached chicken
$^1/_3$ *cup sliced green onion*

Shredded Barbecued Chicken Pizza

This is a great way to give leftover chicken a makeover. You can also substitute duck or turkey for the chicken, or do a quick fix by purchasing already-roasted chicken at the supermarket.

✳   ✳   ✳

1. Roll or press pizza dough into two 12-inch circles, slightly thicker at the edges than in the center. If using pizza pans, sprinkle the bottom with cornmeal or coat with olive oil and place dough in pan. If using a pizza stone, sprinkle with cornmeal and place stone in oven. Preheat oven to 400°.

2. Spread ¾ cup barbecue sauce in the center of each pizza, leaving edges bare.

3. Sprinkle 1 cup Cheddar or Colby over the sauce on each pizza. Distribute 1 cup Monterey jack evenly over each pizza, leaving edges bare.

4. Toss remaining ½ cup barbecue sauce with shredded chicken. Spread chicken evenly over the cheese on each pizza. Sprinkle sliced green onions over each pizza.

5. If using a hot stone or tiles, use a well-floured pizza peel to carefully lift one pizza from preparation surface and place on stone. If using pizza pans, place first pizza in the center of the oven. Bake for 15 to 20 minutes or until the crust is lightly browned and toppings are bubbly.

6. Remove pizza from oven carefully (use peel if baking with a stone). Set aside to rest briefly before slicing. Repeat baking process with second pie.

Hawaiian Pizza

*Chicken breast that's been grilled over hot coals gives the pizza
a wonderful smoky-sweet flavor. Next time you cook out,
make extra for pizza the next day.*

❋   ❋   ❋

Makes two 12-inch pizzas

*¹/₂ recipe Classic Crust dough
   (page 16) or Bread
   Machine Crust dough
   (page 17)
2 tablespoons cornmeal or
   1 tablespoon olive oil
2 cups Speed-Scratch Tomato
   Sauce (page 40)
1 tablespoon brown sugar
1 tablespoon soy sauce
2 cups shredded Colby cheese
2 cups shredded mozzarella
   cheese
2 cups diced grilled or pan-
   seared chicken breast
1 cup diced green bell pepper
1 cup diced fresh or canned
   pineapple
¹/₂ cup diced red onion
¹/₄ cup minced parsley*

1. Roll or press pizza dough into two 12-inch circles, slightly thicker at the edges than in the center. If using pizza pans, sprinkle the bottom with cornmeal or coat with olive oil and place dough in pan. If using a pizza stone, sprinkle with cornmeal and place stone in oven. Preheat oven to 400°.

2. In a bowl, combine tomato sauce, brown sugar, and soy sauce. Whisk to blend. Spread half the sauce in the center of each pizza, leaving edges bare.

3. Sprinkle 1 cup Colby over the sauce on each pizza. Distribute 1 cup mozzarella evenly over each pizza, leaving one inch around the edges bare.

4. Dot each pizza with 1 cup diced chicken breast, followed by ½ cup bell pepper and ½ cup pineapple. Sprinkle onion and parsley over each pizza.

5. If baking on a hot stone or tiles, use a well-floured pizza peel to carefully lift one pizza from preparation surface and place on stone. If using pizza pans, place first pizza in the center of the oven. Bake for 15 to 20 minutes or until the crust is lightly browned and toppings are bubbly.

6. Remove pizza from oven carefully (use peel if baking with a stone). Set aside to rest briefly before slicing. Repeat baking process with second pie.

1 tablespoon vegetable oil
2 tablespoons Thai green
    curry paste
1 (12-ounce) can coconut milk
1 tablespoon Thai fish sauce
1 tablespoon lime juice
2 raw, boneless chicken
    breast halves, cut into
    strips
1 cup sliced mushrooms
$^1/_2$ recipe Classic Crust dough
    (page 16) or Bread
    Machine Crust dough
    (page 17)
2 tablespoons cornmeal or
    1 tablespoon olive oil
$^2/_3$ cup matchstick-cut
    bamboo shoots
1 tablespoon lime zest
1 large red bell pepper, cored
    and cut into strips
1 small sweet onion, trimmed
    and cut into strips
2 tablespoons minced
    cilantro
3 cups shredded mozzarella
    cheese

Thai Chicken Pizza

*Prepared Thai curry paste makes it easy to get the complex
flavors of Thai cuisine in a relatively quick-to-fix dish.*

✳   ✳   ✳

1. In a large skillet or Dutch oven, combine oil and curry paste. Cook over medium-high heat for 2 to 3 minutes, stirring constantly. Add coconut milk, fish sauce, and lime juice. Reduce heat to medium and cook, stirring occasionally, for 15 minutes.

2. Add chicken and mushrooms to coconut milk and cook just until chicken turns opaque, about 3 to 5 minutes. Remove from heat.

3. Roll or press pizza dough into two 12-inch circles, slightly thicker at the edges than in the center. If using pizza pans, sprinkle the bottom with cornmeal or coat with olive oil and place dough in pan. If using a pizza stone, sprinkle with cornmeal and place stone in oven. Preheat oven to 400°.

4. Divide chicken and mushroom mixture over the two pizza crusts, spreading evenly. Distribute ⅓ cup of bamboo shoots over each pizza. Sprinkle each with a little lime zest, then distribute bell pepper and sweet onion over the tops, followed by cilantro.

5. Spread 1½ cups mozzarella over each pizza. If using a hot stone or tiles, use a well-floured pizza peel to carefully lift one pizza from preparation surface and place on stone. If using pizza pans, place first pizza in the center of the oven. Bake for 15 to 20 minutes or until the crust is lightly browned and toppings are bubbly.

6. Remove pizza from oven carefully (use peel if baking with a stone). Set aside to rest briefly before slicing. Repeat baking process with second pie.

Southwest Chicken Pizza

Serve this whole-meal pizza with a dollop of sour cream and extra picante sauce on the side. Use ready-to-eat mesquite-flavored or smoked chicken from the supermarket to save time.

Makes two 12-inch pizzas

$^1/_2$ recipe Cornmeal Crust dough (page 25) or Pepper Crust dough (page 30)

2 tablespoons cornmeal or 1 tablespoon olive oil

$1^1/_2$ cups Picante Sauce (page 48)

2 cups shredded Cheddar or Colby cheese

2 cups shredded Monterey jack cheese

3 cups diced mesquite-grilled or smoked chicken breast

1 cup diced tomatoes

1 cup black beans, drained

1 cup roasted corn

1 cup diced red or green bell pepper

1 cup finely chopped red onion

$^1/_3$ cup minced cilantro

1. Roll or press pizza dough into two 12-inch circles, slightly thicker at the edges than in the center. If using pizza pans, sprinkle the bottom with cornmeal or coat with olive oil and place dough in pan. If using a pizza stone, sprinkle with cornmeal and place stone in oven. Preheat oven to 400°.

2. Spread ¾ cup picante sauce in the center of each pizza, leaving edges bare.

3. Sprinkle 1 cup Cheddar or Colby over the sauce on each pizza. Distribute 1 cup Monterey jack evenly over each pizza, leaving one inch around the edges bare.

4. Spread chicken evenly over the cheese on each pizza. Sprinkle tomatoes, black beans, corn, bell pepper, onion, and cilantro over the chicken.

5. If baking on a hot stone or tiles, use a well-floured pizza peel to carefully lift one pizza from preparation surface and place on stone. If using pizza pans, place first pizza in the center of the oven. Bake for 15 to 20 minutes or until the crust is lightly browned and toppings are bubbly.

6. Remove pizza from oven carefully (use peel if baking with a stone). Set aside to rest briefly before slicing. Repeat baking process with second pie.

½ recipe California Thin Crust
   dough (page 21)
2 tablespoons olive oil
2 tablespoons cornmeal
2 cups Pesto Sauce (page 43)
2 cups shredded mozzarella
   cheese
3 grilled boneless chicken
   breast halves, sliced
   crosswise
½ cup toasted pine nuts
¼ cup fresh basil ribbons
1 cup shredded Parmesan
   cheese
½ cup shredded Asiago
   cheese

Grilled Chicken Pesto Pizza

*This pizza features classic fresh basil pesto sauce. If you prefer
a pesto made with other herbs, or even a sun-dried-tomato
pesto, feel free to experiment.*

✳   ✳   ✳

1. Roll or press pizza dough into two thin 12-inch circles, slightly thicker at the edges than in the center. Spread 1 tablespoon olive oil over the bottom of two pizza pans or large quiche pans. Sprinkle cornmeal over the oil, 1 table-spoon on each pan.

2. Preheat oven to 400°. Place pizza pans in oven and prick in several places with a fork. Bake until crust is lightly browned, about 7 minutes. Remove from oven and spoon or brush 1 cup pesto sauce over each pizza.

3. Divide mozzarella evenly over each pizza, followed by chicken breast slices, pine nuts, and basil ribbons.

4. Combine shredded Parmesan and Asiago cheeses. Sprinkle evenly over the pizzas.

5. Return pizzas to the oven and bake until shredded cheese has melted and crusts darken slightly, about 5 to 7 minutes. Let pizzas rest briefly, then slice with a sharp knife or pizza wheel. If oven won't accommodate both pans easily, bake pizzas one at a time.

Fresh Sauces
Pesto and other sauces made with uncooked ingredients generally taste better and retain more of their original texture when just warmed or barely cooked. Baking pizza crusts "blind" or uncovered for a few minutes helps ensure a cooked crust without overcooking your fresh sauce.

Spicy Fried Chicken Pizza

Serve this pizza in place of Buffalo Wings when you need a snack for your favorite couch-coaches during football or NASCAR season.

1. Line a baking sheet with nonstick foil. Lightly dip each chicken nugget or strip in Buffalo Wing sauce and arrange in a single layer on the foil. Place in a preheated oven. For frozen chicken, follow package baking instructions, turning chicken pieces at least once during baking. For fresh fried chicken, bake at 350° for 5 to 7 minutes. Remove from oven.

2. Roll or press pizza dough into two 12-inch circles, slightly thicker at the edges than in the center. If using pizza pans, sprinkle the bottom with cornmeal or coat with olive oil and place dough in pan. If using a pizza stone, sprinkle with cornmeal and place stone in oven. Preheat oven to 400°.

3. In a bowl, combine tomato sauce, Tabasco, and sugar. Whisk to blend. Spread half the sauce in the center of each pizza, leaving edges bare.

4. Combine Colby and mozzarella cheeses. Sprinkle 1½ cups over the sauce on each pizza, leaving edges bare.

5. Dot each pizza with fried chicken pieces, followed by celery and onion. Sprinkle onion and parsley over each pizza. Divide crumbled bleu cheese over the pizzas.

6. If baking on a hot stone or tiles, use a well-floured pizza peel to carefully lift one pizza from preparation surface and place on stone. If using pizza pans, place first pizza in the center of the oven. Bake for 15 to 20 minutes or until the crust is lightly browned and toppings are bubbly.

7. Remove pizza from oven carefully (use peel if baking with a stone). Set aside to rest briefly before slicing. Repeat baking process with second pie.

1 pound fried chicken nuggets or strips, fresh or frozen
1 cup Buffalo Wing sauce
½ recipe Classic Crust dough (page 16) or Honey-Wheat Crust dough (page 23)
2 tablespoons cornmeal or 1 tablespoon olive oil
2 cups Speed-Scratch Tomato Sauce (page 40)
1 teaspoon Tabasco sauce
2 teaspoons sugar
1 cup shredded Colby cheese
2 cups shredded mozzarella cheese
1 cup sliced celery
½ cup diced red onion
1 cup crumbled bleu cheese

*Makes one 11 x 16-inch
pizza*

½ recipe Sicilian Crust dough
    (page 18)
2 tablespoons olive oil
2 tablespoons cornmeal
2 cups Mustard Cream Sauce
    (page 51)
2 tablespoons butter
1 pound sliced white or
    Portobello mushrooms
2 cloves garlic, minced
½ cup parsley, minced
3 cups shredded poached
    chicken
Black pepper to taste
1 cup shredded Parmesan
    cheese
1 cup shredded Asiago cheese
2 cups shredded mozzarella
    cheese

Chicken and Mushroom Pizza

*Although Sicilian pizzas usually are served with red sauce, the
thick crust also makes a wonderful foil for creamy pizza sauces.*

✳   ✳   ✳

1. On a floured board, roll pizza dough into a rectangle. Coat
   an 11" × 16" oblong metal baking dish with olive oil and
   sprinkle with cornmeal. Press dough into pan, spreading it
   to the corners.

2. Spread Mustard Cream Sauce over the top of the dough.

3. In a large skillet or Dutch oven, heat butter over medium-
   high heat. Add mushrooms and garlic and sauté 3 to 5
   minutes. Add parsley and remove from heat. Spread shredded chicken evenly over the sauce, followed by the cooked
   mushrooms. Add black pepper to taste.

4. Combine Parmesan, Asiago, and mozzarella cheeses.
   Spread evenly over the top of the chicken and mushrooms.
   Preheat oven to 400°. Bake 20 to 25 minutes or until top is
   browned and bubbly. Cut into square slices with a sharp
   knife.

Dark or Light?

*Although most diners profess to prefer chicken breast meat,
the truth is, dark meat is often juicier and more flavorful.
Boneless, skinless chicken thighs, trimmed of any excess fat
and cut into small pieces, stand up well to spicy sauces and
coatings. When added to a shredded chicken mix, dark
meat gives the chicken a richer flavor than breast meat
alone.*

Chicken Piquant Pizza

Unlike the Spanish Picante sauce, this French sauce gets its spark from pepper and slow-cooked tomatoes, without vinegar. It's often used for game and seafood stews in South Louisiana.

※　※　※

1. Roll out two circles of pizza dough. Spread olive oil in two 12" deep-dish pizza or pie pans. Press dough circles into pans and prick bottoms a few times with a fork.

2. Ladle two cups of Sauce Piquant into each pan, followed by ½ cup of Cheddar cheese and ½ cup of mozzarella cheese. Divide chicken evenly over sauce in each pan.

3. Divide remaining 1½ cups of Cheddar and 3½ cups mozzarella over the chicken. Bake at 400° until browned and bubbly, about 20 minutes. Let stand 5 minutes, then serve wedges with forks.

Doctored Piquant
Sauce Piquant has plenty of green bell peppers, celery, onions, tomatoes, and herbs simmered into the mix. However, if you prefer to have a pizza with more crunchy peppers or onions, by all means add a handful of raw veggies in with the chicken.

Makes two 12-inch pizzas

$^1/_2$ recipe Chicago Deep-Dish Crust dough (page 19)
2 tablespoons olive oil
4 cups Sauce Piquant (page 49)
2 cups shredded Cheddar cheese
4 cups shredded mozzarella cheese
4 cups finely diced boneless chicken

1/2 recipe California Thin Crust
   dough (page 21)
2 tablespoons olive oil
2 tablespoons cornmeal
2 cups Sesame-Soy Sauce
   (page 47)
2 cups shredded mozzarella
   cheese
2 pan-seared boneless
   chicken breast halves,
   sliced crosswise
2 tablespoons soy sauce
2 cups small broccoli florets,
   blanched
1/4 cup minced green onion
2 teaspoons sesame seeds
1 cup finely diced smoked
   Gouda cheese

Chicken and Broccoli Pizza

Chinese-American chicken and broccoli is the inspiration for this dish. It can easily be made dairy-free by omitting the cheese and adding diced tofu or more chicken to the pies.

✳   ✳   ✳

1. Roll or press pizza dough into two thin 12-inch circles, slightly thicker at the edges than in the center. Spread 1 tablespoon olive oil over the bottom of two pizza pans or large quiche pans. Sprinkle cornmeal over the oil, 1 tablespoon on each pan.

2. Preheat oven to 400°. Spread 1 cup Sesame-Soy Sauce over each crust, leaving edges bare. Divide mozzarella evenly over each pizza.

3. Toss chicken breast slices in soy sauce and divide chicken over each pizza, followed by broccoli florets and green onion.

4. Sprinkle pizzas with sesame seeds and dot with diced smoked Gouda.

5. Place pizzas in the oven and bake until cheese has melted and crusts are browned, about 10 to 12 minutes. Let pizzas rest briefly, then slice with a sharp knife or pizza wheel. If oven won't accommodate both pans easily, bake pizzas one at a time.

Chicken Alfredo Pizza

Mushrooms give this pizza added substance. If you'd rather not have them, feel free to add another vegetable or more chicken to the pizza.

✳   ✳   ✳

Makes two 12-inch pizzas

$^1/_2$ recipe Pan Pizza Crust
    dough (page 20)
2 tablespoons olive oil
2 cups Cheesy Cream Sauce
    (page 44)
3 chicken breast halves,
    poached and diced
1 teaspoon minced garlic
1 tablespoon butter
2 cups coarsely chopped
    white mushrooms
$1^1/_2$ cups Parmesan cheese
$2^1/_2$ cups mozzarella cheese
Freshly ground black pepper

1. Roll pizza dough into two circles large enough to cover bottom and sides of two 12" pizza or quiche pans. Spread a tablespoon of olive oil over the bottom of each pan, then press dough circles into the pans.

2. Ladle 1 cup of sauce into each pan and spread evenly over the crust. Divide diced chicken and distribute over each pizza.

3. In a large, flat-bottomed wok or Dutch oven, combine garlic, butter, and mushrooms. Sauté 3 to 5 minutes or until mushrooms soften. Remove mushrooms with a slotted spoon and spread over chicken.

4. Spread Parmesan cheese over each pizza, then do the same with the mozzarella. Add freshly ground black pepper to taste. Bake pans in a preheated oven at 400° until crust has browned and cheese is bubbly, about 20 minutes.

Whither Alfredo?
Around 1914, Roman restaurateur Alfredo di Lelio created a dish of supremely thin, tender egg noodles, extra-rich butter, and freshly grated Parmesan cheese. He served it with a flourish, brandishing golden cutlery, and named it Fettuccine all'Alfredo. Eventually, the rest of the world began calling any white Parmesan sauce-laced dish "Alfredo." However, in Rome, the name still refers to a specific dish.

½ recipe Classic Crust dough
    (page 16) or Pepper Crust
    dough (page 30)
2 tablespoons cornmeal or
    1 tablespoon olive oil
2 cups Refried Bean Spread
    (page 50)
1 cup Picante Sauce (page 48)
2 cups shredded Cheddar or
    Colby cheese
2 cups shredded Monterey
    jack cheese
4 grilled chicken breasts,
    sliced into thin strips
1 small green bell pepper,
    cored and cut into strips
1 small red bell pepper, cored
    and cut into strips
1 sweet onion, trimmed and
    cut into strips
1 cup diced tomatoes
¼ cup minced cilantro
1 cup crème fraiche

Chicken Fajita Pizza

*If you have time, place halved peppers and onions on the
grill for a few minutes to get the slightly charred,
smoky flavor of fajita veggies.*

✳   ✳   ✳

1. Roll or press pizza dough into two 12-inch circles, slightly thicker at the edges than in the center. If using pizza pans, sprinkle the bottom with cornmeal or coat with olive oil and place dough in pan. If using a pizza stone, sprinkle with cornmeal and place stone in oven. Preheat oven to 400°.

2. Spread 1 cup Refried Bean Spread in the center of each pizza, leaving edges bare. Top bean spread with Picante Sauce.

3. Sprinkle 1 cup Cheddar or Colby over the sauce on each pizza. Distribute 1 cup Monterey jack evenly over each pizza, leaving one inch around the edges bare.

4. Spread chicken evenly over the cheese on each pizza. Sprinkle peppers, onions, and diced tomatoes over the pizza, followed by cilantro.

5. If baking on a hot stone or tiles, use a well-floured pizza peel to carefully lift one pizza from preparation surface and place on stone. If using pizza pans, place first pizza in the center of the oven. Bake for 15 to 20 minutes or until the crust is lightly browned and toppings are bubbly.

6. Remove pizza from oven carefully (use peel if baking with a stone). Set aside to rest briefly before slicing. Repeat baking process with second pie. Crisscross slices with drizzles of crème fraiche just before serving.

Jerk Chicken Pizza

*Fiery, aromatic jerk seasoning gives this super-simple pizza a kick.
The papaya slices offer a cooling sweetness.*

✳   ✳   ✳

Makes two 12-inch pizzas

4 boneless chicken breast
   halves
2 tablespoons vegetable oil
2 tablespoons jerk seasoning
   blend
1 tablespoon sauce and gravy
   flour
1/2 recipe California Thin Crust
   dough (page 21)
2 tablespoons cornmeal or
   1 tablespoon oil
2/3 cup Garlic and Oil Sauce
   (page 44)
2 cups shredded mozzarella
   cheese
1 medium papaya, peeled,
   seeded, and sliced
1/2 cup golden raisins
1 cup diced Port Salut cheese

1. Coat chicken breast halves with vegetable oil. Combine jerk seasoning and flour and stir until evenly mixed. Rub spice-flour mixture over the chicken breasts. Grill chicken breasts over medium-high heat until cooked through, about 10 to 15 minutes. (Or sear in a nonstick skillet coated with a little oil or cooking spray.) Set aside.

2. Roll or press pizza dough into two very thin 12-inch circles, slightly thicker at the edges than in the center. If using pizza pans, sprinkle the bottom with cornmeal or coat with oil and place dough in pan. If using a pizza stone, sprinkle with cornmeal and place rolled dough directly on stone. Preheat oven to 425°.

3. Spread Garlic and Oil Sauce evenly over each pizza. Sprinkle each with 1 cup mozzarella cheese. Cut jerk chicken into thin slices and distribute over the two pizzas, alternating with papaya slices. Dot pizzas with golden raisins and Port Salut cheese.

4. Place one pizza in the oven at 425°. Bake 10 to 12 minutes or until crust is browned and cheese is melted. Repeat with remaining pizza. Let pizzas rest briefly, then slice with a sharp knife or pizza wheel.

Everybody Loves a Jerk

Authentic Jamaican jerk seasoning is a paste made from Scotch bonnet peppers, allspice berries, green onions, thyme, garlic, cinnamon, nutmeg, salt, and sometimes other ingredients. Locals pride themselves on their recipes, with fiery heat being the common denominator. Dried versions are readily available in supermarkets. After being coated with the spices, meats are generally grilled or roasted.

½ recipe Classic Crust dough
   (page 16) or Herb-Laced
   Crust dough (page 28)
2 tablespoons cornmeal or
   1 tablespoon olive oil
2 cups Slow-Simmered
   Tomato Sauce (page 40)
2 cups shredded Gruyère
   cheese
2 cups shredded mozzarella
   cheese
3 cups thinly sliced smoked
   chicken sausage
1 cup diced green bell pepper
1 cup diced red onion

Smoked Chicken Sausage Pizza

*Chicken sausages come in a wide variety of flavors,
ranging from those that mimic pork sausage to versions
laced with spinach, sun-dried tomatoes, jalapeños,
and maple flavoring. Pick your favorite.*

✳   ✳   ✳

1. Roll or press pizza dough into two 12-inch circles, slightly thicker at the edges than in the center. If using pizza pans, sprinkle the bottom with cornmeal or coat with olive oil and place dough in pan. If using a pizza stone, sprinkle with cornmeal and place stone in oven. Preheat oven to 400°.

2. Spread 1 cup of the sauce in the center of each pizza, leaving edges bare.

3. Sprinkle 1 cup Gruyère over the sauce on each pizza, followed by 1 cup mozzarella, leaving edges bare.

4. Spread chicken sausage slices over each pizza, followed by ½ cup bell pepper and ½ cup onion.

5. If baking on a hot stone or tiles, use a well-floured pizza peel to carefully lift one pizza from preparation surface and place on stone. If using pizza pans, place first pizza in the center of the oven. Bake for 15 to 20 minutes or until the crust is lightly browned and toppings are bubbly.

6. Remove pizza from oven carefully (use peel if baking with a stone). Set aside to rest briefly before slicing. Repeat baking process with second pie.

Chicken and Granny Smith Apple Pizza

That's right, this pizza is Waldorf Salad on a warm, edible plate.
Serve with a glass of Chardonnay or fruit tea for lunch.

❊   ❊   ❊

Makes two 12-inch pizzas

$^1/_2$ recipe California Thin Crust
   dough (page 21)
2 tablespoons olive oil
2 tablespoons cornmeal
1$^1/_2$ cups mayonnaise
1 tablespoon coarse mustard
2 cups diced poached chicken
   breast
2 cups cored and diced
   Granny Smith apples
1 cup sliced celery
1 cup walnut halves
Salt and pepper to taste
2 cups finely shredded sharp
   Cheddar cheese

1. Roll or press pizza dough into two thin 12-inch circles, slightly thicker at the edges than in the center. Spread 1 tablespoon olive oil over the bottom of two pizza pans or large quiche pans. Sprinkle cornmeal over the oil, 1 tablespoon on each pan.

2. Preheat oven to 400°. Place pizza pans in the oven and prick in several places with a fork. Bake until crust is browned, about 8 to 10 minutes. Remove from the oven.

3. Whisk together mayonnaise and mustard. In a large bowl, combine mayonnaise mixture with chicken, apples, celery, and walnuts. Add salt and pepper to taste and mix well.

4. Spoon chicken salad evenly over the pizza crusts and sprinkle each with 1 cup of Cheddar cheese.

5. Return pizzas to the oven and bake just until shredded cheese has melted, about 5 minutes. Slice with a sharp knife or pizza wheel and serve immediately. If oven won't accommodate both pans easily, bake pizzas one at a time.

Safety Tip

Warmed mayonnaise dishes should be eaten promptly and leftovers either quickly refrigerated or discarded. If you aren't sure you'll need two chicken salad pizzas, leave the extra salad in the refrigerator. You can always spread it on the extra pizza crust and have more pizza in a few minutes.

1 large head garlic
*3 tablespoons extra virgin
   olive oil*
2 tablespoons butter
3 cups diced cooked chicken
*1/2 recipe Spinach Crust dough
   (page 29) or Classic Crust
   dough (page 16)*
*2 tablespoons cornmeal or
   2 tablespoons olive oil*
*1 1/2 cups whole-milk ricotta
   cheese*
*2 teaspoons fresh chopped
   basil or 1 teaspoon dried
   oregano*
*3 cups shredded mozzarella
   cheese*
1 cup diced tomatoes
1/3 cup minced parsley

Garlic Chicken Pizza

Roasted garlic gives this pizza an unexpected sweetness.

✳   ✳   ✳

1. Remove one layer of papery outer skin from the garlic head. Leaving the head intact, coat the outside with 1 tablespoon extra virgin olive oil. Wrap the garlic in foil, or place in a covered terracotta dish, and bake at 350° for 1 hour. Set aside until cool enough to handle.

2. Place butter in a large skillet over medium heat. Separate the garlic cloves and press the roasted garlic from the cloves into the skillet. With a wooden spoon or whisk, stir the garlic into the butter until well combined. Add diced chicken and toss until well coated with garlic butter. Remove from heat.

3. Roll or press pizza dough into two 12-inch circles, slightly thicker at the edges than in the center. If using pizza pans, sprinkle the bottom with cornmeal or coat with olive oil and place dough in pan. If using a pizza stone, sprinkle with cornmeal and place stone in oven. Preheat oven to 400°.

4. Brush remaining extra virgin olive oil over each pizza crust, leaving edges bare. Combine ricotta with basil or oregano. Spread ¾ cup ricotta over each pizza, leaving edges bare. Sprinkle 1½ cups mozzarella over each pizza, followed by tomatoes, garlic-coated chicken, and parsley.

5. If baking on a hot stone or tiles, use a well-floured pizza peel to carefully lift one pizza from preparation surface and place on stone. If using pizza pans, place first pizza in the center of the oven. Bake for 15 to 20 minutes or until the crust is lightly browned and toppings are bubbly.

6. Remove pizza from oven carefully (use peel if baking with a stone). Set aside to rest briefly before slicing. Repeat baking process with second pie.

Chicken and Andouille Pizza

Chicken and andouille is a classic combination in Cajun cooking. It turns up in jambalayas, gumbos, and stuffings. Why not pizza?

✳   ✳   ✳

Makes two 12-inch pizzas

$^1/_2$ recipe Classic Crust dough
(page 16) or Herb-Laced
Crust dough (page 28)
2 tablespoons cornmeal or
1 tablespoon olive oil
2 cups Slow-Simmered
Tomato Sauce (page 40)
$^1/_2$ teaspoon dried thyme
2 cups shredded Colby cheese
2 cups shredded mozzarella
cheese
2 cooked chicken breast
halves, thinly sliced
1$^1/_2$ cups diced andouille
sausage
1 cup diced green bell pepper
$^1/_3$ cup minced green onion

1. Roll or press pizza dough into two 12-inch circles, slightly thicker at the edges than in the center. If using pizza pans, sprinkle the bottom with cornmeal or coat with olive oil and place dough in pan. If using a pizza stone, sprinkle with cornmeal and place stone in oven. Preheat oven to 400°.

2. Mix thyme into pizza sauce. Spread 1 cup of the sauce in the center of each pizza, leaving one inch around the edges bare.

3. Sprinkle 1 cup Colby cheese over the sauce on each pizza, followed by 1 cup mozzarella, leaving edges bare.

4. Spread chicken breast slices over each pizza, followed by the diced andouille. Distribute bell pepper and minced green onion over pizzas.

5. If baking on a hot stone or tiles, use a well-floured pizza peel to carefully lift one pizza from preparation surface and place on stone. If using pizza pans, place first pizza in the center of the oven. Bake for 15 to 20 minutes or until the crust is lightly browned and toppings are bubbly.

6. Remove pizza from oven carefully (use peel if baking with a stone). Set aside to rest briefly before slicing. Repeat baking process with second pie.

Authentic Andouille

True South Louisiana-style andouille is a thick sausage made with coarsely chopped pork butt, fat, and spices. The distinctive flavor comes from slow-smoking the sausage ropes over sugar cane and local hardwoods. Although a similarly named sausage hails from France, that product is made from tripe.

Makes two 12-inch pizzas

½ recipe Pan Pizza Crust dough (page 20)
2 tablespoons olive oil
2 cups Sesame-Soy Sauce (page 47)
2 tablespoons sesame oil
2 tablespoons vegetable oil
1 pound ground chicken
4 Asian eggplants, trimmed and cut into julienne strips
4 cloves garlic, minced
⅓ cup soy sauce
½ cup minced green onion
Freshly ground black pepper
2 cups diced fresh mozzarella cheese

Chicken and Eggplant Pizza

Fresh mozzarella cheese gives this savory, Asian-accented pizza a touch of creaminess. For an alternative presentation, skip the cheese and sprinkle thin fried noodles on top of this pie.

❊ ❊ ❊

1. Roll pizza dough into two circles large enough to cover bottom and sides of two 12" pizza or quiche pans. Spread a tablespoon of olive oil over the bottom of each pan, then press dough circles into the pans.
2. Ladle 1 cup of sauce into each pan and spread evenly over the crust.
3. In a large, flat-bottomed wok or Dutch oven, combine sesame and vegetable oils and ground chicken. Cook, stirring constantly, until chicken is no longer pink. Add eggplant, garlic, and soy sauce and continue cooking until eggplant is tender. Remove mixture from pan with a slotted spoon, draining as much liquid as possible.
4. Distribute chicken and eggplant mixture over each pizza crust, then sprinkle green onions evenly over pizzas. Add black pepper to taste, then dot each pizza with 1 cup of diced cheese.
5. Bake pizzas in a preheated oven at 400° until crust has browned and cheese is melted, about 20 minutes.

Chicken and Leek Pizza

Leeks should be cleaned carefully to remove any sand within the stalks, and only the white bulb and 2 inches of pale green stalk should be used.

✳   ✳   ✳

Makes two 12-inch pizzas

3 young leeks, well trimmed
2 tablespoons butter
$^1/_2$ recipe California Thin Crust
    dough (page 21)
2 tablespoons olive oil
2 tablespoons cornmeal
1 cup Garlic and Oil Sauce
    (page 44)
2 cups shredded mozzarella
    cheese
2 grilled boneless chicken
    breast halves, sliced
    crosswise
$^1/_2$ cup crumbled crisp bacon
1 cup shredded Parmesan
    cheese
$^1/_2$ cup shredded Asiago
    cheese

1. Thinly slice trimmed and cleaned leeks. In a large skillet over medium-high heat, melt butter and add leeks. Sauté for 2 to 3 minutes, then remove from heat.

2. Roll or press pizza dough into two thin 12-inch circles, slightly thicker at the edges than in the center. Spread 1 tablespoon olive oil over the bottom of two pizza pans or large quiche pans. Sprinkle cornmeal over the oil, 1 tablespoon on each pan.

3. Preheat oven to 400°. Brush ½ cup Oil and Garlic Sauce over each crust. Divide mozzarella evenly over each pizza, followed by chicken breast slices, sautéed leeks, and crumbled bacon.

4. Combine shredded Parmesan and Asiago cheeses. Sprinkle evenly over the pizzas.

5. Bake pizzas until shredded cheese has melted and crusts darken slightly, about 10 to 12 minutes. Let pizzas rest briefly, then slice with a sharp knife or pizza wheel. If oven won't accommodate both pans easily, bake pizzas one at a time.

Makes two 12-inch pizzas

1/2 recipe Classic Crust dough
    (page 16) or Cornmeal
    Crust dough (page 25)
2 tablespoons cornmeal or
    1 tablespoon olive oil
1 cup prepared whole-berry
    cranberry sauce
1 cup Horseradish Sauce
    (page 45)
2 cups shredded Colby cheese
2 cups shredded mozzarella
    cheese
2 cups shredded cooked
    chicken breast
1 green bell pepper, cored
    and cut into thin strips
1/2 cup diced red onion
1/4 cup minced parsley

Chicken and Cranberry Pizza

*Cranberries and horseradish combine here to make
a spicy-sweet base. This recipe also works very well
with shredded turkey or duck.*

✳   ✳   ✳

1. Roll or press pizza dough into two 12-inch circles, slightly thicker at the edges than in the center. If using pizza pans, sprinkle the bottom with cornmeal or coat with olive oil and place dough in pan. If using a pizza stone, sprinkle with cornmeal and place stone in oven. Preheat oven to 400°.

2. In a bowl, combine cranberry sauce and Horseradish Sauce. Whisk to blend. Spread half the sauce in the center of each pizza, leaving one inch around the edges bare.

3. Sprinkle 1 cup Colby over the sauce on each pizza. Distribute 1 cup mozzarella evenly over each pizza, leaving the edges bare.

4. Dot each pizza with 1 cup shredded chicken breast, followed by bell pepper and onion. Sprinkle parsley over each pizza.

5. If baking on a hot stone or tiles, use a well-floured pizza peel to carefully lift one pizza from preparation surface and place on stone. If using pizza pans, place first pizza in the center of the oven. Bake for 15 to 20 minutes or until the crust is lightly browned and toppings are bubbly.

6. Remove pizza from oven carefully (use peel if baking with a stone). Set aside to rest briefly before slicing. Repeat baking process with second pie.

Chicken and Fresh Tomato Pizza

This pizza captures some of the favorite flavors of summer—grilled chicken, fresh tomatoes, and fresh herbs—on a dense bread crust.

1. Roll focaccia dough into two 12-inch circles. Grease deep-dish pizza pans with olive oil and press dough into the pans. Bake at 400° for 15 minutes, or until focaccias have just begun to brown.

2. Remove from oven and spread Pesto Sauce over each crust. Sprinkle with the Parmesan cheese. Distribute 1 cup diced fresh mozzarella evenly over the pizzas. Dot pizzas with grape tomato halves, followed by the diced chicken, basil ribbons, and the remainder of the mozzarella.

3. Add freshly ground black pepper to taste. Return pans to oven and bake for 10 minutes, or just long enough for mozzarella to melt and tomatoes to soften. Remove from oven and let stand for a few minutes before slicing.

Makes two 12-inch pizzas

---

¹/₂ recipe Focaccia Crust
   dough (page 32)
2 tablespoons olive oil
1 cup Pesto Sauce (page 43)
1 cup shredded Parmesan
   cheese
3 cups diced fresh mozzarella
   cheese
3 cups grape tomatoes,
   halved lengthwise
2 grilled chicken breast halves,
   diced
¹/₄ cup fresh basil ribbons
Freshly ground black pepper
   to taste

¹/₂ recipe Pepper Crust dough (page 30) or Spinach Crust dough (page 29)
2 tablespoons cornmeal or 1 tablespoon olive oil
1¹/₂ cups Slow-Simmered Tomato Sauce (page 40)
1 cup shredded Parmesan cheese
1 cup shredded mozzarella cheese
8 cooked artichoke hearts, quartered
2 cups cooked, diced chicken
1 cup pitted and chopped kalamata olives
2 cups finely diced feta cheese
Freshly ground black pepper to taste

Chicken, Artichoke, and Kalamata Olive Pizza

Feta and kalamata olives make this intensely flavored pizza an acquired taste for some, a revelation for others.

✳ ✳ ✳

1. Roll or press pizza dough into two 12-inch circles, slightly thicker at the edges than in the center. If using pizza pans, sprinkle the bottom with cornmeal or coat with olive oil and place dough in pan. If using a pizza stone, sprinkle with cornmeal and place stone in oven. Preheat oven to 400°.

2. Spread ¾ cup sauce in the center of each pizza, leaving one inch around the edges bare.

3. Combine Parmesan and mozzarella cheeses. Sprinkle 1 cup over the sauce on each pizza. Distribute artichoke heart quarters evenly over each pizza, leaving edges bare. Top with diced chicken and chopped olives. Sprinkle 1 cup diced feta over each pizza. Add pepper to taste.

4. If baking with a hot stone or tiles, use a well-floured pizza peel to carefully lift one pizza from preparation surface and place on stone. If using pizza pans, place first pizza in the center of the oven. Bake for 15 to 20 minutes or until the crust is lightly browned and cheese is melted.

5. Remove pizza from oven carefully (use peel if baking with a stone). Set aside to rest briefly before slicing. Repeat baking process with second pie.

Feta Facts
Feta cheese originated in Greece thousands of years ago. Shepherds curdled sheep's milk in bags, then cut and salted the resulting soft cheese and stored it in brine. Today fresh feta is still brine packed, but it's often made with cow's milk.

Cashew Chicken Pizza

Nuts give pizzas texture and an earthy flavor. For variety, try substituting Lemon Cream Sauce for the Sesame-Soy and slivered almonds for the cashews.

1. Roll or press pizza dough into two very thin 12-inch circles, slightly thicker at the edges than in the center. If using pizza pans, sprinkle the bottom with cornmeal or coat with oil and place dough in pan. If using a pizza stone, sprinkle with cornmeal and place rolled dough directly on stone.

2. Spread ½ cup Sesame-Soy Sauce evenly over each pizza. Sprinkle cilantro over the sauce.

3. Distribute the chicken, cashews, and celery over the sauce on each pizza. Sprinkle with freshly ground black pepper, followed by the mozzarella cheese.

4. Place one pizza in the oven at 425°. Bake 10 to 12 minutes or until crust is browned and cheese is melted. Repeat with remaining pizza.

5. Let pizzas rest briefly, then slice with a sharp knife or pizza wheel.

Makes two 12-inch pizzas

½ recipe California Thin Crust dough (page 21)
2 tablespoons cornmeal or 1 tablespoon oil
1 cup Sesame-Soy Sauce (page 47)
¼ cup chopped fresh cilantro
2 chicken breast halves, cooked and diced
1 cup roasted cashews
1 cup sliced celery
Freshly ground black pepper to taste
3 cups shredded mozzarella cheese

4 uncooked chicken breast
    halves
1¹⁄₂ cups balsamic vinegar
    dressing
2 cups mixed fresh herbs,
    chopped
¹⁄₂ recipe Chicago Deep-Dish
    Crust dough (page 19)
2 tablespoons olive oil
4 cups Chunky Tomato Sauce
    (page 41)
2 cups shredded Parmesan
    cheese
4 cups shredded mozzarella
    cheese

Herbed Chicken Pizza

Combine standbys like green onions, garlic, and parsley with fresh lemon thyme, purple basil, chervil, pineapple sage, and other fresh herbs to make this pizza special.

✳   ✳   ✳

1. Place chicken breast halves in a resealable plastic bag. Whisk 1 cup of herb mixture into the vinegar dressing and pour dressing over the chicken. Seal bag and refrigerate for 6 hours or overnight.

2. Remove chicken from marinade and discard marinade. Grill or pan-sear chicken until cooked through. Thinly slice chicken breasts and toss with remaining 1 cup of mixed herbs.

3. Roll out two circles of pizza dough. Spread olive oil in two 12" deep-dish pizza or pie pans. Press dough circles into pans and prick bottoms a few times with a fork. Ladle 2 cups of tomato sauce into each pan, followed by ½ cup of Parmesan cheese and ½ cup of mozzarella cheese.

4. Arrange herb-coated chicken slices over the cheese. Divide remaining 1 cup of Parmesan and 3 cups of mozzarella over the chicken slices. Bake at 400° until browned and bubbly, about 20 minutes.

About Marinades

Marinades tenderize tough protein fibers while adding flavor to the meat. The best marinades have a high acid content from vinegar or fruit juices, plus aromatic flavoring agents. Since marinades have come in contact with raw meats, drained marinade must be discarded or, if to be used as a sauce or baste, brought to a full boil to kill bacteria before using.

CHAPTER 7
Sizzling Seafood Pies

½ recipe Pan Pizza Crust
    dough (page 20)
2 tablespoons olive oil
2 cups Cheesy Cream Sauce
    (page 44)
2 pounds medium cooked
    shrimp, peeled and
    deveined
1 teaspoon minced garlic
1 tablespoon butter
2 cups coarsely chopped
    white mushrooms
1½ cups Parmesan cheese
2½ cups mozzarella cheese
Freshly ground black pepper

Shrimp Pizza Alfredo

Raw shrimp release a good bit of water while cooking. Lightly sautéing or poaching them before adding to the pizza keeps the shrimp from diluting the sauce or making the pizza soggy.

✳   ✳   ✳

1. Roll pizza dough into two circles large enough to cover bottom and sides of two 12" pizza or quiche pans. Spread a tablespoon of olive oil over the bottom of each pan, then press dough circles into the pans.

2. Ladle 1 cup of sauce into each pan and spread evenly over the crust. Divide the shrimp and distribute over each pizza.

3. In a large, flat-bottomed wok or Dutch oven, combine garlic, butter, and mushrooms. Sauté 3 to 5 minutes or until mushrooms soften. Remove mushrooms with a slotted spoon and spread over chicken.

4. Spread Parmesan cheese over each pizza, then do the same with the mozzarella. Add freshly ground black pepper to taste. Bake pizzas in a preheated oven at 400° until crust has browned and cheese is bubbly, about 20 minutes.

Clams Marinara Pizza

The clams marinara used in this dish is much thicker than the variety most people ladle over spaghetti. Use your favorite homemade or commercial variety of marinara to flavor the clams.

1. In a large bowl, combine clams, marinara sauce, and pressed garlic. Stir well to combine.

2. Roll out two circles of pizza dough. Spread olive oil in two 12" deep-dish pizza or pie pans. Press dough circles into pans and prick bottoms a few times with a fork. Ladle 2 cups tomato sauce into each pan, followed by ½ cup Parmesan cheese and ½ cup mozzarella cheese.

3. With a slotted spoon, scoop sauced clams into the two crusts, allowing excess liquid to remain in the bowl. Divide remaining 1 cup Parmesan and 3 cups mozzarella over the clams. Bake at 400° until browned and bubbly, about 20 minutes.

Clam Varieties

There are dozens of varieties of clams available. Littleneck and Cherrystone clams are two popular types for chowders and sauces and work well on pizzas. Although they may be tender enough to eat whole, chopping the clams disperses the flavor throughout the pizza sauce.

Makes two 12-inch pizzas

3 cups chopped steamed clams
1 cup prepared marinara sauce
2 cloves garlic, pressed
½ recipe Chicago Deep-Dish Crust dough (page 19)
2 tablespoons olive oil
4 cups Chunky Tomato Sauce (page 41)
2 cups shredded Parmesan cheese
4 cups shredded mozzarella cheese

2 tablespoons vegetable oil
2 tablespoons sesame oil
4 cloves garlic, minced
1 tablespoon honey or maple
   syrup
1 tablespoon lemon juice
1/4 teaspoon hot chile paste
1/2 cup soy sauce
1 pound thick tuna steaks
3 tablespoons sesame seeds
1/2 recipe Classic Crust dough
   (page 16) or Bread
   Machine Crust dough
   (page 17)
2 tablespoons cornmeal or
   1 tablespoon olive oil
2 cups Sesame-Soy Sauce
   (page 47)
3 cups shredded mozzarella
   cheese
1 cup blanched snow peas
1/4 cup minced fresh cilantro

Sesame-Seared Tuna Pizza

Tuna slices are added to this pizza halfway through baking in order to keep the slices moist and slightly pink.

* * *

1. In a large, heavy skillet over high heat, combine vegetable and sesame oils. In a large bowl, whisk together garlic, honey or syrup, lemon juice, hot chile paste, and soy sauce.

2. Add tuna steaks to the skillet and cook, turning once, until the steaks are nicely browned outside but still pink inside, about 3 minutes. Pour soy sauce mixture over steaks and turn to coat. Sprinkle with sesame seeds and remove from heat.

3. Roll or press pizza dough into two 12-inch circles, slightly thicker at the edges than in the center. If using pizza pans, sprinkle the bottom with cornmeal or coat with olive oil and place dough in pan. If using a pizza stone, sprinkle with cornmeal and place stone in oven. Preheat oven to 400°.

4. Spread 1 cup of sauce, followed by 1½ cups mozzarella, over each pizza. If baking on a hot stone or tiles, use a well-floured pizza peel to carefully lift one pizza from preparation surface and place on stone. If using pizza pans, place one or both pizzas in the oven. Bake for 10 minutes or until the crust begins to brown.

5. While the crust is baking, cut tuna steaks into thin slices. Once crust begins to brown, lay the tuna slices in a circular pattern over the top of the pizzas, alternating with snow peas. Sprinkle with minced cilantro. Continue baking for another 10 minutes.

6. Remove pizza from oven carefully (use peel if baking with a stone). Set aside to rest briefly before slicing. Repeat with second pie if both don't fit in the oven at the same time.

Crab and Spinach Pizza

The spinach in this pizza comes from the rich spinach sauce. If you'd like even more spinach flavor, add a cup of lightly steamed and drained spinach to the top of the pies before the mozzarella cheese.

1/2 recipe California Thin Crust dough (page 21)
2 tablespoons olive oil
2 tablespoons cornmeal
2 cups Spinach Sauce (page 46)
2 cups shredded mozzarella cheese
1 pound lump crabmeat, rinsed and picked for shells
2/3 cup finely diced red bell pepper
1/4 cup fresh basil ribbons
1 cup shredded Parmesan cheese
1/2 cup shredded Asiago cheese

1. Roll or press pizza dough into two thin 12-inch circles, slightly thicker at the edges than in the center. Spread 1 tablespoon olive oil over the bottom of two pizza pans or large quiche pans. Sprinkle cornmeal over the oil, 1 tablespoon on each pan.

2. Preheat oven to 400°. Place pizza pans in the oven and prick in several places with a fork. Bake until crust is lightly browned, about 7 minutes. Remove from the oven and spoon or brush 1 cup of spinach sauce over each pizza.

3. Divide mozzarella evenly over each pizza, followed by crabmeat, bell pepper, and basil ribbons.

4. Combine shredded Parmesan and Asiago cheeses. Sprinkle evenly over pizzas.

5. Return pizzas to the oven and bake until shredded cheese has melted and crusts darken slightly, about 5 to 7 minutes. Let pizzas rest briefly, then slice with a sharp knife or pizza wheel. If oven won't accommodate both pans easily, bake pizzas one at a time.

1¹/₂ pounds catfish fillets,
   cut into strips
2 cups seasoned cornmeal
   fish fry
Vegetable oil for frying
¹/₂ recipe Classic Crust dough
   (page 16) or Cornmeal
   Crust dough (page 25)
2 tablespoons cornmeal or
   1 tablespoon olive oil
2 cups Speed-Scratch Tomato
   Sauce (page 40)
1 teaspoon Tabasco sauce
2 cups shredded Colby cheese
2 cups shredded mozzarella
   cheese
1 cup chopped toasted
   pecans
¹/₂ cup diced red onion

Fried Catfish Pizza

If you feel the urge to gild this water-lily, make up a batch of Horseradish Sauce (page 45) and pour it into a squirt bottle. Before serving the pizzas, drizzle a few lines of the sauce over the top.

✳   ✳   ✳

1. Dredge raw catfish strips in cornmeal fish fry. In a large, heavy skillet, pour vegetable oil about 2 inches deep and heat until a drop of water sizzles. Fry catfish strips until just browned, about 3 to 4 minutes. Place on paper towels to drain.

2. Roll or press pizza dough into two 12-inch circles, slightly thicker at the edges than in the center. If using pizza pans, sprinkle the bottom with cornmeal or coat with olive oil and place dough in pan. If using a pizza stone, sprinkle with cornmeal and place stone in oven. Preheat oven to 400°.

3. In a bowl, combine tomato sauce and Tabasco. Whisk to blend. Spread half the sauce in the center of each pizza, leaving edges bare.

4. Combine Colby and mozzarella cheeses. Sprinkle 1½ cups over the sauce on each pizza, leaving edges bare.

5. Divide fried catfish pieces over each pizza, followed by pecans and onion.

6. If baking on a hot stone or tiles, use a well-floured pizza peel to carefully lift one pizza from preparation surface and place on stone. If using pizza pans, place first pizza in the center of the oven. Bake for 15 to 20 minutes or until the crust is lightly browned and toppings are bubbly.

7. Remove pizza from oven carefully (use peel if baking with a stone). Set aside to rest briefly before slicing. Repeat baking process with second pie.

Lobster and Chanterelles Pizza

For lobster pizza, you can use either Maine lobster tail and claw meat or just chop up the tails of Florida or spiny lobster, which is less expensive.

✳   ✳   ✳

Makes two 12-inch pizzas

½ recipe Classic Crust dough (page 16) or Bread Machine Crust dough (page 17)

2 tablespoons cornmeal or 1 tablespoon olive oil

1½ cups Lemon Cream Sauce (page 51) or Slow-Simmered Tomato Sauce (page 40)

2 tablespoons unsalted butter

2 cloves garlic, minced

1 pound chanterelle mushrooms, well cleaned

¼ cup minced fresh parsley

1 cup shredded Gruyère cheese

3 cups shredded mozzarella cheese

3 cups cooked, chopped lobster meat

¼ cup chopped fresh tarragon

1. Roll or press pizza dough into two 12-inch circles, slightly thicker at the edges than in the center. If using pizza pans, sprinkle the bottom with cornmeal or coat with olive oil and place dough in pan. If using a pizza stone, sprinkle with cornmeal and place stone in oven. Preheat oven to 400°.

2. Spread ¾ cup sauce in the center of each pizza, leaving edges bare.

3. In a large skillet, heat 2 tablespoons butter until bubbling. Add garlic and mushrooms and sauté until mushrooms are crisp-tender. Sprinkle with parsley.

4. With a slotted spoon, remove mushrooms from the skillet, draining as much liquid as possible.

5. Sprinkle ½ cup Gruyère cheese over each pizza. Then spread 1½ cups mozzarella evenly over each pizza, leaving edges bare. Distribute mushrooms evenly over cheese, followed by lobster pieces and fresh tarragon.

6. If using a hot stone or tiles, use a well-floured pizza peel to carefully lift one pizza from preparation surface and place on stone. If using pizza pans, place first pizza in the center of the oven. Bake for 15 to 20 minutes or until the crust is lightly browned and cheese is melted.

7. Remove pizza from oven carefully (use peel if baking with a stone). Set aside to rest briefly before slicing. Repeat baking process with second pie.

Makes two 12-inch pizzas

½ recipe Pan Pizza Crust
   dough (page 20)
2 tablespoons olive oil
2 cups Lemon Cream Sauce
   (page 51)
2 pounds cooked shrimp,
   peeled and deveined
3 cups quartered cooked
   artichoke hearts
1½ cups Parmesan cheese
2½ cups mozzarella cheese
Freshly ground black pepper

Shrimp and Artichoke Pizza

*If you purchase large shrimp, halve them lengthwise before adding
them to the pizza. This ensures that every bite will be deliciously shrimpy.*

❋   ❋   ❋

1. Roll pizza dough into two circles large enough to cover
   bottom and sides of two 12" pizza or quiche pans. Spread
   a tablespoon of olive oil over the bottom of each pan, then
   press dough circles into the pans.

2. Ladle 1 cup of sauce into each pan and spread evenly over
   the crust.

3. Distribute cooked shrimp evenly over each pizza crust, then
   sprinkle artichokes evenly over the pizzas.

4. Spread Parmesan cheese over each pizza, then do the same
   with the mozzarella. Add black pepper to taste. Bake at 400°
   until browned and bubbly, about 20 minutes.

Makes two 12-inch pizzas

½ recipe Chicago Deep-Dish
   Crust dough (page 19)
2 tablespoons olive oil
4 cups Sauce Piquant
   (page 49)
4 cups cooked, diced shrimp
2 cups shredded Cheddar
   cheese
4 cups shredded mozzarella
   cheese

Shrimp Pizza Diablo

*Sauce Piquant has all the onions, peppers, and herbs one
might want in this pizza, plus the kick of cayenne.*

❋   ❋   ❋

1. Roll out two circles of pizza dough. Spread olive oil in two
   12" deep-dish pizza or pie pans. Press dough circles into
   pans and prick bottoms a few times with a fork.

2. Ladle 2 cups of Sauce Piquant into each pan, followed by
   ½ cup of Cheddar cheese and ½ cup of mozzarella cheese.
   Divide shrimp evenly over cheese in each pan.

3. Divide remaining 1 cup of Cheddar and 3 cups of mozzarella over the shrimp. Bake at 400° until browned and bubbly, about 20 minutes. Let stand 5 minutes, then serve.

Shrimp and Andouille Pizza

*To go full-Cajun with this pizza, add some chopped or
shredded chicken in with the shrimp and sausage.*

✳   ✳   ✳

1. Roll or press pizza dough into two 12-inch circles, slightly thicker at the edges than in the center. If using pizza pans, sprinkle the bottom with cornmeal or coat with olive oil and place dough in pan. If using a pizza stone, sprinkle with cornmeal and place stone in oven. Preheat oven to 400°.

2. Mix thyme into pizza sauce. Spread 1 cup of the sauce in the center of each pizza, leaving one inch around the edges bare.

3. Sprinkle 1 cup Colby cheese over the sauce on each pizza, followed by 1 cup mozzarella.

4. Slice shrimp lengthwise and distribute over each pizza, followed by the diced andouille. Distribute bell pepper and minced green onion over pizzas.

5. If baking on a hot stone or tiles, use a well-floured pizza peel to carefully lift one pizza from preparation surface and place on stone. If using pizza pans, place first pizza in the center of the oven. Bake for 15 to 20 minutes or until the crust is lightly browned and toppings are bubbly.

6. Remove pizza from oven carefully (use peel if baking with a stone). Set aside to rest briefly before slicing. Repeat baking process with second pie.

Makes two 12-inch pizzas

$1/2$ recipe Classic Crust dough
  (page 16) or Herb-Laced
  Crust dough (page 28)
2 tablespoons cornmeal or
  1 tablespoon olive oil
2 cups Slow-Simmered
  Tomato Sauce (page 40)
$1/2$ teaspoon dried thyme
2 cups shredded Colby cheese
2 cups shredded mozzarella
  cheese
4 cups cooked shrimp, peeled
  and deveined
$1^1/2$ cups diced andouille
  sausage
1 cup diced green bell pepper
$1/3$ cup minced green onion

2 pounds raw fillet of grouper
1¹/₂ cups herb vinaigrette
　salad dressing
²/₃ cup minced fresh chives
¹/₂ recipe Chicago Deep-Dish
　Crust dough (page 19)
2 tablespoons olive oil
4 cups Chunky Tomato Sauce
　(page 41)
2 cups shredded Monterey
　jack cheese
4 cups shredded mozzarella
　cheese

Grouper and Chive Pizza

Thick, meaty grouper stands up well to chunky tomatoes and herbs in this simple deep-dish pizza.

❊　　❊　　❊

1. Place grouper in a resealable plastic bag. Pour dressing over the fish. Seal bag and refrigerate for 30 minutes. Remove grouper from marinade and grill over a hot grill or in a heavy skillet over high heat for 3 to 5 minutes, turning once.

2. With a very sharp knife, slice grouper fillet crosswise. Sprinkle with fresh chives. (Don't worry if fish isn't cooked through—it will finish cooking inside the deep-dish crust.)

3. Roll out two circles of pizza dough. Spread olive oil in two 12" deep-dish pizza or pie pans. Press dough circles into pans and prick bottoms a few times with a fork.

4. Ladle 2 cups of tomato sauce into each pan, followed by ½ cup of Monterey jack cheese and ½ cup of mozzarella cheese.

5. Arrange the grouper slices over the cheese. Divide remaining 1 cup of Monterey jack and 3 cups of mozzarella over the chicken slices. Bake at 400° until browned and bubbly, about 20 minutes.

Crab and Asparagus Pizza

King crab legs sold at most supermarket fish counters have been cooked, flash-frozen, and thawed. So don't be reluctant to buy frozen crabmeat directly from the freezer case.

❋ ❋ ❋

1. Cut about 2 inches from the bottom of the asparagus spears. Discard or reserve ends for broth. Cut remaining stalks in half. In a large skillet over medium-high heat, melt butter and add asparagus spears. Sauté for 1 to 2 minutes, then remove from heat. Reserve spear tips and slice middle sections into smaller pieces.

2. Roll or press pizza dough into two thin 12-inch circles, slightly thicker at the edges than in the center. Spread 1 tablespoon olive oil over the bottom of two pizza pans or large quiche pans. Sprinkle cornmeal over the oil, 1 tablespoon on each pan.

3. Preheat oven to 400°. Brush ½ cup Garlic and Oil Sauce over each crust. Divide mozzarella evenly over each pizza, followed by Gruyère, crabmeat, and sliced asparagus. Arrange spear tips decoratively around the pizzas and dot with tomatoes.

4. Sprinkle Butterkase cheese evenly over the pizzas and top with basil.

5. Bake pizzas until shredded cheese has melted and crusts darken slightly, about 10 to 12 minutes. Let pizzas rest briefly, then slice with a sharp knife or pizza wheel. If oven won't accommodate both pans easily, bake pizzas one at a time.

Makes two 12-inch pizzas

1 pound fresh asparagus
2 tablespoons butter
½ recipe California Thin Crust dough (page 21)
2 tablespoons olive oil
2 tablespoons cornmeal
1 cup Garlic and Oil Sauce (page 44)
2 cups shredded mozzarella cheese
1 cup shredded Gruyère cheese
1 pound sliced king crab leg meat
1 cup grape tomatoes, halved lengthwise
1 cup crumbled Butterkase cheese
¼ cup fresh basil ribbons

½ recipe Cornmeal Crust
  dough (page 25) or
  Multigrain Crust dough
  (page 24)
2 tablespoons cornmeal or
  1 tablespoon olive oil
1½ cups Picante Sauce
  (page 48)
2 cups shredded Cheddar or
  Colby cheese
2 cups shredded Monterey
  jack cheese
2 pounds tilapia fillets, cut in
  strips
1 tablespoon sauce and gravy
  flour
1 teaspoon each salt, garlic
  powder, and cumin
2 tablespoons vegetable oil
1 cup diced tomatoes
1 cup sliced black olives
1 cup diced red or green bell
  pepper
1 cup finely chopped red
  onion
⅓ cup minced cilantro

Tilapia Picante Pizza

*Serve this pizza with slices of ripe avocado, lime wedges, and
sour cream. Icy Mexican beer, fruity sangria, or
tropical iced tea would be perfect libations.*

✳   ✳   ✳

1. Roll or press pizza dough into two 12-inch circles, slightly thicker at the edges than in the center. If using pizza pans, sprinkle the bottom with cornmeal or coat with olive oil and place dough in pan. If using a pizza stone, sprinkle with cornmeal and place stone in oven. Preheat oven to 400°.

2. Spread ¾ cup picante sauce in the center of each pizza, leaving edges bare. Sprinkle 1 cup Cheddar or Colby over the sauce on each pizza. Distribute 1 cup Monterey jack evenly over each pizza, leaving edges bare.

3. Place tilapia strips in a bowl. Mix flour, salt, garlic powder, and cumin. Sprinkle over the fish and toss to coat. In a heavy skillet over high heat, heat vegetable oil until hot. Add fish and sauté until fish strips turn opaque. Remove from heat.

4. Spread fish evenly over the cheese on each pizza. Sprinkle tomatoes, black olives, bell pepper, onion, and cilantro over the fish.

5. If baking on a hot stone or tiles, use a well-floured pizza peel to carefully lift one pizza from preparation surface and place on stone. If using pizza pans, place first pizza in the center of the oven. Bake for 15 to 20 minutes or until the crust is lightly browned and toppings are bubbly.

6. Remove pizza from oven carefully (use peel if baking with a stone). Set aside to rest briefly before slicing. Repeat baking process with second pie.

Shrimp and Plum Tomato Pizza

This pizza resembles a hot, open-faced seafood sandwich. For variety, add crumbled bacon or a few bay scallops to the mix.

❊ ❊ ❊

Makes two 12-inch pizzas

$^{1}/_{2}$ recipe Focaccia Crust
  dough (page 32)
2 tablespoons olive oil
$1^{1}/_{2}$ cup Pesto Sauce (page 43)
  or Garlic and Oil Sauce
  (page 44)
1 cup shredded Parmesan
  cheese
3 cups diced fresh mozzarella
  cheese
8 large plum tomatoes,
  thinly sliced
2 pounds cooked, diced
  shrimp
$^{1}/_{4}$ cup fresh basil ribbons
Freshly ground black pepper
  to taste

1. Roll focaccia dough into two 12-inch circles. Grease deep-dish pizza pans with olive oil and press dough into the pans. Bake at 400° for 15 minutes, or until focaccias have just begun to brown.

2. Remove from oven and carefully spread Pesto Sauce or Garlic and Oil Sauce over each crust. Sprinkle with Parmesan cheese. Distribute 1 cup diced fresh mozzarella evenly over the pizzas. Arrange tomato slices in overlapping concentric circles over the cheese, then sprinkle diced shrimp over the tomatoes.

3. Top shrimp with basil ribbons and add freshly ground black pepper to taste. Add remaining mozzarella to pizzas.

4. Return pans to oven and bake for 10 minutes, or just long enough for mozzarella to melt and tomato slices to become warm and soft.

5. Remove from oven and let stand for a few minutes before slicing.

Hearty Fare
Focaccia pizzas hold up to a wide array of ingredients, including moist fresh tomatoes. Serve these pies for a simple luncheon entrée with a glass of sparkling wine or Soave.

½ cup butter

1 cup finely chopped onion

1 small green bell pepper, cored and diced

½ cup chopped parsley

2 large cloves garlic, minced

2 pounds peeled crawfish tails

1 cup water

¼ teaspoon cayenne pepper

¼ teaspoon black pepper

⅛ teaspoon dried thyme leaves

Salt to taste

2 tablespoons cold water

2 teaspoons cornstarch

½ recipe Chicago Deep-Dish Crust dough (page 19)

2 tablespoons olive oil

2 cups shredded Colby cheese

4 cups shredded mozzarella cheese

Crawfish Etouffee Pizza

This pizza doesn't include a separate pizza sauce. Instead, the etouffee sauce serves as the pizza sauce.

❋　❋　❋

1. In a large saucepan or Dutch oven over medium-high heat, melt butter. Add onion, bell pepper, parsley, and garlic. Sauté until onion softens, about 5 minutes. Add crawfish tails, 1 cup of water, cayenne and black pepper, thyme, and salt. Reduce heat to medium and simmer 20 minutes, stirring often.

2. Dissolve cornstarch in 2 tablespoons of cold water. Stir cornstarch into crawfish mixture and simmer 2 to 3 minutes or until thickened. Remove from heat and allow to cool slightly.

3. Roll out two circles of pizza dough. Spread olive oil in two 12" deep-dish pizza or pie pans. Press dough circles into pans and prick bottoms a few times with a fork.

4. With a slotted spoon, divide the crawfish evenly into each pan, adding as much sauce as desired. Divide the Colby and mozzarella over the crawfish. Bake at 400° until browned and bubbly, about 20 minutes. Let stand 5 minutes, then serve wedges with forks.

Authentic Etouffee

In Cajun and Creole parlance, "etouffee" means smothered. It refers to seafood and poultry cooked slowly in butter or oil with seasonings and aromatic vegetables and occasional additions of water or broth. The pot is often partially covered—hence the smothered aspect. Some cooks thicken etouffee with cornstarch, while others use a roux.

Popcorn Crawfish Pizza

It takes 7 to 8 pounds of whole crawfish to make 1 pound of crawfish tails. Look for sealed packs of peeled, blanched crawfish in your fish market freezer case. In the fall and spring, fresh peeled tails may also be available.

❈   ❈   ❈

Makes two 12-inch pizzas

1½ pounds crawfish tails, rinsed and drained
½ cup sauce and gravy flour
Salt and cayenne pepper to taste
2 eggs
½ cup milk
3 cups corn flour
Vegetable oil for frying
½ recipe Classic Crust dough (page 16) or Bread Machine Crust dough (page 17)
2 tablespoons cornmeal or 2 tablespoons olive oil
1½ cups Slow-Simmered Tomato Sauce (page 40)
1 cup shredded Cheddar cheese
3 cups shredded mozzarella cheese

1. Place crawfish in a large bowl. Combine sauce flour with salt and pepper. Sprinkle over crawfish and toss to coat.

2. Whisk together eggs and milk. Place corn flour on a large plate. Dip crawfish tails in egg batter, then dredge in corn flour.

3. In a large skillet, pour oil to a depth of about 2 inches. Heat over medium-high heat until a drop of water sizzles in the oil. Fry crawfish tails, a batch at a time, until coating is crisp and golden. Drain on paper towels.

4. Roll or press pizza dough into two 12-inch circles, slightly thicker at the edges than in the center. If using pizza pans, sprinkle the bottom with cornmeal or coat with oil and place dough in pan. If using a pizza stone, sprinkle with cornmeal and place in a 400° oven.

5. Spread ¾ cup of pizza sauce onto each crust, followed by ½ cup of Cheddar cheese and 1½ cups of mozzarella.

6. Arrange fried crawfish over the cheese, lightly pressing crawfish into the cheese. If using a pizza stone, carefully place the first pizza onto the stone using a pizza peel. If using pans, place the first pizza in the center of the oven. Bake at 400° until browned and bubbly, about 15 to 20 minutes. Remove from the oven and repeat with the remaining pizza. Let pizzas stand for 5 minutes before cutting with a sharp knife or pizza wheel.

1 pound lump crabmeat
1 tablespoon mayonnaise
1 tablespoon Dijon mustard
1 egg
1 teaspoon Old Bay
    seasoning
2 slices white bread
Oil for frying
$^1/_2$ recipe California Thin Crust
    dough (page 21)
2 tablespoons olive oil
1$^1/_2$ cups Slow-Simmered
    Tomato Sauce (page 40)
3 cups shredded mozzarella
    cheese

Crabcake Pizza

The trick to making great crabcakes is a gentle hand. Be very careful not to break up delicate lumps of crabmeat when mixing and shaping the ingredients.

* * *

1. Place lump crabmeat in a bowl and carefully check for shell bits. In a small bowl, whisk together mayonnaise, mustard, egg, and Old Bay. Pour mixture over crab meat.

2. Place the bread in a food processor and pulse to form soft crumbs. Add to the crabmeat mixture and mix lightly with hands.

3. Refrigerate crabmeat mixture for an hour. Shape mixture into cocktail-sized crabcakes, about 1½ inches across. Pour about 2 inches of oil into a large, deep skillet and place over medium-high heat. When oil is hot, fry crabcakes quickly, a few at a time, until browned on both sides. Drain on paper towels.

4. Coat two 12" pizza pans with olive oil. Roll out or press dough into pans to cover the bottoms. Spread ¾ cup sauce over each pizza, then sprinkle each pizza with 1½ cups mozzarella.

5. Bake pizzas in a preheated 400° oven for 10 minutes. Add fried crabcakes to pizzas. Continue baking pizzas for another 5 to 10 minutes or until crust is browned.

Roasted Oyster Pizza

*Mushrooms and onions make a nice foil for simple roasted
oysters in this lemon-accented pizza.*

* * *

1. In a large skillet or Dutch oven, combine onions, mushrooms, butter, and garlic. Cook over medium heat, stirring often, until onions and mushrooms are tender.

2. Roll dough into two 12-inch circles, slightly thicker at the edges than in the center. If using pizza pans, sprinkle the bottom with cornmeal or coat with olive oil and place dough in pan. If using a pizza stone, sprinkle with cornmeal and place stone in oven. Preheat oven to 400°.

3. Spread a thin layer of lemon cream sauce over each crust, leaving one inch around the edges bare. Sprinkle pizzas with Asiago cheese. Spread onions and mushrooms over the sauce.

4. Bake pizzas, one at a time if necessary, at 400° in the center of the oven for 10 minutes. Add a dozen oysters to each pizza, topped by pepper and parsley. Bake 5 minutes longer. Remove from oven and let stand for 5 minutes, then slice and serve.

Low Country Feast

To roast oysters, place scrubbed oysters in the shell in a Dutch oven or on a grill. Roast at high heat until shells open slightly. Remove and shuck. Some cooks prefer to place a wet towel or sack over the oysters to promote steam. Drawn butter and cocktail sauce are the best accompaniments.

Makes two 12-inch pizzas

1 large Vidalia onion, sliced
1 pound Portobello
   mushrooms, sliced
3 tablespoons butter
2 cloves garlic, minced
$^1/_2$ recipe California Thin Crust
   dough (page 21)
2 tablespoons cornmeal or
   2 tablespoons olive oil
1 cup Lemon Cream Sauce
   (page 51)
2 cups Asiago cheese
24 oven- or grill-roasted
   oysters, shucked
Freshly ground black pepper
   to taste
$^1/_4$ cup minced fresh parsley

1/2 recipe California Thin Crust
    dough (page 21)
2 tablespoons cornmeal or
    1 tablespoon oil
1 cup Garlic and Oil Sauce
    (page 44)
1 cup shredded Manchego
    cheese
2 cups shredded mozzarella
    cheese
24 large scallops, briefly
    pan-seared
1/4 cup minced fresh parsley
4 tablespoons grated lemon
    zest
Freshly ground black pepper
    to taste

Scallop and Lemon Zest Pizza

*For moist scallops, just brown the top and bottom in a skillet.
Don't cook them all the way through. They'll finish
cooking on the pizzas.*

❊   ❊   ❊

1. Roll or press pizza dough into two very thin 12-inch circles,
    slightly thicker at the edges than in the center. If using pizza
    pans, sprinkle the bottom with cornmeal or coat with oil
    and place dough in pan. If using a pizza stone, sprinkle with
    cornmeal and place rolled dough directly on stone.

2. Spread ½ cup Garlic and Oil Sauce evenly over each pizza.
    Combine the cheeses and spread over the sauce.

3. Arrange a dozen scallops over each pizza and sprinkle the
    tops with parsley and lemon zest. Add pepper to taste.

4. Place one pizza in the oven at 425°. Bake 10 to 12 minutes
    or until crust is browned and cheese is melted. Repeat with
    remaining pizza. Let pizzas rest briefly, then slice with a
    sharp knife or pizza wheel.

Shrimp Croquette Pizza

Shrimp croquettes can be deep-fried in oil. Or, as in this recipe, they can be baked. Add a drizzle or spray of oil to ensure a crisp, brown exterior.

✳   ✳   ✳

1. Finely chop shrimp by pulsing in a food processor. In a large bowl, combine chopped shrimp, eggs, soft bread crumbs, mayonnaise, green onions, parsley, and seafood seasoning. Work together with hands until ingredients are well blended and evenly distributed.

2. Roll the shrimp mixture into small balls, about 1 inch in diameter. Roll each ball in dry bread crumbs. Place on a baking sheet lined with nonstick foil. Lightly spray with cooking spray. Bake at 350°, turning occasionally, until croquettes are cooked through, about 10 minutes. Remove from oven.

3. Roll out two circles of pizza dough. Spread olive oil in two 12" deep-dish pizza or pie pans. Press dough circles into pans and prick bottoms a few times with a fork.

4. Ladle 2 cups of sauce into each pan, followed by ½ cup of fontina cheese and ½ cup of mozzarella cheese. Divide the croquettes evenly over sauce and cheese in each pan.

5. Divide remaining 1 cup of fontina and 3 cups of mozzarella over the pizzas. Bake at 400° until browned and bubbly, about 20 minutes. Let stand 5 minutes, then serve with forks.

Crazy for Croquettes
Croquettes can be made from a variety of ingredients, including chopped ham, salmon, and assorted vegetables. Some cooks use mashed potatoes or rice as binders in place of the bread. Warm croquettes can be served as a tapa or cocktail-hour munchie, or dropped into deep-dish pizza.

Makes two 12-inch pizzas

1½ pounds cooked, peeled shrimp
2 eggs
1 cup soft bread crumbs
1 tablespoon mayonnaise
2 green onions, minced
¼ cup fresh parsley leaves, minced
1 tablespoon seafood seasoning
1 cup fine bread crumbs
Olive oil cooking spray
½ recipe Chicago Deep-Dish Crust dough (page 19)
2 tablespoons olive oil
4 cups Chunky Tomato Sauce (page 41)
2 cups shredded fontina cheese
4 cups shredded mozzarella cheese

1/2 recipe Classic Crust dough
   (page 16) or Spinach
   Crust dough (page 29)
2 tablespoons cornmeal or
   1 tablespoon olive oil
1 1/2 cups Slow-Simmered
   Tomato Sauce (page 40)
1 1/2 cups shredded mozzarella
   cheese
1/2 cup shredded provolone
   cheese
1/2 cup shredded Asiago
   cheese
1/2 cup shredded Parmesan
   cheese
1/2 cup shredded Romano
   cheese
1 pound salmon fillet,
   poached
1 small green bell pepper,
   cored and cut into strips
1 small yellow bell pepper,
   cored and cut into strips

Salmon Pipperade Pizza

Salmon works well in this recipe because the flavor is distinctive and the fish flakes easily. However, any fresh, firm fish can be substituted.

✳ ✳ ✳

1. Roll or press pizza dough into two 12-inch circles, slightly thicker at the edges than in the center. If using pizza pans, sprinkle the bottom with cornmeal or coat with olive oil and place dough in pan. If using a pizza stone, sprinkle with cornmeal and place stone in oven. Preheat oven to 400°.

2. Spread ¾ cup sauce in the center of each pizza, leaving one inch around the edges bare.

3. In a large bowl, combine all the cheeses and toss gently to mix. Sprinkle half the cheese blend over the sauce on each pizza, leaving edges bare.

4. Gently flake salmon with a fork, removing any skin and bones. Sprinkle salmon over the cheese, followed by pepper strips.

5. If using a hot stone or tiles, use a well-floured pizza peel to carefully lift one pizza from preparation surface and place on stone. If using pizza pans, place first pizza in the center of the oven. Bake for 15 to 20 minutes or until the crust is lightly browned and cheese is melted.

6. Remove pizza from oven carefully (use peel if baking with a stone). Set aside to rest briefly before slicing. Repeat baking process with second pie.

Fresh Catch

Delicate fish like flounder and sole may be favored for entrees, but on a saucy pizza that delicate flavor can be overwhelmed. The fish can also turn to mush from overhandling and overcooking. Look for firm, meaty fish to add to your pizzas.

Smoked Salmon Pizza

*Think of this as a brunch pizza, with smoked salmon and
all the trimmings over a warm, crispy crust.*

1. Roll or press pizza dough into two very thin 12-inch circles, slightly thicker at the edges than in the center. If using pizza pans, sprinkle the bottom with cornmeal or coat with oil and place dough in pan. If using a pizza stone, sprinkle with cornmeal and place rolled dough directly on stone.

2. Spread ½ cup Lemon Cream Sauce evenly over each pizza. Sprinkle Gouda and Farmer cheese over the sauce.

3. Place pizzas in the oven at 425°. Bake 10 to 12 minutes or until crust is browned and cheese is melted. Remove from the oven and let rest briefly.

4. Divide salmon over each pizza, followed by capers, cucumbers, and tomatoes. Sprinkle with pepper to taste, cut into wedges, and serve immediately.

Makes two 12-inch pizzas

½ recipe California Thin Crust
  dough (page 21)
2 tablespoons cornmeal or
  1 tablespoon oil
1 cup Lemon Cream Sauce
  (page 51)
1 cup finely diced Gouda
  cheese
1 cup crumbled Farmer
  cheese
12 ounces Nova Scotia
  salmon, cut in strips
2 tablespoons capers
1 seedless cucumber, peeled
  and diced
2 plum tomatoes, diced
Freshly ground black pepper
  to taste

*½ recipe California Thin Crust
    dough (page 21)*
3 tablespoons olive oil
2 tablespoons cornmeal
*2 cups Fresh Tomato Sauce
    (page 42)*
*1 tablespoon prepared
    horseradish*
*2 pounds cooked shrimp,
    peeled and deveined*
⅓ cup finely diced red onion
4 cups mozzarella crumbles

Shrimp Cocktail Pizza

*Buy refrigerated prepared horseradish for this dish and check the
"use by" date. Or, for a really pungent treat, grind fresh horseradish
root in a food processor, then mix with 2 or 3 tablespoons of
lemon juice or vinegar and a pinch of salt.*

* * *

1. Roll or press pizza dough into two thin 12-inch circles,
    slightly thicker at the edges than in the center. Spread
    1 tablespoon olive oil over the bottom of two pizza pans or
    large quiche pans. Sprinkle cornmeal over the oil, 1 table-
    spoon on each pan.

2. Preheat oven to 400°. Place pizza pans in the oven and bake
    until crust is lightly browned, about 7 minutes. Remove from
    the oven. Stir horseradish into the tomato sauce. Spoon
    1 cup of sauce over each pizza.

3. Divide shrimp over the tomatoes on each pizza. Sprinkle
    with diced onion. Top each pizza with 2 cups of mozzarella
    crumbles.

4. Return pizzas to the oven and bake until shredded cheese
    has melted and crusts darken slightly, about 5 to 7 minutes.
    Let pizzas rest briefly, then slice with a sharp knife or pizza
    wheel.

Fried Calamari Pizza

Calamari can be tough as rubber bands, and homemade calamari
takes a lot of time to prepare. Buy a good frozen brand,
where the tenderizing has been done for you.

❋   ❋   ❋

1. Fry calamari according to package directions. Drain on paper towels.

2. On a floured board, roll pizza dough into a rectangle. Coat an 11" × 16" oblong metal baking dish with olive oil and sprinkle with cornmeal. Press dough into pan, spreading it to the corners.

3. Spread tomato sauce over the top of the dough. Distribute peppers and fried calamari over the sauce, then sprinkle with black pepper to taste. Combine Parmesan, Asiago, and mozzarella cheeses. Spread evenly over the pizza.

4. Preheat oven to 400°. Bake 20 to 25 minutes or until top is browned and bubbly. Cut into square slices with a sharp knife.

1 pound frozen breaded
    calamari
Vegetable oil for frying
$1/2$ recipe Sicilian Crust dough
    (page 18)
2 tablespoons olive oil
2 tablespoons cornmeal
2 cups Slow-Simmered
    Tomato Sauce (page 40)
1 green bell pepper, cored
    and thinly sliced
1 red bell pepper, cored and
    thinly sliced
Black pepper to taste
1 cup shredded Parmesan
    cheese
1 cup shredded Asiago cheese
2 cups shredded mozzarella
    cheese

1 recipe Chicago Deep-Dish
    Crust dough (page 19)
2 pounds sliced mozzarella
    cheese
1 tablespoon Pernod
4 cups Chunky Tomato Sauce
    (page 41)
36 small steamed mussels,
    shucked
1 cup shredded Parmesan
    cheese

Mussels Marinara Pizza

*Sliced mozzarella gives Chicago-style pizza an even blanket of
cheese layered within the rich crust and sauce.*

✳   ✳   ✳

1. Coat two 12" deep-dish pizza or pie pans with olive oil.
   Divide dough and press into pans, making sure dough goes
   all the way up the sides of the pans. Preheat oven to 450°.

2. Lay mozzarella slices over the crust of each pizza, using
   about half the mozzarella. Stir Pernod into sauce. Pour 1½
   cups sauce in the center of each pizza and spread evenly
   over the mozzarella. Distribute 18 mussels over sauce on
   each pizza.

3. Lay remaining mozzarella slices evenly over the mussels.
   Spread remaining sauce over the cheese layer, dividing
   evenly over the two pizzas. Sprinkle ½ cup Parmesan over
   the top of each pizza.

4. Reduce heat to 400° and bake pizzas for 20 to 25 minutes
   or until crust is light brown and centers are browned and
   bubbly.

Mad for Mussels

*Atlantic Blue mussels are the most common variety available
in North America, and clean, tender farmed mussels are sold
in fish markets and supermarkets. Look for mussels with
tightly closed shells or shells that close when tapped. Clean
mussels in the shell can be steamed in a tomato-wine-saffron
broth or dropped into paella or cioppino. When cooked, the
mussel shells open.*

CHAPTER 8
Hearty Meat Pizzas

½ recipe Chicago Deep-Dish
   Crust dough (page 19)
2 pounds sliced mozzarella
   cheese
4 cups Chunky Tomato Sauce
   (page 41)
½ pound ground beef,
   browned
½ pound bulk sausage,
   browned
½ pound finely diced ham
½ pound finely diced
   pepperoni
2 cups shredded Parmesan
   cheese

Carnivore's Delight

*This hearty pizza isn't for the faint of heart. Serve it on a
cold day with forks and plenty of napkins.*

✻   ✻   ✻

1. Coat two 12" deep-dish pizza or pie pans with olive oil.
   Divide dough and press into pans, making sure dough goes
   all the way up the sides of the pans. Preheat oven to 450°.

2. Lay mozzarella slices over the crust of each pizza, using
   about half the mozzarella. Pour 1½ cups sauce in the center
   of each pizza and spread evenly over the mozzarella. Sprinkle the meats, in the order listed, evenly over the sauce.

3. Lay remaining mozzarella slices evenly over the meats.
   Spread remaining sauce over the cheese layer, dividing
   evenly over the two pizzas.

4. Sprinkle 1 cup Parmesan over the top of each pizza.

5. Reduce heat to 400° and bake pizzas for 20 to 25 minutes
   or until crust is light brown and centers are browned and
   bubbly.

Sausage Savvy

*Most sausage labeled "Italian sausage" or "breakfast
sausage" and some chorizos are fresh sausages, which
means they're very perishable and must be cooked
thoroughly before using. Never add uncooked fresh sausage
to pizzas. Even if the pizza is in the oven long enough to
cook the sausage, you'll wind up with plenty of unwanted
grease on your pie.*

Andouille Sausage, Vidalia Onion, and Pepper Pizza

Authentic andouille is quite spicy, giving this pizza a hot, smoky kick.
The sweetness of the onion and peppers makes a nice counterbalance.

✳   ✳   ✳

1. Roll or press pizza dough into two 12-inch circles, slightly thicker at the edges than in the center. If using pizza pans, sprinkle the bottom with cornmeal or coat with olive oil and place dough in pan. If using a pizza stone, sprinkle with cornmeal and place stone in oven. Preheat oven to 400°.

2. Spread ¾ cup sauce in the center of each pizza, leaving one inch around the edges bare.

3. In a large bowl, combine all the cheeses and toss gently to mix. Sprinkle half the cheese blend over the sauce on each pizza, leaving edges bare.

4. Sprinkle the diced andouille evenly over each pizza. Separate onion rings and lay onions over the pizzas, followed by bell pepper strips.

5. If using a hot stone or tiles, use a well-floured pizza peel to carefully lift one pizza from preparation surface and place on stone. If using pizza pans, place first pizza in the center of the oven. Bake for 15 to 20 minutes or until the crust is lightly browned and cheese is melted.

6. Remove pizza from oven carefully (use peel if baking with a stone). Set aside to rest briefly before slicing. Repeat baking process with second pie.

Makes two 12-inch pizzas

½ recipe Classic Crust dough (page 16) or Bread Machine Crust dough (page 17)
2 tablespoons cornmeal or 1 tablespoon olive oil
1½ cups Slow-Simmered Tomato Sauce (page 40) or Sauce Piquant (page 49)
1½ cups shredded mozzarella cheese
1 cup shredded provolone cheese
½ cup shredded white Cheddar cheese
1 pound andouille sausage, diced
1 Vidalia onion, thinly sliced
1 green bell pepper, cored and cut into strips
1 yellow bell pepper, cored and cut into strips

Makes two 12-inch pizzas

1/2 recipe Classic Crust dough (page 16) or Cornmeal Crust dough (page 25)
2 tablespoons cornmeal or 1 tablespoon olive oil
1 1/2 cups Slow-Simmered Tomato Sauce (page 40)
2 tablespoons unsalted butter
2 cloves garlic, minced
2 cups fresh or rehydrated morels, coarsely chopped
1 pound coarsely ground venison, browned
1/4 cup minced fresh parsley
Freshly ground black pepper to taste
1 cup shredded Asiago cheese
3 cups shredded mozzarella cheese

Venison and Morel Pizza

American morel mushrooms grow wild in Michigan, Oregon, and several other states. Fresh morels are available in the spring, and dried can be purchased year-round. They have a wonderful earthy flavor.

✳ ✳ ✳

1. Roll or press pizza dough into two 12-inch circles, slightly thicker at the edges than in the center. If using pizza pans, sprinkle the bottom with cornmeal or coat with olive oil and place dough in pan. If using a pizza stone, sprinkle with cornmeal and place stone in oven. Preheat oven to 400°.

2. Spread ¾ cup sauce in the center of each pizza, leaving edges bare.

3. In a large skillet, heat 2 tablespoons butter until bubbling. Add garlic and morels and sauté until mushrooms are tender.

4. With a slotted spoon, remove mushrooms from the skillet, draining as much liquid as possible. Distribute mushrooms evenly over pizza sauce. Spread ground venison over each pizza, followed by parsley and black pepper.

5. Sprinkle ½ cup Asiago cheese over the mushrooms and venison on each pizza. Then spread 1½ cups mozzarella evenly over each pizza, leaving edges bare.

6. If using a hot stone or tiles, use a well-floured pizza peel to carefully lift one pizza from preparation surface and place on stone. If using pizza pans, place first pizza in the center of the oven. Bake for 15 to 20 minutes or until the crust is lightly browned and cheese is melted.

7. Remove pizza from oven carefully (use peel if baking with a stone). Set aside to rest briefly before slicing. Repeat baking process with second pie.

Szechwan Shredded Pork Pizza

This pizza can easily go cheeseless for those who prefer a dairy-free pie. Inexpensive cuts of slow-cooked pork shred easily and work best in this recipe.

✳   ✳   ✳

1. In a large, flat-bottomed wok over high heat, combine sesame and vegetable oils, garlic, and ginger. Stir-fry for 10 seconds before adding water chestnuts, mushrooms, bamboo shoots, and green onion. Stir-fry until vegetables are crisp-tender, about 5 minutes. Reduce heat and add pork. Combine soy sauce, hot chile paste, and syrup. Add to wok and simmer just until most liquid has evaporated, stirring often.

2. Roll or press pizza dough into two very thin 12-inch circles, slightly thicker at the edges than in the center. If using pizza pans, sprinkle the bottom with cornmeal or coat with oil and place dough in pan. If using a pizza stone, sprinkle with cornmeal and place rolled dough directly on stone.

3. Paint each crust with Sesame-Soy Sauce. Divide pork mixture evenly over each crust and sprinkle with mozzarella, if desired. Place one pizza in the oven at 425°. Bake 10 to 12 minutes or until crust is browned. Repeat with remaining pizza. Let pizzas rest briefly, then slice with a sharp knife or pizza wheel.

Makes two 12-inch pizzas

2 tablespoons dark sesame oil
1 tablespoon vegetable oil
2 cloves garlic, minced
1 teaspoon minced fresh ginger
1 cup chopped water chestnuts
1 cup matchstick-sliced mushrooms
1/2 cup fine julienne bamboo shoots
2 green onions, minced
3 cups shredded roasted pork shoulder
1/2 cup soy sauce
1 tablespoon hot chile paste
1 tablespoon maple syrup
1/2 recipe California Thin Crust dough (page 21)
2 tablespoons cornmeal or 1 tablespoon oil
1 cup Sesame-Soy Sauce (page 47)
1 cup shredded mozzarella cheese

1/2 recipe Classic Crust dough
  (page 16) or Bread
  Machine Crust dough
  (page 17)
2 tablespoons cornmeal or
  2 tablespoons olive oil
1 1/2 cups Slow-Simmered
  Tomato Sauce (page 40)
  or Speed-Scratch Tomato
  Sauce (page 40)
1 1/2 cups shredded mozzarella
  cheese
1 cup shredded provolone
  cheese
1 pound very rare sirloin or
  New York strip steak,
  thinly sliced
2 cups diced plum tomatoes
1 cup crumbled bleu cheese
Freshly ground black pepper
  to taste

Steak and Tomato Pizza

To turn this pizza into warm steak salad on a crust, cover just-cooked pizza with shredded lettuce and drizzle a bit of creamy dressing over the top.

✳   ✳   ✳

1. Roll or press pizza dough into two 12-inch circles, slightly thicker at the edges than in the center. If using pizza pans, sprinkle the bottom with cornmeal or coat with olive oil and place dough in pan. If using a pizza stone, sprinkle with cornmeal and place stone in oven. Preheat oven to 400°.

2. Spread ¾ cup sauce in the center of each pizza, leaving one inch around the edges bare.

3. In a large bowl, combine mozzarella and provolone cheeses and toss gently to mix. Sprinkle half the cheese blend over the sauce on each pizza, leaving edges bare. Arrange steak strips in circular pattern over each pizza. Distribute tomatoes over each pizza, followed by crumbled bleu cheese and pepper.

4. If using a hot stone or tiles, use a well-floured pizza peel to carefully lift one pizza from preparation surface and place on stone. If using pizza pans, place first pizza in the center of the oven. Bake for 15 to 20 minutes or until the crust is lightly browned and cheese is melted.

5. Remove pizza from oven carefully (use peel if baking with a stone). Set aside to rest briefly before slicing. Repeat baking process with second pie.

Bison Meatball Pizza

Bison is leaner, and some would say more flavorful, than beef. It's farmed in the U.S. and available at many supermarket meat counters.

Makes two 12-inch pizzas

1 pound ground bison
1 egg
1 cup soft bread crumbs
1 tablespoon Worcestershire sauce
2 green onions, minced
1/4 cup fresh parsley leaves, minced
Salt and pepper to taste
1/2 recipe Chicago Deep-Dish Crust dough (page 19)
2 tablespoons olive oil
4 cups Chunky Tomato Sauce (page 41)
2 cups shredded Cheddar cheese
4 cups shredded mozzarella cheese

✳   ✳   ✳

1. In a large bowl, combine bison, egg, bread crumbs, Worcestershire sauce, green onions, and parsley. Add salt and pepper to taste. Work together with hands until well blended and ingredients have been evenly distributed in the meat. (If mixture seems dry, add a small amount of water or club soda to moisten.)

2. Roll the bison mixture into small meatballs, about 1 inch in diameter. Place meatballs on a baking sheet lined with nonstick foil. Bake at 350°, turning occasionally, until meatballs are cooked through, about 15 minutes. Remove from oven.

3. Roll out two circles of pizza dough. Spread olive oil in two 12" deep-dish pizza or pie pans. Press dough circles into pans and prick bottoms a few times with a fork.

4. Ladle 2 cups of sauce into each pan, followed by ½ cup of Cheddar cheese and ½ cup of mozzarella cheese. Divide the meatballs evenly over sauce and cheese in each pan.

5. Divide remaining 1 cup of Cheddar and 3 cups of mozzarella over the pizzas. Bake at 400° until browned and bubbly, about 20 minutes. Let stand 5 minutes, then serve with forks.

Home on the Range
Farmed game meats, such as bison or buffalo (which are the same thing), elk, venison, and boar, make an interesting alternative to the usual beef and pork. Some cuts can be found at large supermarkets or specialty meat markets. If you want a larger selection of cuts and quantities, there are multiple online sources that ship anywhere.

1/2 recipe Classic Crust dough
  (page 16) or Bread
  Machine Crust dough
  (page 17)
2 tablespoons cornmeal or
  1 tablespoon olive oil
1 1/2 cups Slow-Simmered
  Tomato Sauce (page 40)
1 cup shredded Parmesan
  cheese
3 cups shredded mozzarella
  cheese
8 ounces pepperoni, sliced

Pepperoni Pizza

*If you're a real pepperoni lover, feel free to increase the amount
used on each pizza. Buy freshly sliced pepperoni from a deli
counter rather than prepackaged slices.*

❋　❋　❋

1. Roll or press pizza dough into two 12-inch circles, slightly
   thicker at the edges than in the center. If using pizza pans,
   sprinkle the bottom with cornmeal or coat with olive oil
   and place dough in pan. If using a pizza stone, sprinkle with
   cornmeal and place stone in oven. Preheat oven to 400°.

2. Spread ¾ cup sauce in the center of each pizza, leaving one
   inch around the edges bare.

3. Sprinkle ½ cup Parmesan over the sauce on each pizza.
   Distribute 1½ cups mozzarella evenly over each pizza, leaving edges bare. Distribute pepperoni slices evenly over each
   pizza.

4. If baking on a hot stone or tiles, use a well-floured pizza
   peel to carefully lift one pizza from preparation surface and
   place on stone. If using pizza pans, place first pizza in the
   center of the oven. Bake for 15 to 20 minutes or until the
   crust is lightly browned and cheese is melted.

5. Remove pizza from oven carefully (use peel if baking with a
   stone). Set aside to rest briefly before slicing. Repeat baking
   process with second pie.

Passion for Pepperoni
*Pepperoni is by far America's favorite pizza topping, accounting
for more than a third of pizzas ordered. Pepperoni is a dry
salami, made from beef, pork, veal, and spices. It's available in
small- or large-diameter rolls and with varying levels of spiciness
and moisture. Try several varieties to find your favorite.*

Canadian Bacon and Pineapple Pizza

Of course you can top this pizza with the usual red sauce. But the slightly sweet Mustard Cream Sauce makes a nice complement to the smoky bacon and sweet-tart pineapple.

✳   ✳   ✳

Makes two 12-inch pizzas

¹/₂ recipe Classic Crust dough
(page 16) or Bread
Machine Crust dough
(page 17)
2 tablespoons cornmeal or
1 tablespoon olive oil
2 cups Mustard Cream Sauce
(page 51)
1 tablespoon honey
2 cups shredded Emmentaler
cheese
2 cups shredded mozzarella
cheese
8 ounces Canadian bacon
slices, quartered
1 cup diced green bell pepper
1¹/₂ cups quartered pineapple
slices
¹/₂ cup diced red onion
¹/₄ cup minced parsley

1. Roll or press pizza dough into two 12-inch circles, slightly thicker at the edges than in the center. If using pizza pans, sprinkle the bottom with cornmeal or coat with olive oil and place dough in pan. If using a pizza stone, sprinkle with cornmeal and place stone in oven. Preheat oven to 400°.

2. In a bowl, whisk together mustard cream sauce and honey. Spread half the sauce in the center of each pizza, leaving one inch around the edges bare.

3. Sprinkle 1 cup Emmentaler over the sauce on each pizza. Distribute 1 cup mozzarella evenly over each pizza, leaving edges bare.

4. Dot each pizza with half the Canadian bacon, followed by half the bell pepper and half the pineapple. Sprinkle onion and parsley over each pizza.

5. If baking on a hot stone or tiles, use a well-floured pizza peel to carefully lift one pizza from preparation surface and place on stone. If using pizza pans, place first pizza in the center of the oven. Bake for 15 to 20 minutes or until the crust is lightly browned and toppings are bubbly.

6. Remove pizza from oven carefully (use peel if baking with a stone). Set aside to rest briefly before slicing. Repeat baking process with second pie.

¹/₂ recipe Pan Pizza Crust
     dough (page 20)
2 tablespoons olive oil
2 cups Slow-Simmered
     Tomato Sauce (page 40)
3 cups shredded Cheddar
     cheese
1 pound ground beef, cooked
3 cups mozzarella cheese
1 cup crumbled bacon
1 cup chopped onion
Freshly ground black pepper

Double Cheeseburger Pizza

*If you have a passion for mushroom burgers, just add a layer of
sautéed white mushrooms over the ground beef.*

✳   ✳   ✳

1. Roll pizza dough into two circles large enough to cover
   bottoms and sides of two 12" pizza or quiche pans. Spread
   a tablespoon of olive oil over the bottom of each pan, then
   press dough circles into the pans.

2. Ladle 1 cup sauce into each pan and spread evenly over the
   crust. Top sauce with 1 cup Cheddar, followed by ground
   beef.

3. Combine remaining cup of Cheddar with mozzarella.
   Spread evenly over ground beef on each pizza.

4. Dot cheese with crumbled bacon and onion. Add freshly
   ground black pepper to taste. Bake pizzas in a preheated
   oven at 400° until crust has browned and cheese is bubbly,
   about 20 minutes.

Mini Pan Pies

*Serve your guests their own individual pizzas straight from
the oven. Personal-size pizza pans can be purchased at
kitchen supply stores, or you can simply use individual tart
or crème brûlée pans. Bake at 400°. Your pies should be
nicely browned in 10 to 12 minutes. Serve the mini-pizzas
with a thatch of mixed greens tossed with a simple dressing
and fresh fruit.*

Veal Parmesan Pizza

Good veal is, of course, expensive. If you prefer, this dish can be made with thinly sliced pork or turkey breast slices.

* * *

1. Salt and pepper veal, then lightly coat each slice with flour.

2. Whisk together eggs and milk. Pour bread crumbs onto a large plate or pie pan. Dip each veal slice in egg mixture and coat lightly with seasoned bread crumbs.

3. In a large skillet, pour oil to a depth of about 2 inches. Heat over medium-high heat until a drop of water sizzles in the oil. Fry veal slices, a few at a time, until browned. Drain on paper towels.

4. Roll out two circles of pizza dough. Spread olive oil in two 12" deep-dish pizza or pie pans. Press dough circles into pans and prick bottoms a few times with a fork. Ladle 2 cups of tomato sauce into each pan, followed by ½ cup of Parmesan cheese and ½ cup of mozzarella cheese.

5. Arrange fried veal slices over the cheese, overlapping as necessary. Divide remaining 1 cup of Parmesan and 3 cups of mozzarella over the veal slices. Bake at 400° until browned and bubbly, about 20 minutes.

Makes two 12-inch pizzas

1 pound thinly sliced veal cutlets
Salt and pepper to taste
½ cup granulated flour
2 eggs
¼ cup milk
4 cups Italian-style seasoned bread crumbs
Vegetable oil for frying
½ recipe Chicago Deep-Dish Crust dough (page 19)
2 tablespoons olive oil
4 cups Chunky Tomato Sauce (page 41)
2 cups shredded Parmesan cheese
4 cups shredded mozzarella cheese

*¹/₂ recipe Classic Crust dough
(page 16) or Bread
Machine Crust dough
(page 17)*

*2 tablespoons cornmeal or
1 tablespoon olive oil*

*1¹/₂ cups Slow-Simmered
Tomato Sauce (page 40)*

*1 cup shredded Parmesan
cheese*

*3 cups shredded mozzarella
cheese*

*1 pound hot or mild Italian
sausage, browned and
sliced diagonally*

*12 ounces white mushrooms,
sliced*

*1 green bell pepper, cored
and diced*

¹/₂ teaspoon dried oregano

Italian Sausage, Pepper, and Mushroom Pizza

*It's possible to buy five different brands of Italian sausage and get
five different spice blends. Each purveyor follows its own recipe.
Sample until you find one that suits you.*

✳   ✳   ✳

1. Roll or press pizza dough into two 12-inch circles, slightly thicker at the edges than in the center. If using pizza pans, sprinkle the bottom with cornmeal or coat with olive oil and place dough in pan. If using a pizza stone, sprinkle with cornmeal and place stone in oven. Preheat oven to 400°.

2. Spread ¾ cup sauce in the center of each pizza, leaving edges bare.

3. Sprinkle ½ cup Parmesan over the sauce on each pizza. Distribute 1½ cups mozzarella evenly over each pizza, leaving one inch around the edges bare.

4. Arrange sausage slices evenly over cheese on each pizza. Distribute mushrooms over pies, followed by bell pepper and a sprinkle of oregano.

5. If using a hot stone or tiles, use a well-floured pizza peel to carefully lift one pizza from preparation surface and place on stone. If using pizza pans, place first pizza in the center of the oven. Bake for 15 to 20 minutes or until the crust is lightly browned and cheese is melted.

6. Remove pizza from oven carefully (use peel if baking with a stone). Set aside to rest briefly before slicing. Repeat baking process with second pie.

Sesame Pork and Eggplant Pizza

Long, thin Asian-style eggplants hold their shape better and tend to be less bitter than Italian-style eggplant. They don't require salting before cooking.

❋ ❋ ❋

1. In a large, flat-bottomed wok over medium-high heat, combine vegetable and sesame oils. In a large bowl, whisk together garlic, honey or syrup, lemon juice, hot chile paste, and soy sauce. Toss diced pork and eggplant in soy sauce mixture to coat.

2. Add pork and eggplant to wok and cook until pork is no longer pink, about 3 to 5 minutes. Remove from heat.

3. Roll or press pizza dough into two 12-inch circles, slightly thicker at the edges than in the center. If using pizza pans, sprinkle the bottom with cornmeal or coat with olive oil and place dough in pan. If using a pizza stone, sprinkle with cornmeal and place stone in oven. Preheat oven to 400°.

4. Divide pork and eggplant mixture over the two pizza crusts, spreading evenly. Distribute ⅓ cup bamboo shoots over each pizza, followed by the bell pepper. Sprinkle each with green onions.

5. Spread 1½ cups mozzarella over each pizza. If using a hot stone or tiles, use a well-floured pizza peel to carefully lift one pizza from preparation surface and place on stone. If using pizza pans, place first pizza in the center of the oven. Bake for 15 to 20 minutes or until the crust is lightly browned and toppings are bubbly.

6. Remove pizza from oven carefully (use peel if baking with a stone). Set aside to rest briefly before slicing. Repeat baking process with second pie.

Makes two 12-inch pizzas

2 tablespoons vegetable oil
2 tablespoons sesame oil
4 cloves garlic, minced
1 tablespoon honey or maple syrup
1 tablespoon lemon juice
¼ teaspoon hot chile paste
½ cup soy sauce
12 ounces boneless pork, diced
2 Asian eggplants, trimmed and diced
½ recipe Classic Crust dough (page 16) or Bread Machine Crust dough (page 17)
2 cups Sesame-Soy Sauce (page 47)
2 tablespoons cornmeal or 1 tablespoon olive oil
⅔ cup matchstick-cut bamboo shoots
1 large red bell pepper, cored and diced
2 green onions, minced
3 cups shredded mozzarella cheese

1/2 recipe Focaccia Crust
    dough (page 32)
2 tablespoons olive oil
1 cup Pesto Sauce (page 43)
    or Garlic and Oil Sauce
    (page 44)
1/2 cup shredded Parmesan
    cheese
1/2 pound provolone cheese,
    thinly sliced
1/4 pound Genoa salami,
    thinly sliced
1/4 pound ham, thinly sliced
1/4 pound pepperoni, thinly
    sliced
1/2 pound mozzarella cheese,
    thinly sliced
3 plum tomatoes, sliced
1 cup sliced cherry peppers
1 cup sliced green olives
1/4 cup fresh basil ribbons
Freshly ground black pepper
    to taste

Antipasto Pizza

*Think of this pizza as a warm antipasto to go. It's perfect for
serving on the patio during warm weather or as an
offering on a party buffet.*

❉   ❉   ❉

1. Roll focaccia dough into two 12-inch circles. Grease deep-dish pizza pans with olive oil and press dough into the pans. Bake at 400° for 15 minutes, or until focaccias have just begun to brown.

2. Remove from oven and spread Pesto Sauce or Garlic and Oil Sauce over each crust. Sprinkle with Parmesan cheese. Distribute provolone, salami, ham, pepperoni, and mozzarella in alternating layers over each crust. Top each pizza with sliced plum tomatoes, cherry peppers, and olives.

3. Sprinkle basil ribbons over each pizza and add freshly ground black pepper to taste. Return pans to oven and bake for 10 minutes, or just long enough for cheese to melt and tomato slices to become warm and soft.

4. Remove from oven and let stand for a few minutes before slicing.

Antipasto Platters

If you love real antipasto platters, complete with capicolla, hard salami, and pickled vegetables, you can always vary the selection on your Antipasto Pizza. Antipasto really means "before the pasta" and is served as a first course at Italian meals.

Beef Taco Pizza

Taco-seasoned ground beef is available in ready-to-use tubs at supermarkets. Or make your own in 10 minutes with a packet of taco seasoning and ground beef. Just follow package directions.

1. Roll or press pizza dough into two 12-inch circles, slightly thicker at the edges than in the center. If using pizza pans, sprinkle the bottom with cornmeal or coat with olive oil and place dough in pan. If using a pizza stone, sprinkle with cornmeal and place stone in oven. Preheat oven to 400°.

2. Spread 1 cup sauce in the center of each pizza, leaving one inch around the edges bare.

3. Sprinkle 1 cup Cheddar over the sauce on each pizza. Distribute 1 cup Monterey jack evenly over each pizza, leaving edges bare.

4. Spread beef evenly over the cheese on each pizza. Sprinkle sliced green onions over each pizza.

5. If using a hot stone or tiles, use a well-floured pizza peel to carefully lift one pizza from preparation surface and place on stone. If using pizza pans, place first pizza in the center of the oven. Bake for 15 to 20 minutes or until the crust is lightly browned and toppings are bubbly.

6. Remove pizza from oven carefully (use peel if baking with a stone). Set aside to rest briefly before slicing. Repeat baking process with second pie. Just before serving, top pizzas with shredded lettuce and tomatoes. Serve with sour cream.

Makes two 12-inch pizzas

$^1/_2$ recipe Classic Crust dough (page 16) or Cornmeal Crust dough (page 25)
2 tablespoons cornmeal or 1 tablespoon olive oil
2 cups Picante Sauce (page 48)
2 cups shredded Cheddar cheese
2 cups shredded Monterey jack cheese
3 cups cooked, taco-seasoned ground beef
$^1/_3$ cup sliced green onion
4 cups shredded iceberg lettuce
2 cups diced tomatoes
1 cup sour cream

½ recipe Asiago Cheese
   Crust dough (page 33)
   or Classic Crust dough
   (page 16)
2 tablespoons cornmeal or
   1 tablespoon olive oil
1½ cups Lemon Cream Sauce
   (page 51)
2 cups shredded mozzarella
   cheese
½ cup shredded Asiago
   cheese
½ cup shredded Parmesan
   cheese
1 pound spinach, cleaned
   and lightly steamed
1 pound roasted pork
   tenderloin, thinly sliced
½ cup finely chopped sun-
   dried tomatoes

Roast Pork and Spinach Pizza

Fresh spinach has a wonderful, aromatic flavor. But it also harbors a lot of water that can make pizzas and other dishes soggy. Be sure to squeeze liquid from spinach before adding to other dishes.

❋   ❋   ❋

1. Roll or press pizza dough into two 12-inch circles, slightly thicker at the edges than in the center. If using pizza pans, sprinkle the bottom with cornmeal or coat with olive oil and place dough in pan. If using a pizza stone, sprinkle with cornmeal and place stone in oven. Preheat oven to 400°.

2. Spread ¾ cup sauce in the center of each pizza, leaving edges bare.

3. In a large bowl, combine all the cheeses and toss gently to mix. Sprinkle half the cheese blend over the sauce on each pizza, leaving edges bare.

4. Press as much water as possible from steamed spinach. Coarsely chop spinach and distribute evenly over cheese on pizzas. Top cheese and spinach with sliced pork. Sprinkle with sun-dried tomatoes.

5. If baking with a hot stone or tiles, use a well-floured pizza peel to carefully lift one pizza from preparation surface and place on stone. If using pizza pans, place first pizza in the center of the oven. Bake for 15 to 20 minutes or until the crust is lightly browned and cheese is melted.

6. Remove pizza from oven carefully (use peel if baking with a stone). Set aside to rest briefly before slicing. Repeat baking process with second pie.

Hot Italian Sausage and Fennel Pizza

This thick pie travels well and still tastes great at room temperature.

❋ ❋ ❋

1. On a floured board, roll pizza dough into a rectangle. Coat an 11" × 16" oblong metal baking dish with olive oil and sprinkle with cornmeal. Press dough into pan, spreading it to the corners.

2. Spread sauce over the dough, followed by browned sausage.

3. In a large skillet or Dutch oven, heat butter over medium-high heat. Add fennel, mushrooms, and garlic and sauté 3 minutes. Add parsley and remove from heat. Spread mixture over pizza.

4. Combine Parmesan, Asiago, and mozzarella cheeses. Spread evenly over the top of the sausage and vegetables. Preheat oven to 400°. Bake 20 to 25 minutes or until top is browned and bubbly. Cut into square slices with a sharp knife.

Makes one 11 x 16-inch pizza

¹/₂ recipe Sicilian Crust dough (page 18)
2 tablespoons olive oil
2 tablespoons cornmeal
2 cups Slow-Simmered Tomato Sauce (page 40)
1 pound bulk hot Italian sausage, browned
1 tablespoon butter
2 cups sliced fennel bulb
1 pound sliced white or Portobello mushrooms
2 cloves garlic, minced
¹/₂ cup parsley, minced
Black pepper to taste
1 cup shredded Parmesan cheese
1 cup shredded Asiago cheese
2 cups shredded mozzarella cheese

Chopped Ham and Smoked Edam Pizza

Two sauces give this pizza an extra kick.

❋ ❋ ❋

1. Roll dough into two 12-inch circles, slightly thicker at the edges than in the center. If using pizza pans, sprinkle the bottom with cornmeal or coat with olive oil and place dough in pan. If using a pizza stone, sprinkle with cornmeal and place stone in oven. Preheat oven to 400°.

2. Spread a thin layer of Cilantro Pesto sauce over each crust. Follow with a layer of tomato sauce. Sprinkle pizzas with chopped ham. Spread cheese over the pizzas. Top with ground black pepper.

3. Bake pizzas at 400° in the center of the oven for 15 minutes or until browned. Remove and let stand for 5 minutes, then serve.

Makes two 12-inch pizzas

¹/₂ recipe California Thin Crust dough (page 21)
2 tablespoons cornmeal or 2 tablespoons olive oil
1 cup Cilantro Pesto (page 43)
1 cup Fresh Tomato Sauce (page 41)
2 cups chopped ham
3 cups shredded smoked Edam cheese
Freshly ground black pepper to taste

$^1/_2$ recipe Classic Crust dough
(page 16) or Bread
Machine Crust dough
(page 17)
2 tablespoons cornmeal or
1 tablespoon olive oil
$1^1/_2$ cups Slow-Simmered
Tomato Sauce (page 40)
or Speed-Scratch Tomato
Sauce (page 40)
$1^1/_2$ cups shredded mozzarella
cheese
$1^1/_2$ cups shredded Cheddar
cheese
$^1/_2$ pound Lebanon bologna
slices, quartered

Lebanon Bologna Pizza

Lebanon bologna is a smoky, intensely flavored Pennsylvania Dutch-country cold cut that bears little resemblance to ordinary bologna. Buy it at your supermarket deli counter.

✳   ✳   ✳

1. Roll or press pizza dough into two 12-inch circles, slightly thicker at the edges than in the center. If using pizza pans, sprinkle the bottom with cornmeal or coat with olive oil and place dough in pan. If using a pizza stone, sprinkle with cornmeal and place stone in oven. Preheat oven to 400°.

2. Spread ¾ cup sauce in the center of each pizza, leaving one inch around the edges bare.

3. Combine the mozzarella and Cheddar cheeses and toss gently to mix. Sprinkle half the cheese blend over the sauce on each pizza, leaving edges bare. Distribute Lebanon bologna over the cheese.

4. If using a hot stone or tiles, use a well-floured pizza peel to carefully lift one pizza from preparation surface and place on stone. If using pizza pans, place first pizza in the center of the oven. Bake for 15 to 20 minutes or until the crust is lightly browned and cheese is melted.

5. Remove pizza from oven carefully. Use peel if baking with a stone. Set aside to rest briefly before slicing. Repeat baking process with second pie.

Pizza for a Crowd
When introducing friends to pizza made with unusual toppings, like Lebanon bologna or Moo-Shu Tofu, always prepare a traditional cheese or meat pizza to go along. When it comes to pizza, diners either love variety or really don't care for it.

Matchstick Beef and Caramelized Onion Pizza

This sweet-and-savory pie gets a spicy kick from the Horseradish Sauce. Leftover roast beef works perfectly in this dish.

❊　❊　❊

Makes two 12-inch pizzas

2 tablespoons vegetable oil
2 cloves garlic, pressed
1 tablespoon Worcestershire
　sauce
1 tablespoon prepared
　mustard
1 tablespoon lemon juice
2 tablespoons ketchup
$1/2$ teaspoon cumin
$1/2$ pound roasted beef, cut
　into matchstick pieces
2 large sweet onions, thinly
　sliced
3 tablespoons butter
$1/2$ teaspoon sugar
$1/2$ recipe California Thin Crust
　dough (page 21)
2 tablespoons olive oil
2 tablespoons cornmeal
$1^1/2$ cups Horseradish Sauce
　(page 45)
2 cups shredded mozzarella
　cheese
1 cup shredded Asiago cheese

1. In a large bowl, combine oil, garlic, Worcestershire sauce, mustard, lemon juice, ketchup, and cumin. Add matchstick beef and toss well to coat. Set aside.

2. In a large skillet or Dutch oven, combine onions, butter, and sugar. Cook over medium heat, stirring often, until onions reach a uniform deep brown color.

3. Roll or press pizza dough into two thin 12-inch circles, slightly thicker at the edges than in the center. Divide 1 tablespoon olive oil over the bottoms of two pizza pans or large quiche pans. Sprinkle cornmeal over the oil, 1 tablespoon on each pan.

4. Preheat oven to 400°. Spread Horseradish Sauce over each pizza, leaving edges bare. Combine mozzarella and Asiago cheeses and spread evenly over the sauce.

5. Top cheese on pizzas with a generous tangle of caramelized onions, followed by seasoned matchstick beef.

6. Place pizzas in the oven and bake until shredded cheese has melted and crusts darken slightly, about 10 to 12 minutes. Let pizzas rest briefly, then slice with a sharp knife or pizza wheel. If oven won't accommodate both pans easily, bake pizzas one at a time.

1/2 recipe Sicilian Crust dough
    (page 18)
2 tablespoons olive oil
2 tablespoons cornmeal
2 cups Slow-Simmered
    Tomato Sauce (page 40)
1 cup shredded Parmesan
    cheese
2 tablespoons butter
1 pound sliced small
    Portobello mushrooms
2 cloves garlic, minced
1/2 cup parsley, minced
1/2 pound ground beef,
    browned
1/2 pound ham, finely diced
Black pepper to taste
1 cup shredded Asiago cheese
2 cups shredded mozzarella
    cheese

Beef, Ham, and Mushroom Pizza

Serve this meaty pizza at your next tailgate party. The thick crust makes you feel like you're eating an open-faced, hot sandwich.

✳   ✳   ✳

1. On a floured board, roll pizza dough into a rectangle. Coat an 11" × 16" oblong metal baking dish with olive oil and sprinkle with cornmeal. Press dough into the pan, spreading it to the corners.

2. Spread sauce over the top of the dough. Sprinkle evenly with Parmesan cheese.

3. In a large skillet or Dutch oven, heat butter over medium-high heat. Add mushrooms and garlic and sauté 3 to 5 minutes. Add parsley and remove from heat. Spread beef and ham evenly over the sauce, followed by the cooked mushrooms. Add black pepper to taste.

4. Combine Asiago and mozzarella cheeses. Spread evenly over the top of the beef, ham, and mushrooms. Preheat oven to 400°. Bake 20 to 25 minutes or until top is browned and bubbly. Cut into square slices with a sharp knife.

Prosciutto, Pear, and Gorgonzola Pizza

Pick pears that are ripe, but not too soft, for this pizza. Bartlett or Comice pears work well, or try three or four tiny Seckels if they're available.

1. Roll or press pizza dough into two very thin 12-inch circles, slightly thicker at the edges than in the center. If using pizza pans, sprinkle the bottom with cornmeal or coat with oil and place dough in pan. If using a pizza stone, sprinkle with cornmeal and place rolled dough directly on stone.

2. Spread Garlic and Oil Sauce evenly over each pizza. Arrange pear slices in a circular pattern over the pizzas. Cut prosciutto into slivers and spread over pear slices. Sprinkle Gorgonzola over the pizzas.

3. Place one pizza in the oven at 425°. Bake 10 to 12 minutes or until crust is browned and cheese is soft. Repeat with remaining pizza.

4. Let pizzas rest briefly, then slice with a sharp knife or pizza wheel.

The Fruits of Your Labor

Firm fruits like apples, pears, and quince make a great addition to pizzas featuring smoky meats and intense cheeses. Be sure to slice fruits thinly enough that they soften slightly during baking. You probably want to remove the peels on most fruits, too, as the peels will dry up as the fruit cooks.

Makes two 12-inch pizzas

$^1/_2$ recipe California Thin Crust dough (page 21)
2 tablespoons cornmeal or 1 tablespoon oil
1 cup Garlic and Oil Sauce (page 44)
2 small pears, peeled, cored, and sliced
4 ounces thinly sliced prosciutto
1 cup crumbled Gorgonzola cheese

*1/2 recipe Classic Crust dough
  (page 16)*
*2 tablespoons cornmeal or
  2 tablespoons olive oil*
*1 1/2 cups whole-milk ricotta
  cheese*
1 tablespoon plain yogurt
2 green onions, minced
2 cloves garlic, pressed
1/4 cup minced parsley
Black pepper to taste
*3 cups shredded mozzarella
  cheese*
1 cup diced tomatoes
8 ounces gyro meat, chopped

Gyro Pizza

Gyro meat is a dense loaf of minced and spiced pork, lamb, or beef that's spit-roasted. Many supermarkets carry it in the freezer section. A few carry fresh gyro meat in the deli section.

✳   ✳   ✳

1. Roll or press pizza dough into two 12-inch circles, slightly thicker at the edges than in the center. If using pizza pans, sprinkle the bottom with cornmeal or coat with olive oil and place dough in pan. If using a pizza stone, sprinkle with cornmeal and place stone in oven. Preheat oven to 400°.

2. Combine ricotta with yogurt, green onion, garlic, and parsley. Add black pepper to taste. Spread ricotta mixture over each pizza, leaving edges bare. Sprinkle 1½ cups mozzarella over each pizza, followed by tomatoes and gyro meat.

3. If baking on a hot stone or tiles, use a well-floured pizza peel to carefully lift one pizza from preparation surface and place on stone. If using pizza pans, place first pizza in the center of the oven. Bake for 15 to 20 minutes or until the crust is lightly browned and toppings are bubbly.

4. Remove pizza from oven carefully (use peel if baking with a stone). Set aside to rest briefly before slicing. Repeat baking process with second pie.

Ground Pork, Black Olive, and Feta Pizza

Ground turkey or even ground chicken can easily substitute for the ground pork in this recipe. Or, for a real Greek homage, try ground or chopped lamb.

❈　❈　❈

1. Roll or press pizza dough into two 12-inch circles, slightly thicker at the edges than in the center. If using pizza pans, sprinkle the bottom with cornmeal or coat with olive oil and place dough in pan. If using a pizza stone, sprinkle with cornmeal and place stone in oven. Preheat oven to 400°.

2. Spread ¾ cup sauce in the center of each pizza, leaving one inch around the edges bare.

3. Sprinkle ¾ cup mozzarella cheese over the sauce on each pizza. Distribute 1 cup crumbled feta evenly over each pizza, leaving edges bare. Evenly distribute pork, olives, and oregano leaves, then grind black pepper to taste over each pizza.

4. If using a hot stone or tiles, use a well floured pizza peel to carefully lift one pizza from preparation surface and place on stone. If using pizza pans, place first pizza in the center of the oven. Bake for 15 to 20 minutes or until the crust is lightly browned and cheese is melted.

5. Remove pizza from oven carefully (use peel if baking with a stone). Set aside to rest briefly before slicing. Repeat baking process with second pie.

Makes two 12-inch pizzas

½ recipe Spinach Crust dough (page 29) or Bread Machine Crust dough (page 17)
2 tablespoons cornmeal or 2 tablespoons olive oil
1½ cups Slow-Simmered Tomato Sauce (page 40)
1½ cups shredded mozzarella cheese
2 cups crumbled feta cheese
½ pound cooked ground pork
1 cup chopped black olives
¼ cup fresh oregano leaves
Black pepper to taste

½ recipe Sicilian Crust dough
    (page 18)
2 tablespoons olive oil
2 tablespoons cornmeal
2 cups Slow-Simmered
    Tomato Sauce (page 40)
1 tablespoon butter
1 pound rib eye, sliced
    paper-thin
2 cloves garlic, minced
½ cup parsley, minced
Black pepper to taste
2 cups shredded provolone
    cheese
2 cups shredded mozzarella
    cheese

Cheesesteak Pizza

Cheesesteak lovers fall into two camps: those who think cheesesteaks taste best with real provolone, and those who prefer a melted cheese sauce drizzled on top. If you fall into the latter camp, just replace the provolone with diced processed cheese.

✳   ✳   ✳

1. On a floured board, roll pizza dough into a rectangle. Coat an 11" × 16" oblong metal baking dish with olive oil and sprinkle with cornmeal. Press dough into the pan, spreading it to the corners.

2. Spread the sauce over the top of the dough.

3. In a large skillet or Dutch oven, heat butter over high heat. Add sliced steak and garlic and sauté 3 to 5 minutes until beef is cooked. Add parsley and black pepper and remove from heat. Arrange steak over the top of the pizza.

4. Combine provolone and mozzarella cheeses. Spread evenly over the top of the steak. Preheat oven to 400°. Bake 20 to 25 minutes or until top is browned and bubbly. Cut into square slices with a sharp knife.

King of Steaks

At Pat's Steaks in South Philadelphia, steak sandwiches were created when the owners of a hot dog stand on the site decided to grill up steak sandwiches for their own supper. Regulars got a whiff and wanted the steaks too. The next day, steak sandwiches were all the rage. It took a few more years for the cheese to be added.

CHAPTER 9
Breaking with Tradition: Alternative Pizzas

2 shelf-stable 12-inch pizza
crusts (Boboli or other)
1 cup jarred pizza sauce or
thick pasta sauce
4 cups preshredded Italian
six-cheese blend
2 cups sliced pepperoni

Semi-Homemade Pizza

The toppings for this quick-fix pie can be varied according to your tastes or what's in the fridge. Even though the prep is done for you, you'll still have the great smell of fresh-baked pizza in the house.

✳ ✳ ✳

1. Place one ready-to-top crust on a perforated pizza pan or pizza stone. Spread half the sauce over the top of the pizza, leaving the edges of the crust bare. Sprinkle 2 cups cheese evenly over the sauce. Distribute 1 cup pepperoni slices over the cheese.

2. Bake at 450° for 12 minutes or until cheese is melted and bubbly. Remove from oven and let rest briefly before slicing. Repeat procedure with remaining ingredients to make second pie.

Convenience Rules
Yes, from-scratch cooking yields many rewards—both psychic and gastronomic. But even if you don't have time to do it all yourself, you don't have to resort to take-out food. Supermarkets are full of products like ready-to-top pizza crusts, preshredded cheese, cooked meats, and prechopped veggies. In general, these items are higher quality than the cardboard-tasting versions of a decade ago.

Pita Pizza

Hummus makes a great, unexpected topping for these herb-laced pizzas. If you want a full Mediterranean experience, add a little tabbouleh to the toppings.

✻   ✻   ✻

1. Place whole pita loaves, uncut, on a baking sheet lined with non-stick foil. Spread pesto sauce over each loaf. With a small spoon, place little dabs of hummus over each loaf and lightly press with the back of the spoon to spread.

2. Sprinkle a cup of cheese over each loaf. Bake pita pizzas at 350° for 10 minutes until cheese is melted and pitas are toasty. Let stand for a few minutes before serving. Allow one pita pizza per person.

Makes four 6-inch pizzas

---

4 white or whole-wheat pita loaves
1 cup prepared pesto sauce
1 cup prepared hummus
4 cups shredded mozzarella cheese

English Muffin Pizza

This is the quintessential afternoon snack pizza, easily assembled from ingredients most people have on hand.

✻   ✻   ✻

1. Split English muffins and toast the halves, either in a toaster or in the oven. Place muffin halves soft-side up on a baking sheet. Spread pasta sauce over each muffin half. Combine the cheeses and sprinkle over the sauce on each muffin pizza.

2. Place muffins in a 350° oven and bake for 12 minutes or until cheese is bubbly and browned. Let stand briefly before serving.

Makes 6 small pizzas

---

3 English muffins
1 cup thick pasta sauce
2 cups shredded mozzarella cheese
1 cup shredded Parmesan cheese

12 (6-inch) soft corn tortillas
2 cups warm queso dip
2 cups taco-seasoned ground
    beef
1 cup chunky salsa
4 cups shredded Mexican
    cheese blend
Sour cream

Nacho Tortilla Pizza

*Use commercially prepared queso for this recipe, or make up a
batch of that old favorite, Ro-Tel Dip. Just melt a pound of
Velveeta cheese with a can of Ro-Tel tomatoes and green chiles.*

✲   ✲   ✲

1. Cover a large baking sheet with nonstick foil. Place four
    tortillas on the sheet. Spread some of the queso over each,
    followed by a sprinkle of ground beef. Top each with
    another tortilla. Divide the remaining queso and beef over
    the second tortilla layer. Top each tortilla pizza with another
    tortilla.

2. Spread salsa over the top of each tortilla stack, followed by
    1 cup of shredded cheese. Bake tortilla pizzas at 350° for
    12 minutes or until shredded cheese is melted and lightly
    browned.

3. Let pizzas stand for a few minutes, then serve with sour
    cream.

Embrace the Mess
*Sometimes the best-tasting foods are the most unwieldy.
Don't shy away from a recipe that could turn into a gooey
mess, particularly if you love saucy, cheesy dishes. Just use
a wide spatula to transfer your mini pizzas onto plates and
serve with forks.*

French Bread Pizza

Whether you buy super-skinny, hard baguettes or slightly larger, softer loaves is a matter of personal taste. Either type of French bread will work for this recipe.

❋ ❋ ❋

1. With a bread knife, slice loaf in half horizontally, then cut pieces in half vertically to create four 6-inch French bread crusts. Place bread soft-side up on a baking sheet covered with nonstick foil. Brush olive oil over the top of each loaf. Place in a 350° oven for 5 to 10 minutes to toast loaves slightly.

2. In a large bowl, combine garlic, parsley, tomatoes, olives, salt, and pepper. Mix well. Remove bread from oven and divide mixture evenly over each loaf. Sprinkle ½ cup of bleu cheese over each loaf.

3. Return pizzas to oven and bake 10 minutes. Let stand briefly before serving.

A World of Breads

French, Italian, Cuban, sourdough—virtually any substantial bread can become a pizza crust. Day-old bread works particularly well, standing up to sauces and moist toppings. Experiment with different loaf styles, including crusty artisan-type breads. Bread pizzas also work well on the grill and, unlike pizzas that start with uncooked dough, can be placed over the coals and removed with ordinary barbecue tongs.

Makes four 6-inch-long pizzas

1 (12-inch) loaf crusty French bread
⅓ cup olive oil
2 teaspoons minced garlic
¼ cup minced parsley
2 cups diced plum tomatoes
1 cup chopped black olives
Salt and black pepper to taste
2 cups crumbled bleu cheese

6 large Portobello mushroom
     caps
2 tablespoons butter
1 garlic clove, minced
$\frac{1}{2}$ cup balsamic vinaigrette
3 plum tomatoes, trimmed
     and sliced
$1\frac{1}{2}$ cups crumbled
     Gorgonzola cheese
1 cup shredded mozzarella
     cheese
1 tablespoon dried oregano
Black pepper to taste

Portobello Mushroom Pizza

*Low-carb dieters can rejoice in this grain-free pizza. It makes
a particularly delicious centerpiece to a salad of
lightly dressed, tossed spring greens.*

✳   ✳   ✳

1. Rinse mushroom caps and pat dry. Melt butter in a heavy
   skillet over medium-high heat. Add garlic. Quickly sear
   mushroom caps top-down in the skillet. Place caps, underside up, on a baking sheet lined with nonstick foil.

2. Brush caps with balsamic vinaigrette. Place tomato slices
   over each mushroom cap, then top with Gorgonzola cheese
   and shredded mozzarella. Season with oregano and black
   pepper.

3. Bake mushrooms at 350° for 10 to 12 minutes or until cheese
   is melted and bubbly. Remove from oven and let stand
   briefly before serving.

Toast Cup Pizzas

Sixties-era hostesses used to serve chicken à la king in little bread cups like these. If you want to get fancy-schmancy, you can use pastry shells instead of toast cups.

❅   ❅   ❅

1. Generously butter the cups of a 12-cup muffin pan. Press one bread slice into each cup, leaving bread corners sticking out in four points. Slices should form a cup shape, with no tears. Bake at 350° for 10 to 15 minutes or until slices are browned and crisp at the edges.

2. In a bowl, combine sauce, pepperoni, sausage, mushrooms, green pepper, and onion. Stir to blend. Spoon mixture into the cups, dividing equally. Sprinkle cheese over each cup.

3. Return muffin pan to the oven and bake at 350° for 10 minutes or until cheese is melted and filling is bubbly. Let stand 5 minutes before serving.

A Bowl of Bread

Crust is nothing more than glorified bread, and the original pizzas were meals on edible bread plates. Experiment with different types of bread-borne pizzas. Crusty rye bread might make a perfect foil for that corned beef and cabbage pizza with Dubliner cheese you've been thinking about for St. Patrick's Day.

Makes 12 cups

1 dozen slices white or soft wheat bread
2 cups pizza sauce
1 cup chopped pepperoni
1 cup browned bulk sausage
1 cup chopped mushrooms
$1/2$ cup finely diced green pepper
$1/2$ cup finely diced onion
4 cups shredded Italian-blend cheese

Makes two 12-inch pizzas

2 (12-inch) ready-to-top pizza
    crusts
1½ cups thick pasta sauce
1 cup browned ground beef
    or chopped meatballs
1 cup chopped chicken or
    ham
1 cup drained peas or
    chopped broccoli
2 green onions, minced
2 teaspoons mixed dried
    herbs
1 pound sliced cheese (any
    varieties)

Leftovers Pizza

Use your imagination, and all those little plastic containers of leftover food, to top this pizza. Recycled leftovers never tasted so good.

✳   ✳   ✳

1. Place one pizza crust on a perforated pizza pan or pizza stone. Spread with half the pasta sauce and top with half the meats and vegetables. Sprinkle with half the green onions and herbs. Place half the cheese slices, overlapping, over the toppings.

2. Bake the pizza in a 450° oven for 10 to 12 minutes or until the cheese is melted and bubbly. Remove from the oven and let stand for a few minutes before slicing. Repeat process with the second crust and remaining ingredients.

Makes 12 servings

1 pound cream cheese,
    softened
2 tablespoons mayonnaise
1 teaspoon Italian seasoning
    blend
½ teaspoon black pepper
1 cup Parmesan cheese
1 cup minced pepperoni
1 cup pizza sauce
3 cups shredded Italian blend
    cheese

Cream Cheese Pizza Dip

This layered dip goes very well with breadsticks and focaccia wedges, as well as the usual chips and crackers.

✳   ✳   ✳

1. In a mixer bowl, combine cream cheese, mayonnaise, Italian seasoning, and black pepper. Mix on low until ingredients are thoroughly blended. Add Parmesan cheese and mix briefly.

2. Fold in minced pepperoni and spread mixture in a lightly greased casserole dish. Spread pizza sauce over the top of the cream cheese and spread shredded cheese over sauce.

3. Bake at 350° until browned and bubbly, about 12 to 15 minutes. Serve with breadsticks, vegetables, and other dippers.

Pepperoni-in-a-Pie-Crust Pizza

This gooey deep-dish pie is for real pepperoni lovers only. However, the basic recipe can be used with other meats and veggies.

❉ ❉ ❉

1. Unfold pie crusts and press into two greased 9" deep-dish pie pans. Layer cheese slices over the crust. Combine pasta sauce and tomatoes and spoon a small amount over the cheese. Top with a layer of sliced pepperoni and chopped pepperoni.

2. Continue to layer cheese, sauce, and pepperoni in the pie crust, until all the ingredients have been used. Sprinkle Parmesan over the top of each pie.

3. Bake pies at 350° for 30 minutes or until pies are browned and bubbly.

Deep Dish, Quick Dish

Ordinary pie crust can be used to create deep-dish pizzas. Or line a pie pan with refrigerated crescent roll or flattened biscuit dough for a springier crust. For a really unusual improvised crust, hollow out a round loaf of hearth-baked artisan bread. Fill it with a small amount of sauce, meats, and cheese and bake until the cheese is melted.

2 refrigerated pie crusts
1 pound mozzarella slices
2 cups thick pasta sauce
1 can chopped tomatoes, drained
2 cups sliced pepperoni
1 cup chopped pepperoni
1 cup shredded Parmesan cheese

2 (1-pound) rolls ready-made
  polenta
2 cups thick pasta sauce
2 cups shredded Italian-blend
  cheese
1 pound Italian sausage,
  browned and sliced
¹/₃ cup minced fresh parsley

Polenta Pizza

*This recipe makes wonderful hors d'oeuvres. Or, for
a kids' party, use cookie cutters to cut the polenta
into fanciful shapes before topping.*

✳   ✳   ✳

1. Slice each polenta roll into 8 slices. Place slices on a cookie
   sheet lined with nonstick foil. Spread each polenta top with
   pasta sauce and sprinkle with shredded cheese. Top with
   sliced sausage and garnish with parsley.

2. Bake at 350° for 12 to 15 minutes or until cheese is melted
   and polenta becomes crisp around the edges. Let stand
   briefly before serving.

Polenta Possibilities

*Ready-made polenta is easy to use and available in the
refrigerator case of most supermarkets. However, if you're
willing to stir a cup of cornmeal into 5 cups of boiling water
for 20 to 30 minutes, you can make your own. The great
thing about homemade polenta is that you control the
consistency—creamy or stiff—and you can flavor it with
cheese, chopped mushrooms, herbs, sun-dried tomatoes, or
whatever else you fancy.*

Grits Pizza

To serve this pizza as a brunch casserole, just top the hot pizza with 8 poached or over-easy eggs and serve each guest an egg-topped slice. For a south-of-the-border turn, replace pizza sauce with salsa and use Monterey jack instead of mozzarella.

Makes one 9 × 13-inch pizza

7 cups water
1 teaspoon salt
1½ cups corn grits
2 tablespoons butter
2 cups shredded Cheddar cheese
1 cup pizza sauce or thick pasta sauce
1 pound sliced mushrooms, sautéed
2 cups finely diced ham
2 cups shredded mozzarella cheese

※　※　※

1. Bring water and salt to a rolling boil in a heavy pot. Slowly pour grits into the water, stirring constantly to keep grains from clumping. Boil for 3 to 5 minutes, stirring, until mixture thickens. Then reduce heat to medium-low and cook grits for 20 to 30 minutes, stirring constantly.

2. When grits are thick enough to hold a spoon standing upright in the pot, add butter and Cheddar cheese. Stir until well blended. Pour grits into a buttered oblong baking dish, smooth top, and let stand for 10 minutes.

3. Top grits with pizza or pasta sauce and cover with sautéed mushrooms, diced ham, and mozzarella cheese. Bake at 350° for 12 minutes, or until cheese is melted and lightly browned. Let stand several minutes before serving.

The Gritty on Grits

Southern breakfasts always include a side of grits, a coarse meal made from ground dried corn. For best flavor, buy yellow stone-ground corn grits, which are made from whole-kernel dried corn. White hominy grits come from dried corn soaked in an alkaline solution to remove the outer husk. Polenta and cornmeal are grits' cousins, made from dried corn that's been more finely ground.

4 large soft spinach tortillas
1 cup pizza sauce or thick
    pasta sauce
$1/2$ cup Alfredo sauce
2 cups shredded cooked
    chicken
1 cup broccoli slaw
2 cups shredded mozzarella
    cheese
1 cup shredded Colby cheese

Pizza Wraps

*Broccoli slaw, available in supermarket bagged-salad sections,
gives these wraps a slight crunch and a nutritional boost.*

✳   ✳   ✳

1. Lay spinach tortillas flat on a work surface. Combine pizza
   or pasta sauce with Alfredo sauce. Spread a layer of sauce
   in the center of each tortilla. Arrange shredded chicken and
   broccoli slaw in a wide strip in the center of each tortilla.
   Sprinkle cheeses over the top of the entire tortilla.

2. Fold the bottom 2 inches of the tortillas over the filling ingredients, leaving a straight edge at the bottom of each wrap.
   Fold the sides of the tortillas inward, overlapping.

3. Place wraps, seam side down, on a baking sheet lined with
   nonstick foil. Bake at 350° for 6 to 7 minutes, just to warm.
   Use a wide spatula to remove each wrap from the baking
   sheet. Serve immediately.

Pizza Omelet

*This baked egg dish is actually more frittata than omelet. But it's
a great way to have eggs for four ready at once.*

* * *

Makes one 12-inch omelet

1 dozen eggs
$1/2$ cup heavy cream
Salt and pepper to taste
1 teaspoon dried mixed
 Italian seasoning
1 cup diced bell pepper
1 cup sliced mushroom
$1/2$ cup chopped onion
$1/2$ pound bacon, cooked crisp
 and crumbled
1 cup pizza or pasta sauce
$1^1/2$ cups shredded mozzarella
 cheese
$1/2$ cup shredded Parmesan
 cheese

1. Place eggs, cream, salt, pepper, and Italian seasoning in a blender. Pulse until thick and well blended.

2. Butter a 12" pizza or quiche pan. Sprinkle bell pepper, mushrooms, onion, and bacon evenly over the pan. Pour egg mixture into the pan and bake at 350° for 20 minutes.

3. Remove omelet from the oven. Spread sauce over the top and sprinkle with mozzarella and Parmesan cheese. Return to the oven and bake another 5 to 6 minutes—just long enough for the cheese to melt. Remove from oven, cut into four wedges, and serve.

Rice Cake Pizza

*This quick snack pizza doesn't even require heating.
Just pile on the ingredients and munch away.*

* * *

Makes 6 pizzas

6 large plain or cheese
 flavored rice cakes
8 ounces cream cheese
$1/3$ cup pizza sauce or pasta
 sauce
Dash Tabasco
6 thin slices ham
6 thin slices turkey
6 slices provolone cheese

1. Combine cream cheese with pizza sauce and Tabasco. Spread over the tops of each rice cake. Top each cake with a slice of ham and a slice of turkey.

2. Top rice cakes with provolone cheese and serve.

Bagel Pizzas

Makes 6 pizzas

3 large bagels, plain, wheat,
    or Asiago cheese
2 cups ricotta cheese
2 plum tomatoes, thinly sliced
1 teaspoon dried oregano
Black pepper to taste
2 cups shredded Italian-blend
    cheese

*This recipe makes a great alternative to ordinary bagels and
cream cheese. For variety, add a slice of smoked salmon
or a slice of salami over the ricotta.*

❊   ❊   ❊

1. Split bagels in half horizontally and toast lightly. Place toasted bagels cut-side up on a baking sheet lined with nonstick foil. Spread each with ⅓ cup ricotta cheese and top with slices of tomato. Sprinkle tomatoes with oregano and black pepper.

2. Top each bagel with ½ cup shredded cheese. Bake at 350° for 8 to 10 minutes or until cheese is melted. Let stand briefly before serving.

Right-Sized Bagels

Bakery bagels—those giant, puffy, chewy-crust wonders—actually represent four servings of bread. According to the U.S.D.A., a standard serving of bagel is half of a 3½-inch version. Our bagel pizzas use the large-size bagels, with one-half of a bagel forming the crust for each. That's two servings of bread, or about what most folks consume at lunch.

Matzo Pizza

*These matzo stacks can be tricky to cut. Use a sharp chef's knife and
cut each stack down the center with a quick, firm motion.
Each stack makes two servings.*

✳   ✳   ✳

Makes 2 pizzas

6 whole matzos
1 cup pesto sauce
1 cup pizza sauce or thick
    pasta sauce
1 cup shredded Parmesan
    cheese
4 plum tomatoes, thinly sliced
2 teaspoons olive oil
2 cups shredded mozzarella
    cheese

1. Place two matzos side by side on a baking sheet lined with non-stick foil. Spread the top of each with pesto sauce, then place another matzo on top of the sauce. Spread the tops of the second matzos with pizza or pasta sauce and top each with ½ cup of Parmesan cheese.

2. Place the remaining matzos on top of each stack and brush with olive oil. Distribute tomato slices over the tops and sprinkle each with a cup of mozzarella cheese. Bake at 350° for 10 to 12 minutes or until cheese is melted and stacks are heated through. Let stand a few minutes, then cut each stack in half and serve.

Pizza Pretzels

*These aromatic pretzels make a great after-school snack.
They also freeze well.*

✳   ✳   ✳

Makes 4 pizza pretzels

1 pound frozen bread dough,
    thawed
½ cup pizza sauce
1 teaspoon dried oregano
Red pepper flakes to taste
4 slices provolone cheese
4 slices mozzarella cheese

1. Allow bread dough to rise until doubled in size. Punch down and divide into four pieces. Roll each piece into a 20-inch rope. Line two baking sheets with nonstick foil. Coil dough ropes into four pretzels, two on each sheet. Let dough rise for about an hour.

2. Gently spoon pizza sauce over the pretzels and sprinkle each with oregano and, if desired, red pepper flakes. Bake at 400° for 10 minutes or until pretzels are golden.

3. Immediately top each pretzel with a slice of provolone and a slice of mozzarella. Let stand until cheese melts over pretzels. Serve.

Makes one 9 × 13-inch
kugel
_____

6 large Idaho-type potatoes,
    peeled
1 medium onion
2 cloves garlic, pressed
1 teaspoon oregano
3 eggs
3 tablespoons olive oil
$^1/_2$ cup flour
1 teaspoon baking powder
1 teaspoon salt
$^1/_2$ teaspoon black pepper
1$^1/_2$ cups thick pasta sauce
4 cups shredded Italian-blend
    cheese

T

Pizza Kugel

*This pizza dish uses potato kugel as a base, since most noodle
kugels tend to be sweet. Serve this as a meat-free main course or
as a side dish with grilled salmon.*

�֍   �֍   �֍

1. In a food processor with a shredding disk, grate potatoes
    and onion. Place shreds in a large bowl with garlic, oregano,
    eggs, and olive oil. Stir until well blended. Combine flour,
    baking powder, salt, and black pepper. Slowly add to potato
    mixture while stirring to form a thick batter.

2. Bake kugel at 350° until firm and browned, about 40 min-
    utes. Remove from oven and spread room-temperature
    pasta sauce over the top of the kugel, followed by shredded
    cheese.

3. Return kugel to the oven and bake 5 to 10 minutes, until
    cheese has melted and sauce is bubbly. Let stand briefly
    before slicing.

Noodling over Kugels
*Fruity, sweet noodle kugels can form the basis for an
unusual dessert pizza. Prepare your favorite sweet dairy
kugel recipe with wide noodles. Combine strawberry yogurt
with sweetened sour cream and pour over the top of the
baked casserole. Top with dried fruit or fresh berries and
shredded coconut.*

Pizza Casserole

This recipe is either pizza without the crust or lasagna without the ground beef. Feel free to layer in other ingredients you may have on hand for a low-fuss, family-friendly midweek supper.

✳   ✳   ✳

1. Cook noodles according to package directions, making sure not to overcook. Drain well and toss with olive oil, salt, and pepper.

2. Arrange a layer of noodles in a buttered baking dish. Top with a cup of sauce, followed by the bell pepper, mushrooms, onion, and sausage. Sprinkle 1 cup of shredded cheese over the sausage layer. Spread another layer of noodles over the casserole, followed by 1 cup of sauce, sliced pepperoni, and another cup of cheese. Add the remaining noodles in an even layer and cover generously with sauce. Distribute dollops of ricotta over the noodles, then spread the remaining cheese over the top of the casserole.

3. Place the dish on a baking sheet to catch drips and bake at 350° for 30 to 35 minutes. Cheese should be nicely browned. Let stand 10 minutes before serving.

Makes one 9 × 13-inch casserole

---

1 (1-pound) bag wide noodles
1 tablespoon olive oil
Salt and pepper to taste
4 cups thick pasta sauce
1 cup green bell pepper, diced
1 pound sliced mushrooms
1 medium onion, diced
$^1/_2$ pound Italian sausage, cooked and sliced
6 cups shredded Italian-blend cheese
$^1/_2$ pound sliced pepperoni
1 cup ricotta cheese

6 large black bean cakes,
    fully cooked
1¹/₂ cups fresh tomato salsa
¹/₂ cup sliced black olives
3 cups shredded Mexican
    blend cheese
Sour cream
Avocado slices

Bean Cake Pizzas

Bean cakes make a flavorful, yielding crust for these little snack pizzas. Cocktail-sized bean cakes can be used to prepare beany-pizza hors d'oeuvres.

❋　　❋　　❋

1. Place bean cakes on a baking sheet lined with nonstick foil. Top each with ¼ cup well-drained salsa, a few black olive slices, and ½ cup shredded cheese.

2. Bake bean cake pizzas at 350° or until cheese is melted. Serve with sour cream and avocado slices.

Bean Burgers

Black bean cakes can be found in supermarket freezer cases, as well as freshly made at gourmet markets. To create your own, drain canned beans and mash with a fork. Stir in chopped peppers, green onion, garlic, salt, pepper, and cumin, plus an egg and enough bread crumbs to make a stiff mixture. Roll the mixture into balls, then flatten the bean balls, coat with cornmeal or bread crumbs, and pan-fry until browned. Some cooks like to add shredded carrots or whole-kernel corn to the mix for color.

CHAPTER 10
Dessert Pizzas

Makes two 12-inch pizzas

½ recipe Chocolate Crust
 dough (page 37)
1 tablespoon melted butter
3 cups Chocolate Ganache
 (page 54)
3 cups coarsely grated white
 chocolate
1 cup coarsely grated milk
 chocolate

Triple-Chocolate Pizza

*Grate good-quality chocolate bars by hand or with a food
processor fitted with a large-hole shredding blade.
However, make sure the chocolate is cold or the friction
will cause it to melt while grating.*

✳   ✳   ✳

1. Roll or press pizza dough into two 12-inch circles, slightly thicker at the edges than in the center. Coat pizza pans with melted butter and place dough in the pans. Bake dough at 375° for 20 minutes. Remove from oven and allow to cool. Remove crusts from pans and place on serving platters.

2. Spread 1½ cups ganache evenly over each pizza. Allow pizzas to cool to warm room temperature. Sprinkle grated chocolate evenly over each pizza and serve immediately.

For the True Chocoholic

A freshly baked chocolate pizza crust is a wonderful thing. But if you're a chocolate purist, you can always melt your favorite chocolate bars—eating-quality chocolate, not baking chocolate—and pour the chocolate into a 12" nonstick pizza pan. Let it cool and harden, then top this pure chocolate "crust" with frosting and your favorite candies.

Peaches and Cream Pizza

Make a small X at the bottom of each fresh peach, then plunge the peach in boiling water for a few seconds. Remove it with a slotted spoon. The skin should slip right off.

* * *

Makes two 12-inch pizzas

$^{1}/_{2}$ recipe Sweet Crust dough
(page 36)
1 tablespoon melted butter
3 cups Sweet Mascarpone
Sauce (page 52)
4 cups peeled, sliced peaches
3 cups confectioners' sugar
$^{1}/_{2}$ cup heavy cream
4 cups whipped cream

1. Roll or press pizza dough into two 12-inch circles, slightly thicker at the edges than in the center. Coat pizza pans with the melted butter and place dough in the pans. Bake dough at 375° for 20 minutes. Remove from oven and allow to cool. Remove crusts from pans and place on racks to cool completely. Transfer to serving platters.

2. Spread 1½ cups sauce evenly over each pizza. Distribute 2 cups sliced peaches over the sauce on each pizza. In a small bowl, whisk confectioners' sugar to remove any lumps, then stir in heavy cream until smooth. Drizzle this glaze in a crosshatch pattern over the peaches. Spoon on mounds of whipped cream just before serving.

½ recipe Chocolate Crust
dough (page 37)
1 tablespoon melted butter
3 cups smooth peanut butter
½ cup heavy cream
1 cup Chocolate Ganache
(page 54)
2 cups coarsely grated white
chocolate
1 cup coarsely grated milk
chocolate
1 cup chopped peanuts

Chocolate Peanut Butter Pizza

Think of this pizza as the best chocolate
peanut butter cup you've ever tasted.

❄   ❄   ❄

1. Roll or press pizza dough into two 12-inch circles, slightly thicker at the edges than in the center. Coat pizza pans with the melted butter and place dough in the pans. Bake dough at 375° for 20 minutes. Remove from oven and allow to cool slightly. Remove crusts from pans and place on racks to cool completely. Transfer to serving platters.

2. Warm peanut butter in the microwave and stir in heavy cream until smooth. Spread half the peanut butter evenly over each pizza. Drizzle ½ cup warm Chocolate Ganache over each pizza. Allow pizzas to cool, then top with grated chocolate and sprinkle with chopped peanuts. Cut in wedges with a sharp knife.

Going Nutty

Although peanut butter is the classic, you can find cashew butter, almond butter, hazelnut butter, and even macadamia butter at most natural foods stores and some supermarkets. Any one can be used in place of peanut butter to add variety to recipes. If you can't find your favorite nut in butter form, just process whole or blanched nuts in your food processor with a tablespoon of peanut or almond oil.

Cheese-Course Pizza

*Fruit, cheese, and bread, all in one package. The slightly sweet crust
makes a nice foil for the creamy, rich cheeses.*

1. Roll or press pizza dough into two 12-inch circles, slightly thicker
    at the edges than in the center. Coat each pizza pan with ½ table-
    spoon melted butter and place dough in the pans. Brush dough
    with remaining butter and top with diced apples. Bake dough at
    375° for 20 minutes. Remove from oven.

2. Arrange sliced cheeses over hot pizza. Either alternate differ-
    ent varieties or devote one-quarter of each pizza to one type of
    cheese. Allow pizzas to cool slightly, then scatter grape halves
    over each. Serve in wedges with glasses of chilled, dry sherry.

Choosing Cheeses

*Cheese courses ideally offer three or four different varieties of
cheese, including firm varieties like Cheddar or aged Manchego,
semisoft cheeses like Port Salut or Gouda, and soft cheese such as
Brie and Camembert. Make sure your selections include strongly
flavored cheeses like bleu cheese and sharp Cheddar, as well as
mild cheese like Butterkase.*

Makes two 12-inch pizzas

$^1/_2$ recipe Sweet Crust dough
(page 36)
2 tablespoons melted butter
3 cups finely diced peeled
apples
$^1/_4$ pound sliced Cheddar
cheese
$^1/_4$ pound sliced Camembert
$^1/_4$ pound sliced Butterkase
$^1/_4$ pound sliced Port Salut
1 cup red grapes, halved

Makes two 12-inch pizzas

½ recipe Chocolate Crust
    dough (page 37)
1 tablespoon melted butter
3 cups Chocolate Ganache
    (page 54)
3 cups coarsely grated white
    chocolate
24 chocolate-dipped whole
    strawberries

Chocolate-Dipped Strawberry Pizza

*Buy already-made chocolate-dipped fresh strawberries or make
your own. Just melt a little dark chocolate with a spoonful of
cream, dip washed strawberries in it, and let the strawberries rest
on waxed paper until the chocolate becomes firm.*

✳   ✳   ✳

1. Roll or press pizza dough into two 12-inch circles, slightly
    thicker at the edges than in the center. Coat pizza pans with
    the melted butter and place dough in the pans. Bake dough
    at 375° for 20 minutes. Remove from oven and allow to cool
    for 5 minutes. Remove crusts from pans and place on serv-
    ing platters.

2. Spread 1½ cups Chocolate Ganache evenly over each pizza.
    Allow pizzas to cool to warm room temperature. Sprinkle
    grated chocolate evenly over each pizza, then garnish with
    chocolate-dipped strawberries and serve immediately.

About Fruit Fondue

*Be sure fresh fruit is completely dry and at room temperature
before dipping in warm chocolate. Plan to serve chocolate-
dipped berries and other fruit the same day you make it—
refrigeration will cause condensation to form and mar the
finish on the chocolate.*

Strawberry Shortcake Pizza

Make your fruit sauce with strawberries for this recipe. If you don't have time to make fruit sauce from scratch, just place coarsely chopped strawberries and a jar of strawberry jam in a saucepan and heat until melted and well blended.

❊　❊　❊

1. Place spongecake shells on serving platters. Carefully spread 2 cups strawberry fruit sauce over each shell. Allow sauce to cool.

2. Pile whipped cream over the sauce on each spongecake and drizzle caramel sauce over each. Garnish each with whole strawberries.

Makes two 10-inch pizzas

2 large spongecake shells
4 cups Fruit Sauce (page 56)
6 cups sweetened whipped
   cream
1 cup Caramel Sauce
   (page 53)
24 whole strawberries

Croissant-Crust Pizza

This rich pie pays homage to Southern chess pies, with the addition of a soft, buttery crust. Serve in thin wedges with fresh berries.

❊　❊　❊

1. Spread croissant dough in a single layer over the bottom and up the sides of two pizza pans. In a large bowl, place cream cheese and butter. With a mixer on medium speed, beat until blended. Add sugar and continue beating until creamy. Beat in eggs one at a time, then add vanilla and almond extract.

2. Pour batter over croissant crust, dividing evenly. Bake pizzas at 375° for 40 minutes or until centers are set. While pizzas are still hot, sprinkle with turbinado sugar and blanched almonds. Allow to cool, then sprinkle fresh raspberries over each.

Makes two 12-inch pizzas

2 cans refrigerated croissant
   dough
1 pound cream cheese
1 cup butter
2 cups sugar
10 eggs
1 teaspoon vanilla
1 teaspoon almond extract
2 tablespoons turbinado
   sugar
3 cups toasted blanched
   almonds
3 cups fresh raspberries

Makes one 12-inch pizza

1 recipe Cookie Pizza Crust
        dough (page 38)
1 cup Chocolate Ganache
        (page 54)
1 quart vanilla or strawberry
        ice cream, softened
1 cup Caramel Sauce
        (page 53)
Whipped cream
Sprinkles or chopped nuts
Maraschino cherries

Ice Cream Sundae Pizza

*This is the perfect dessert to serve when you need something
easy and fabulous for young diners.*

✳   ✳   ✳

1. Prepare Cookie Pizza Crust as directed in recipe. Pour Chocolate Ganache over the baked crust. Let cool completely.

2. Just before serving, spread crust with softened ice cream. Drizzle caramel sauce over the ice cream in a crosshatch pattern. Garnish with whipped cream, sprinkles, or nuts and cherries.

Makes two 12-inch pizzas

$1/2$ recipe Sweet Crust dough
        (page 36)
1 tablespoon melted butter
3 cups Caramel Sauce
        (page 53)
4 cups toasted pecan halves
3 cups confectioners' sugar
$1/2$ cup heavy cream

Caramel Pecan Pizza

*Toast pecans on a baking sheet in the oven, or in a little butter
in a heavy skillet. Turn or shake often and watch carefully
to keep the pecans from burning.*

✳   ✳   ✳

1. Roll or press pizza dough into two 12-inch circles, slightly thicker at the edges than in the center. Coat pizza pans with the melted butter and place dough in the pans. Bake dough at 375° for 20 minutes. Remove from oven and allow to cool. Remove crusts from pans and transfer to serving platters.

2. Spread 1½ cups sauce evenly over each pizza. Distribute 2 cups toasted pecans over the sauce on each pizza. In a small bowl, whisk confectioners' sugar to remove any lumps, then stir in heavy cream until smooth. Drizzle this glaze over the pecans. Serve warm with ice cream.

Pumpkin Pie Pizza

*Try this aromatic pizza at your next holiday gathering.
It's a fun alternative to traditional pumpkin pie.*

✳   ✳   ✳

1. Roll or press pizza dough into two 12-inch circles, slightly thicker at the edges than in the center. Coat each pizza pan with ½ tablespoon melted butter and place dough in the pans. Brush dough with remaining butter. Top each pizza with 1 can of pumpkin pie filling, spread evenly over the crust. Sprinkle each with pecans and brown sugar.

2. Bake pizzas at 375° for 20 minutes. Remove from oven and let stand for a few minutes. Use plastic squirt bottles to add Cream Cheese Sauce and Caramel Sauce to pizzas in a crisscross pattern. Serve warm.

Makes two 12-inch pizzas

½ recipe Sweet Crust dough
   (page 36)
2 tablespoons melted butter
2 (15-ounce) cans pumpkin
   pie filling
1 cup toasted pecans
½ cup brown sugar
1 cup Cream Cheese Sauce
   (page 53)
1 cup Caramel Sauce
   (page 53)

Cookies and Cream Pizza

*This pizza makes no apologies for being chocolaty and super-sweet.
It travels well, making it a great contribution to potlucks and buffets.*

✳   ✳   ✳

1. Prepare brownie batter according to package directions. Pour into a lightly greased pizza pan and bake 12 minutes or until set. Remove from oven and let cool completely.

2. Place butter and marshmallow cream in a medium bowl. Beat with a mixer on medium speed until creamy. Add confectioners' sugar and vanilla. Spread cream over brownie crust.

3. Place 12 whole cookies around the edges of the pizza. Break up the remaining cookies and sprinkle over the pizza. Serve with coffee or icy milk.

Makes one 12-inch pizza

1 package brownie mix, plus
   ingredients to prepare
½ cup butter
1 cup marshmallow cream
3 cups confectioners' sugar
1 teaspoon vanilla
1 (18-ounce) package
   chocolate sandwich
   cookies

½ recipe Sweet Crust dough
(page 36) or Chocolate
Crust dough (page 37)
1 tablespoon melted butter
3 large bananas, sliced
4 cups prepared vanilla
pudding, well chilled
4 cups whipped cream
2 cups coarsely grated white
chocolate

Banana Cream Pizza

*Use your own from-scratch pudding recipe, or make pudding
from a box. Either way, make sure the pudding is cold
before piling it on your pizza.*

❊   ❊   ❊

1. Roll or press pizza dough into two 12-inch circles, slightly
   thicker at the edges than in the center. Coat pizza pans with
   the melted butter and place dough in the pans. Bake dough
   at 375° for 20 minutes. Remove from oven and allow to cool
   slightly. Remove crusts from pans and place on racks to
   cool completely. Transfer to serving platters.

2. Place 1 sliced banana in a layer over the crust on each pizza.
   Top each with 2 cups of pudding. Divide remaining bananas
   over the pudding. Top with whipped cream and grated
   white chocolate. Cut in wedges with a sharp knife.

Banana-Rama

*Homey banana pudding gets its flavor from sliced bananas
being submerged in custard for several hours or even a day
or two. But sliced bananas turn brown quickly, so if you're
serving guests, plan to prepare your bananas just before
serving for the best presentation.*

Banana Split Pizza

This is a great pizza to prepare for your favorite teen and his or her friends. Unless you have freezer space for leftovers, prepare the pizzas one at a time.

1. Roll or press pizza dough into two 12-inch circles, slightly thicker at the edges than in the center. Coat pizza pans with the melted butter and place dough in the pans. Bake dough at 375° for 20 minutes. Remove from oven and allow to cool slightly. Remove crusts from pans and place on racks to cool completely. Transfer to serving platters.

2. Spread 1 cup Chocolate Ganache over each pizza. Cut bananas in half horizontally, then cut each half in quarters. Arrange the banana strips in a spoke pattern over the chocolate. With an ice cream scoop, place alternating scoops of each flavor of ice cream over each of the pizzas. Spoon chopped pineapple, caramel sauce, and strawberries over the scoops, one topping per scoop. Garnish with whipped cream and cherries. Serve immediately.

Makes two 12-inch pizzas

¹/₂ recipe Sweet Crust dough (page 36) or Chocolate Crust dough (page 37)
1 tablespoon melted butter
2 cups Chocolate Ganache (page 54)
6 large bananas
1 pint each chocolate, vanilla, and strawberry ice cream
1 cup chopped fresh pineapple
1 cup caramel sauce
1 cup chopped fresh strawberries
Whipped cream
Maraschino cherries

Makes two 12-inch pizzas

½ recipe Sweet Crust dough
   (page 36)
3 tablespoons melted butter
3 cups Caramel Sauce
   (page 53)
4 cups walnut halves
1 cup maple syrup
1 cup toffee bits
Whipped cream

Maple Walnut Pizza

This pizza makes a great coffee-klatch offering, or serve it with a scoop of white chocolate ice cream for an impressive dessert..

❊   ❊   ❊

1. Roll or press pizza dough into two 12-inch circles, slightly thicker at the edges than in the center. Coat each pizza pan with 1 tablespoon melted butter and place dough in the pans. Bake dough at 375° for 20 minutes. Remove from oven and top each with half the caramel sauce. Remove crusts from pans and transfer to serving platters.

2. In a large, nonstick skillet, combine remaining butter and walnuts. Toast walnuts in butter over medium-high heat, stirring frequently. Once walnuts are toasted, pour maple syrup over walnuts and bring mixture to a boil. Remove from heat and stir well to coat walnuts thoroughly. With a slotted spoon, remove walnuts from pan and spread evenly over pizzas. Sprinkle ½ cup of toffee bits over each pizza. Serve with whipped cream.

Makes one 12-inch pizza

1 recipe Cookie Pizza Crust
   dough (page 38)
1½ cups Nutella
1 cup chocolate chips
1 cup shredded coconut
Whipped cream

Quick Hazelnut Spread Pizza

Make the pizza crust in advance or use packaged cookie dough if you're pressed for time.

❊   ❊   ❊

1. Prepare Cookie Pizza Crust as directed in recipe. Spread Nutella over the baked crust. Spread chocolate chips and coconut over the top.

2. Serve in wedges with whipped cream.

Mango Coconut Pizza

Use mangoes that yield slightly when pressed. Cut the fruit on each side of the large center seed. Discard center and place mango halves on a cutting surface, flesh side up. Score the mango flesh inside the peel, making diagonal cuts with a sharp knife. Pull the peel back and scrape off perfectly diced pieces of fruit.

*　*　*

Makes two 12-inch pizzas

$^1/_2$ recipe Sweet Crust dough
   (page 36)
1 tablespoon melted butter
3 cups Sweet Mascarpone
   Sauce (page 52)
4 cups diced mangoes
2 cups shaved fresh coconut
3 cups confectioners' sugar
$^1/_2$ cup coconut milk

1. Roll or press pizza dough into two 12-inch circles, slightly thicker at the edges than in the center. Coat pizza pans with the melted butter and place dough in the pans. Bake dough at 375° for 20 minutes. Remove from oven and allow to cool. Remove crusts from pans and place on racks to cool completely. Transfer to serving platters.

2. Spread 1½ cups sauce evenly over each pizza. Distribute 2 cups diced mangoes over the sauce on each pizza. Sprinkle with shaved coconut.

3. In a small bowl, whisk confectioners' sugar to remove any lumps, then stir in coconut milk until smooth. Drizzle glaze over the pizzas and serve.

1/2 recipe Sweet Crust dough
    (page 36)
3 tablespoons melted butter
2 cups brown sugar
24 fresh pineapple rings
1 cup pitted cherries
1 cup shredded coconut
    (optional)

Pineapple Pizza

Your favorite pineapple upside-down cake just got flatter, simpler, and a little more intense.

✳   ✳   ✳

1. Roll or press pizza dough into two 12-inch circles, slightly thicker at the edges than in the center. Coat each pizza pan with ½ tablespoon melted butter and place dough in the pans. Brush dough with remaining butter. Top each pizza with half the brown sugar. Layer 12 pineapple rings over each pizza and dot with half the cherries.

2. Bake pizzas at 375° for 20 minutes. Remove from oven and let stand for a few minutes. Sprinkle with shredded coconut, if desired. Serve warm.

Pineapple Particulars

Fresh pineapple contains an enzyme that keeps gelatin from getting firm. The same enzyme, papain, is also found in papaya and it's often used as a meat tenderizer. To use pineapple in dishes thickened with gelatin, be sure to use canned pineapple. The cooking and canning process neutralizes the papain.

Cranberry Apple Pizza

Looking for an alternative to your usual apple pie?
Try this slightly tart pizza at your next fall dinner.

* * *

1. Roll or press pizza dough into two 12-inch circles, slightly thicker at the edges than in the center. Coat each pizza pan with ½ tablespoon melted butter and place dough in the pans. Brush dough with remaining butter. Top each pizza with half the sliced apples and half the cranberries. Sprinkle each with lemon zest and brown sugar.

2. Bake pizzas at 375° for 20 minutes. Remove from oven and let stand for a few minutes. Drizzle with caramel sauce. Serve warm.

Makes two 12-inch pizzas

½ recipe Sweet Crust dough
   (page 36)
2 tablespoons melted butter
4 cups peeled, sliced apples
1 cup dried cranberries
1 tablespoon lemon zest
½ cup brown sugar
1 cup Caramel Sauce
   (page 53)

Raspberry Tea Pizzas

These bite-sized pizzas would look beautiful on a table set for
afternoon tea. Serve them to your book club.

* * *

1. Divide pizza dough in half, then divide each half into twelve pieces. Press each piece of dough into a small circle. Line two baking sheets with nonstick foil and place 12 mini-pizza crusts on each. Brush each circle with melted butter.

2. Place a spoonful of almond paste on each dough circle and smooth down the paste with the back of a spoon. Top each circle with a few raspberries and grated white chocolate. Bake at 375° for 10 to 12 minutes or until crusts are lightly browned. Cool slightly before serving.

Makes 24 mini-pizzas

½ recipe Sweet Crust dough
   (page 36)
3 tablespoons melted butter
2 cups Almond Paste
   (page 55)
2 cups fresh raspberries
2 cups grated white chocolate

Summer Fruit Pizza

Makes two 12-inch pizzas

¹/₂ recipe Sweet Crust dough
(page 36)
2 tablespoons melted butter
1 cup sliced fresh peaches
1 cup sliced fresh nectarines
1 cup sliced fresh plums
1 cup pitted cherries
¹/₂ cup brown sugar

Think of this pizza as a very elegant, streamlined tart. Serve with iced espresso or a glass of Chardonnay.

✳   ✳   ✳

1. Roll or press pizza dough into two 12-inch circles, slightly thicker at the edges than in the center. Coat each pizza pan with ½ tablespoon melted butter and place dough in the pans. Brush dough with remaining butter. Top each pizza with half the sliced fruit and half the cherries. Sprinkle each with brown sugar.

2. Bake pizzas at 350° for 20 minutes. Remove from oven and let stand for a few minutes. Serve warm.

Cheesecake Pizza

Makes two 12-inch pizzas

¹/₂ recipe Sweet Crust dough
(page 36)
2 tablespoons melted butter
2 tubs ready-to-eat
cheesecake filling
2 cups cherry pie filling
2 cups white chocolate curls

Ready-to-eat cheesecake filling makes this pizza a super-quick fix. If you prefer, substitute blackberry or blueberry pie filling for the cherry filling.

✳   ✳   ✳

1. Roll or press pizza dough into two 12-inch circles, slightly thicker at the edges than in the center. Coat each pizza pan with ½ tablespoon melted butter and place dough in the pans. Brush dough with remaining butter.

2. Bake pizza crusts at 350° for 20 minutes. Remove from oven and let stand for a few minutes. Remove to racks to cool completely. Spread cooled crusts with ready-to-eat cheesecake filling, then top cheesecake filling with cherry pie filling. Sprinkle pizzas with white chocolate curls and serve immediately.

CHAPTER 11
Pizza on the Grill

½ recipe Pizza Crust for the
Grill dough (page 35)
Cornmeal and flour for
dusting
Vegetable oil
3 tablespoons olive oil
1 cup Slow-Simmered Tomato
Sauce (page 40)
½ pound sliced mozzarella
cheese
½ pound sliced provolone
cheese
4 cups diced mesquite-
smoked chicken
1 small red bell pepper, cored
and cut in strips
1 small yellow or green bell
pepper, cored and cut
in strips
1 cup Asiago cheese,
shredded

Mesquite-Smoked Chicken and Peppers Pizza

If you're handy with a smoker, by all means make your own smoked chicken in advance of making pizza. Otherwise, buy prepared smoked chicken or substitute grilled chicken.

✳ ✳ ✳

1. On a lightly floured board or on parchment, roll out two 12-inch dough circles. Place one circle of dough on a metal pizza peel or rimless baking sheet generously sprinkled with flour and cornmeal.

2. Prepare a gas or charcoal grill so that one area is hot while another side or corner is medium-hot. Add soaked mesquite chips to the coals or place in a wood chip container for gas grills. Brush the grill rack with vegetable oil. Slide the pizza onto the grill rack over the hot coals or heating element. Close the lid immediately and grill for 2 to 3 minutes or until pizza dough is cooked on the bottom and grill marks appear. Remove dough to peel or baking sheet, turning the grilled side up.

3. Brush the grilled pizza side with half the olive oil, then quickly spread half the pizza sauce. Cover the sauce with half the slices of mozzarella and half the slices of provolone. Top with 2 cups diced smoked chicken and half the pepper strips. Sprinkle with half the Asiago cheese.

4. Carefully slide the pizza back onto the grill, placing it over the medium-hot area. Close grill cover and cook 3 minutes. Check to make sure crust isn't browning too quickly. If it is, move some coals to the opposite side of the grill or lower gas grill thermostat to reduce heat. Continue to cook for another 4 to 5 minutes or until crust is browned and cheese is melted and bubbly. Remove from heat, cool slightly, and serve. Repeat cooking process with second pizza.

Artisan Cheese Grill-Fired Pizza

Look for cheeses from small-batch creameries at gourmet shops and in the specialty cheese case of some supermarkets. Some will have familiar names like Cheddar or Jack, while many of the triple-crème and sheep's milk cheeses have names unique to a specific dairy.

1. On a lightly floured board or on parchment, roll out two 12-inch dough circles. Place one circle of dough on a metal pizza peel or rimless baking sheet generously sprinkled with flour and cornmeal.

2. Prepare a gas or charcoal grill so that one area is hot while another side or corner is medium-hot. Brush the grill rack with vegetable oil. Slide the pizza onto the grill rack over the hot coals or heating element. Close the lid immediately and grill for 2 to 3 minutes or until pizza dough is cooked on the bottom and grill marks appear. Remove dough to peel or baking sheet, turning the grilled side up.

3. Brush the grilled pizza side with half the olive oil, then quickly spoon on half the pizza sauce. Evenly distribute half the cubes of triple-crème cheese, followed by half the slices of Cheddar and half the mozzarella or Manchego. Add black pepper to taste.

4. Carefully slide the pizza back onto the grill, placing it over the medium-hot area. Close grill cover and cook 3 minutes. Check to make sure crust isn't browning too quickly. If it is, move some coals to the opposite side of the grill or lower gas grill thermostat to reduce heat. Continue to cook for another 4 to 5 minutes or until crust is browned and cheese is melted and bubbly. Remove from heat, cool slightly, and serve. Repeat cooking process with second pizza.

Makes two 12-inch pizzas

¹/₂ recipe Pizza Crust for the Grill dough (page 35)
Cornmeal and flour for dusting
Vegetable oil
3 tablespoons olive oil
1 cup Fresh Tomato Sauce (page 42)
1 pound triple-crème-type cheese, rind removed and diced
¹/₂ pound thinly sliced herb-laced Cheddar-type cheese
¹/₂ pound thinly sliced fresh mozzarella or Manchego cheese
Freshly ground black pepper to taste

1/2 recipe Pizza Crust for the
    Grill dough (page 35)
Cornmeal and flour for
    dusting
Vegetable oil
3 tablespoons olive oil
1 cup Barbecue Sauce
    (page 45)
1 teaspoon Tabasco sauce
2 pounds grilled or smoked
    wild boar tenderloin,
    sliced
1 cup minced red onion
1/2 cup minced fresh parsley
1 pound thinly sliced aged
    Manchego cheese
1 pound thinly sliced
    mozzarella

Wild Boar Barbecue Pizza

*Wild boar has a richer, more complex flavor than its domesticated
cousin. You can find wild boar roasts at some gourmet shops
and online, and of course from hunters in various regions.
If you can't easily get wild boar, substitute pork tenderloin.*

✳   ✳   ✳

1. On a lightly floured board or on parchment, roll out two 12-inch dough circles. Place 1 circle of dough on a metal pizza peel or rimless baking sheet generously sprinkled with flour and cornmeal.

2. Prepare a gas or charcoal grill so that one area is hot while another side or corner is medium-hot. Brush the grill rack with vegetable oil. Slide the pizza onto the grill rack over the hot coals or heating element. Close the lid immediately and grill for 2 to 3 minutes or until pizza dough is cooked on the bottom and grill marks appear. Remove dough to peel or baking sheet, turning the grilled side up.

3. Brush the grilled pizza side with half the olive oil. Stir Tabasco sauce into the barbecue sauce, then quickly spread half the sauce over the grilled crust. Cover the sauce with half the wild boar slices, followed by half the red onion and half the parsley. Layer half the Manchego slices and half the mozzarella over the top.

4. Carefully slide the pizza back onto the grill, placing it over the medium-hot area. Close grill cover and cook 3 minutes. Check to make sure crust isn't browning too quickly. If it is, move some coals to the opposite side of the grill or lower gas grill thermostat to reduce heat. Continue to cook for another 4 to 5 minutes or until crust is browned and cheese is melted and bubbly. Remove from heat, cool slightly, and serve. Repeat cooking process with second pizza.

Barbecued Brisket Pizza

Makes two 12-inch pizzas

$^1/_2$ *recipe Pizza Crust for the Grill dough (page 35)*
Cornmeal and flour for dusting
Vegetable oil
3 tablespoons olive oil
2 cups Barbecue Sauce (page 45)
4 cups shredded barbecued beef brisket
1 cup diced green bell pepper
1 minced jalapeño pepper (optional)
$^1/_2$ *pound sliced mozzarella cheese*
$^1/_2$ *pound sliced sharp Cheddar cheese*

*Slow-cooked beef brisket is one of the staples of the barbecue repertoire.
For this dish, leftover brisket—from either the pit or the kitchen—
can be used. If you're really in a hurry, buy prepared brisket
from your local barbecue restaurant.*

1. On a lightly floured board or on parchment, roll out two 12-inch dough circles. Place 1 circle of dough on a metal pizza peel or rimless baking sheet generously sprinkled with flour and cornmeal.

2. Prepare a gas or charcoal grill so that one area is hot while another side or corner is medium-hot. Brush the grill rack with vegetable oil. Slide the pizza onto the grill rack over the hot coals or heating element. Close the lid immediately and grill for 2 to 3 minutes or until pizza dough is cooked on the bottom and grill marks appear. Remove dough to peel or baking sheet, turning the grilled side up.

3. Brush the grilled pizza side with half the olive oil. Spread ½ cup of the sauce over the crust. Mix 1 cup sauce with the shredded brisket and spread half the brisket over the top of the crust. Sprinkle with half the green pepper and half the jalapeño, if desired. Cover the pizza with half the slices of mozzarella and half the slices of Cheddar.

4. Carefully slide the pizza back onto the grill, placing it over the medium-hot area. Close grill cover and cook 3 minutes. Check to make sure crust isn't browning too quickly. If it is, move some coals to the opposite side of the grill or lower gas grill thermostat to reduce heat. Continue to cook for another 4 to 5 minutes or until crust is browned and cheese is melted and bubbly. Remove from heat, cool slightly, and serve. Repeat cooking process with second pizza.

½ *recipe Pizza Crust for the Grill dough (page 35)*
Cornmeal and flour for dusting
Vegetable oil
3 tablespoons olive oil
1 cup Sesame-Soy Sauce (page 47)
2 pounds grilled or smoked duck breast, sliced
2 cups chopped dried plums
½ *cup minced green onion*
1 pound thinly sliced provolone cheese, cut into wide strips

Grilled Duck and Dried Plum Pizza

Dried plums? Don't we mean prunes? Well, yes and no. Prunes are dried plums, but the word "prune" also refers to a specific type of dried plum as well as a method of preparing dried plums. For this recipe, use dry-packed, dehydrated sweet plums.

✳ ✳ ✳

1. On a lightly floured board or on parchment, roll out two 12-inch dough circles. Place one circle of dough on a metal pizza peel or rimless baking sheet generously sprinkled with flour and cornmeal.

2. Prepare a gas or charcoal grill so that one area is hot while another side or corner is medium-hot. Brush the grill rack with vegetable oil. Slide the pizza onto the grill rack over the hot coals or heating element. Close the lid immediately and grill for 2 to 3 minutes or until pizza dough is cooked on the bottom and grill marks appear. Remove dough to peel or baking sheet, turning the grilled side up.

3. Brush the grilled pizza side with half the olive oil. Spread half the sesame-soy sauce over the crust. Cover the sauce with half the duck slices, followed by half the chopped plums and half the green onion. Layer half of the provolone strips in a crosshatch pattern over the top.

4. Carefully slide the pizza back onto the grill, placing it over the medium-hot area. Close grill cover and cook for 3 minutes. Check to make sure crust isn't browning too quickly. If it is, move some coals to the opposite side of the grill or lower gas grill thermostat to reduce heat. Continue to cook for another 4 to 5 minutes or until crust is browned and cheese is melted and bubbly. Remove from heat, cool slightly, and serve. Repeat cooking process with second pizza.

Grilled Veggie Pie

Experiment with different vegetables in the mix. Or for a gourmet touch, use baby zucchini and squash sliced in half lengthwise and slender enoki mushrooms in place of the more common varieties.

✳   ✳   ✳

1. On a lightly floured board or on parchment, roll out two 12-inch dough circles. Place one circle of dough on a metal pizza peel or rimless baking sheet generously sprinkled with flour and cornmeal.

2. Prepare a gas or charcoal grill so that one area is hot while another side or corner is medium-hot. Brush the grill rack with vegetable oil. Slide the pizza onto the grill rack over the hot coals or heating element. Close the lid immediately and grill for 2 to 3 minutes or until pizza dough is cooked on the bottom and grill marks appear. Remove dough to peel or baking sheet, turning the grilled side up.

3. Brush the grilled pizza side with half the olive oil. Spread half the Pesto Sauce over the grilled crust. Cover the sauce with half the bleu or Gorgonzola cheese followed by half the zucchini, half the squash, half the onions, half the tomatoes, and half the mushrooms. Top the pie with half the basil and black pepper to taste.

4. Carefully slide the pizza back onto the grill, placing it over the medium-hot area. Close grill cover and cook 3 minutes. Check to make sure crust isn't browning too quickly. If it is, move some coals to the opposite side of the grill or lower gas grill thermostat to reduce heat. Continue to cook for another 4 to 5 minutes or until crust is browned and cheese is melted. Remove from heat, cool slightly, and serve. Repeat cooking process with second pizza.

Makes two 12-inch pizzas

1/2 recipe Pizza Crust for the Grill dough (page 35)
Cornmeal and flour for dusting
Vegetable oil
3 tablespoons olive oil
1 cup Pesto Sauce (page 43)
1 pound crumbled bleu or Gorgonzola cheese
1 cup grilled zucchini, diced
1 cup grilled yellow or pattypan squash, diced
1 cup grilled sweet onion, diced
1 cup grilled cherry tomatoes, halved
1 cup grilled mushrooms, diced
1/2 cup fresh basil ribbons
Black pepper to taste

Makes two 12-inch pizzas

¹/₂ recipe Pizza Crust for the Grill dough (page 35)
Cornmeal and flour for dusting
Vegetable oil
2 tablespoons olive oil
1 cup Garlic and Oil Sauce (page 44)
4 cups sliced, caramelized onions
¹/₄ cup rinsed and dried anchovy fillets
1 cup pitted niçoise olives
Freshly ground black pepper to taste

Grilled Anchovy and Onion Pie

This cheese-free pizza makes a great cocktail snack or, served with a field-greens salad, a satisfying entrée. The caramelized onions can be prepared a day in advance and stored in the refrigerator.

❋　❋　❋

1. On a lightly floured board or on parchment, roll out two 12-inch dough circles. Place one circle of dough on a metal pizza peel or rimless baking sheet generously sprinkled with flour and cornmeal.

2. Prepare a gas or charcoal grill so that one area is hot while another side or corner is medium-hot. Brush the grill rack with vegetable oil. Slide the pizza onto the grill rack over the hot coals or heating element. Close the lid immediately and grill for 2 to 3 minutes or until pizza dough is cooked on the bottom and grill marks appear. Remove dough to peel or baking sheet, turning the grilled side up.

3. Brush the grilled pizza side with half the olive oil. Spread half the sauce over the grilled crust. Cover the sauce with half the onions. Arrange half the anchovy fillets in a cross-hatch pattern and dot the pie with half the olives. Add black pepper to taste.

4. Carefully slide the pizza back onto the grill, placing it over the medium-hot area. Close grill cover and cook 3 minutes. Check to make sure crust isn't browning too quickly. If it is, move some coals to the opposite side of the grill or lower gas grill thermostat to reduce heat. Continue to cook for another 4 to 5 minutes or until crust is browned. Remove from heat, cool slightly, and serve. Repeat cooking process with second pizza.

Grilled Tomato and Fontina Pizza

Tarragon, basil, oregano, parsley, and garlic chives make great flavorings for this tomato-rich pie. Try to find heirloom tomatoes with a variety of colorings for an eye-appealing dish.

❊   ❊   ❊

Makes two 12-inch pizzas

$^1/_2$ recipe Pizza Crust for the
   Grill dough (page 35)
Cornmeal and flour for
   dusting
Vegetable oil
3 tablespoons olive oil
1 cup Garlic and Oil Sauce
   (page 44) or Pesto Sauce
   (page 43)
1 pound fontina cheese,
   thinly sliced
6 medium heirloom tomatoes,
   trimmed and sliced
1 cup minced mixed fresh
   herbs
1 pound fontina cheese,
   coarsely grated
Freshly ground black pepper
   to taste

1. On a lightly floured board or on parchment, roll out two 12-inch dough circles. Place one circle of dough on a metal pizza peel or rimless baking sheet generously sprinkled with flour and cornmeal.

2. Prepare a gas or charcoal grill so that one area is hot while another side or corner is medium-hot. Brush the grill rack with vegetable oil. Slide the pizza onto the grill rack over the hot coals or heating element. Close the lid immediately and grill for 2 to 3 minutes or until pizza dough is cooked on the bottom and grill marks appear. Remove dough to peel or baking sheet, turning the grilled side up.

3. Brush the grilled pizza side with half the olive oil. Spread half the sauce over the grilled crust. Cover the sauce with half the fontina slices, followed by half the tomato slices, arranged in an overlapping pattern. Sprinkle on half the fresh herbs, followed by half the grated fontina cheese. Add black pepper to taste.

4. Carefully slide the pizza back onto the grill, placing it over the medium-hot area. Close grill cover and cook 3 minutes. Check to make sure crust isn't browning too quickly. If it is, move some coals to the opposite side of the grill or lower gas grill thermostat to reduce heat. Continue to cook for another 4 to 5 minutes or until crust is browned and cheese is melted and bubbly. Remove from heat, cool slightly, and serve. Repeat cooking process with second pizza.

Makes two 12-inch pizzas

¹/₂ recipe Pizza Crust for the
    Grill dough (page 35)
Cornmeal and flour for
    dusting
Vegetable oil
3 tablespoons olive oil
1 cup Lemon Cream Sauce
    (page 51)
1 pound thinly sliced
    Butterkase cheese
1 pound thinly sliced
    mozzarella
2 pounds large cooked
    shrimp, peeled and
    halved lengthwise
2 cups red and yellow grape
    tomatoes, halved
    lengthwise
¹/₄ cup minced fresh parsley
2 tablespoons fresh oregano
    leaves

Grilled Shrimp and Grape Tomato Pizza

Shrimp should be barely cooked for this dish. Raw shrimp would give off too much liquid, but well-done shrimp could become dry and tough. If you're concerned, coat shrimp with a little oil before adding to the pizza.

✳ ✳ ✳

1. On a lightly floured board or on parchment, roll out two 12-inch dough circles. Place one circle of dough on a metal pizza peel or rimless baking sheet generously sprinkled with flour and cornmeal.

2. Prepare a gas or charcoal grill so that one area is hot while another side or corner is medium-hot. Brush the grill rack with vegetable oil. Slide the pizza onto the grill rack over the hot coals or heating element. Close the lid immediately and grill for 2 to 3 minutes or until pizza dough is cooked on the bottom and grill marks appear. Remove dough to peel or baking sheet, turning the grilled side up.

3. Brush the grilled pizza side with half the olive oil. Quickly spread half the sauce over the grilled crust. Cover the sauce with half the cheese slices, followed by half the shrimp, half the grape tomatoes, and half the parsley and oregano.

4. Carefully slide the pizza back onto the grill, placing it over the medium-hot area. Close grill cover and cook 3 minutes. Check to make sure crust isn't browning too quickly. If it is, move some coals to the opposite side of the grill or lower gas grill thermostat to reduce heat. Continue to cook for another 4 to 5 minutes or until crust is browned and cheese is melted and bubbly. Remove from heat, cool slightly, and serve. Repeat cooking process with second pizza.

Grilled Italian Sausage and Peppers Pizza

Thinly slice sausage on the diagonal to create larger slices. Depending on your tastes, hot or mild sausage can be used. Or try a combination of both. Peppers can be added to the pie fresh, or lightly grilled.

❊   ❊   ❊

Makes two 12-inch pizzas

$1/_2$ recipe Pizza Crust for the Grill dough (page 35)
Cornmeal and flour for dusting
Vegetable oil
3 tablespoons olive oil
1 cup Slow-Simmered Tomato Sauce (page 40)
1 pound thinly sliced provolone cheese
1 pound thinly sliced mozzarella
2 pounds grilled Italian sausage, sliced
1 small red bell pepper, cored and sliced
1 small yellow bell pepper, cored and sliced
1 small green bell pepper, cored and sliced
2 tablespoons fresh oregano leaves
1 cup shredded Asiago cheese

1. On a lightly floured board or on parchment, roll out two 12-inch dough circles. Place one circle of dough on a metal pizza peel or rimless baking sheet generously sprinkled with flour and cornmeal.

2. Prepare a gas or charcoal grill so that one area is hot while another side or corner is medium-hot. Brush the grill rack with vegetable oil. Slide the pizza onto the grill rack over the hot coals or heating element. Close the lid immediately and grill for 2 to 3 minutes or until pizza dough is cooked on the bottom and grill marks appear. Remove dough to peel or baking sheet, turning the grilled side up.

3. Brush the grilled pizza side with half the olive oil. Quickly spread half the sauce over the grilled crust. Cover the sauce with half the provolone and mozzarella slices, followed by half the sausage slices, half the peppers, half the oregano, and half the Asiago cheese.

4. Carefully slide the pizza back onto the grill, placing it over the medium-hot area. Close grill cover and cook 3 minutes. Check to make sure crust isn't browning too quickly. If it is, move some coals to the opposite side of the grill or lower gas grill thermostat to reduce heat. Continue to cook for another 4 to 5 minutes or until crust is browned and cheese is melted and bubbly. Remove from heat, cool slightly, and serve. Repeat cooking process with second pizza.

1/2 recipe Pizza Crust for the
    Grill dough (page 35)
Cornmeal and flour for
    dusting
Vegetable oil
3 tablespoons olive oil
1 cup Sesame-Soy Sauce
    (page 47)
2 pounds grilled venison
    tenderloin steaks, thinly
    sliced
1 cup cut baby corn
1 cup dried blueberries
2 teaspoons grated fresh
    ginger
4 green onions, trimmed and
    cut into long, thin strips

Grilled Venison Tenderloin Pizza

*Farm-raised venison is lean and flavorful without being gamey.
It's also readily available at large supermarkets. Or, if you
prefer, substitute sliced beef or pork.*

✳   ✳   ✳

1. On a lightly floured board or on parchment, roll out two
   12-inch dough circles. Place one circle of dough on a metal
   pizza peel or rimless baking sheet generously sprinkled
   with flour and cornmeal.

2. Prepare a gas or charcoal grill so that one area is hot while
   another side or corner is medium-hot. Brush the grill rack
   with vegetable oil. Slide the pizza onto the grill rack over the
   hot coals or heating element. Close the lid immediately and
   grill for 2 to 3 minutes or until pizza dough is cooked on the
   bottom and grill marks appear. Remove dough to peel or
   baking sheet, turning the grilled side up.

3. Brush the grilled pizza side with half the olive oil. Toss the
   sliced venison with 2 tablespoons of the Sesame-Soy Sauce,
   then spread half the remaining sauce over the grilled crust.
   Cover the sauce with half the venison slices, followed by
   half the corn, half the blueberries, and 1 tablespoon of
   the grated ginger. Top the pizza with half the green onion
   strips.

4. Carefully slide the pizza back onto the grill, placing it over
   the medium-hot area. Close grill cover and cook 3 minutes.
   Check to make sure crust isn't browning too quickly. If it is,
   move some coals to the opposite side of the grill or lower
   gas grill thermostat to reduce heat. Continue to cook for
   another 4 to 5 minutes or until crust is browned. Remove
   from heat, cool slightly, and serve. Repeat cooking process
   with second pizza.

Grilled Potato Cheese Pizza

This unusual pizza makes a great brunch dish. Serve it with scrambled eggs, pan-seared tomato slices, and a salad of spring greens vinaigrette.

1. On a lightly floured board or on parchment, roll out two 12-inch dough circles. Place one circle of dough on a metal pizza peel or rimless baking sheet generously sprinkled with flour and cornmeal.

2. Prepare a gas or charcoal grill so that one area is hot while another side or corner is medium-hot. Brush the grill rack with vegetable oil. Slide the pizza onto the grill rack over the hot coals or heating element. Close the lid immediately and grill for 2 to 3 minutes or until pizza dough is cooked on the bottom and grill marks appear. Remove dough to peel or baking sheet, turning the grilled side up.

3. Brush the grilled pizza side with half the olive oil. Quickly spread half the sauce over the grilled crust. Cover the sauce with half the Cheddar and Butterkase slices, followed by half the potato slices arranged in overlapping circles. Drizzle a tablespoon of melted butter over the potatoes, then sprinkle with salt and pepper and top with half the rosemary. Sprinkle half the shredded Monterey jack cheese over the potatoes.

4. Carefully slide the pizza back onto the grill, placing it over the medium-hot area. Close grill cover and cook 3 minutes. Check to make sure crust isn't browning too quickly. If it is, move some coals to the opposite side of the grill or lower gas grill thermostat to reduce heat. Continue to cook for another 4 to 5 minutes or until crust is browned and cheese is melted and bubbly. Remove from heat, cool slightly, and serve. Repeat cooking process with second pizza.

Makes two 12-inch pizzas

1/2 recipe Pizza Crust for the Grill dough (page 35)
Cornmeal and flour for dusting
Vegetable oil
3 tablespoons olive oil
1/2 cup Garlic and Oil Sauce (page 44)
1 pound thinly sliced Cheddar cheese
1 pound thinly sliced smoked Butterkase cheese
6 Idaho potatoes, peeled, cooked, and thinly sliced
2 tablespoons melted butter
Salt and pepper to taste
1/4 cup fresh rosemary leaves
2 cups shredded Monterey jack cheese

1/2 recipe Pizza Crust for the
    Grill dough (page 35)
Cornmeal and flour for
    dusting
Vegetable oil
3 tablespoons olive oil
1 cup Slow-Simmered Tomato
    Sauce (page 40)
1/2 pound thinly sliced Gruyère
    cheese
1/2 pound thinly sliced
    mozzarella cheese
2 pounds Portobello
    mushrooms, grilled and
    sliced
1/4 cup minced fresh basil
2 tablespoons fresh oregano
    leaves
1 cup crumbled Gorgonzola
    cheese

Grilled Mushroom Pizza

Meaty Portobello mushrooms hold up to the smoky flavor of the grill. Give large caps a few turns on the grill before slicing. A brush of balsamic vinaigrette will add flavor.

✴   ✴   ✴

1. On a lightly floured board or on parchment, roll out two 12-inch dough circles. Place one circle of dough on a metal pizza peel or rimless baking sheet generously sprinkled with flour and cornmeal.

2. Prepare a gas or charcoal grill so that one area is hot while another side or corner is medium-hot. Brush the grill rack with vegetable oil. Slide the pizza onto the grill rack over the hot coals or heating element. Close the lid immediately and grill for 2 to 3 minutes or until pizza dough is cooked on the bottom and grill marks appear. Remove dough to peel or baking sheet, turning the grilled side up.

3. Brush the grilled pizza side with half the olive oil. Quickly spread half the sauce over the grilled crust. Cover the sauce with half the Gruyère and mozzarella cheese slices, followed by half the mushroom slices, half the basil and oregano, and half the Gorgonzola crumbles.

4. Carefully slide the pizza back onto the grill, placing it over the medium-hot area. Close grill cover and cook 3 minutes. Check to make sure crust isn't browning too quickly. If it is, move some coals to the opposite side of the grill or lower gas grill thermostat to reduce heat. Continue to cook for another 4 to 5 minutes or until crust is browned and cheese is melted and bubbly. Remove from heat, cool slightly, and serve. Repeat cooking process with second pizza.

Seared Swordfish Pizza

*Swordfish is meaty and strongly flavored, making it an acquired taste
for some. Combine the fish with vibrant ingredients like
black olives and capers for a balanced pizza.*

1. On a lightly floured board or on parchment, roll out two 12-inch dough circles. Place one circle of dough on a metal pizza peel or rimless baking sheet generously sprinkled with flour and cornmeal.

2. Prepare a gas or charcoal grill so that one area is hot while another side or corner is medium-hot. Brush the grill rack with vegetable oil. Slide the pizza onto the grill rack over the hot coals or heating element. Close the lid immediately and grill for 2 to 3 minutes or until pizza dough is cooked on the bottom and grill marks appear. Remove dough to peel or baking sheet, turning the grilled side up.

3. Brush the grilled pizza side with half the olive oil. Quickly spread half the sauce over the grilled crust. Cover the sauce with half of the diced swordfish, followed by half of the black olives, half of the capers, all of the parsley, and half of the lemon zest. Combine the provolone and mozzarella cheeses and sprinkle half of the mixture over the pizza.

4. Carefully slide the pizza back onto the grill, placing it over the medium-hot area. Close grill cover and cook 3 minutes. Check to make sure crust isn't browning too quickly. If it is, move some coals to the opposite side of the grill or lower gas grill thermostat to reduce heat. Continue to cook for another 4 to 5 minutes or until crust is browned and cheese is melted and bubbly. Remove from heat, cool slightly, and serve. Repeat cooking process with second pizza.

Makes two 12-inch pizzas

---

*$1/2$ recipe Pizza Crust for the
   Grill dough (page 35)
Cornmeal and flour for
   dusting
Vegetable oil
3 tablespoons olive oil
1 cup Fresh Tomato Sauce
   (page 42)
1 pound skinned, seared
   swordfish steaks, diced
1 cup sliced black olives
2 tablespoons capers
$1/4$ cup minced fresh parsley
2 tablespoons lemon zest
$1/2$ pound thinly sliced
   provolone cheese
$1/2$ pound thinly sliced
   mozzarella cheese*

$^1/_2$ recipe Pizza Crust for the
    Grill dough (page 35)
Cornmeal and flour for
    dusting
Vegetable oil
3 tablespoons olive oil
1 cup Cilantro Pesto (page 43)
2 pounds sea scallops,
    pan-seared and
    quartered
$1^1/_2$ cups sliced kumquats
$^1/_2$ cup minced green onion
1 teaspoon cumin
Black pepper to taste
1 cup shredded Monterey
    jack cheese
1 cup shredded Manchego
    cheese

Scallop and Kumquat Pizza

Kumquats add bright color and a sweet-tart zing to this grilled pizza. Sear scallops quickly over high heat to caramelize the surface. The creamy disks will continue cooking on the pizza.

✳   ✳   ✳

1. On a lightly floured board or on parchment, roll out two 12-inch dough circles. Place one circle of dough on a metal pizza peel or rimless baking sheet generously sprinkled with flour and cornmeal.

2. Prepare a gas or charcoal grill so that one area is hot while another side or corner is medium-hot. Brush the grill rack with vegetable oil. Slide the pizza onto the grill rack over the hot coals or heating element. Close the lid immediately and grill for 2 to 3 minutes or until pizza dough is cooked on the bottom and grill marks appear. Remove dough to peel or baking sheet, turning the grilled side up.

3. Brush the grilled pizza side with half the olive oil. Quickly spread half the Cilantro Pesto over the grilled crust. Cover the sauce with half the scallops and kumquat slices, followed by half the green onion. Sprinkle with cumin and pepper. Combine the Monterey jack and Manchego cheeses and distribute half over the top of the pizza.

4. Carefully slide the pizza back onto the grill, placing it over the medium-hot area. Close grill cover and cook 3 minutes. Check to make sure crust isn't browning too quickly. If it is, move some coals to the opposite side of the grill or lower gas grill thermostat to reduce heat. Continue to cook for another 4 to 5 minutes or until crust is browned and cheese is melted and bubbly. Remove from heat, cool slightly, and serve. Repeat cooking process with second pizza.

Grilled Focaccia Pie

Buy flat, round loaves of focaccia at your favorite bakery or specialty bread store. This is a super-easy recipe for impromptu entertaining.

Makes two 12-inch pies

2 baked focaccia loaves
1½ cups Pesto Sauce
    (page 43)
Vegetable oil
1 cup roasted red pepper
    strips
½ cup toasted pine nuts
Freshly ground black pepper
    to taste
2 cups shredded Asiago
    cheese

* * *

1. Place focaccias on a work surface. With a serving fork, pierce several holes in the top. Slowly spoon half the pesto over each loaf, allowing some of the sauce to seep into the holes in the bread.

2. Prepare a gas or charcoal grill so the cooking surface is medium-hot. Brush the grill rack with vegetable oil. Layer roasted pepper strips and pine nuts over each focaccia loaf and sprinkle with Asiago cheese. Slide both loaves onto the grill rack. Close the lid immediately and grill for 3 to 5 minutes, or until grill marks appear on the loaf and cheese is melted.

3. Remove from heat. Cool slightly, cut into wedges, and serve with wine and cocktails.

Makes two 12-inch-long turnovers

$^{1}/_{2}$ recipe Pizza Crust for the
    Grill dough (page 35)
Cornmeal and flour for
    dusting
Vegetable oil
1$^{1}/_{2}$ cups Slow-Simmered
    Tomato Sauce (page 40)
6 cups finely diced cooked
    ham
Black pepper to taste
$^{1}/_{2}$ pound sliced mozzarella
    cheese
$^{1}/_{2}$ pound sliced provolone
    cheese

Grilled Ham Turnovers

This recipe makes two large turnovers designed to be sliced and shared. If you prefer, the pizza dough can be made into four or six smaller circles for individual turnovers.

✳   ✳   ✳

1. On a lightly floured board or on parchment, roll out two 12-inch dough circles. Place each circle of dough on a metal pizza peel or rimless baking sheet generously sprinkled with flour and cornmeal.

2. In a large bowl, stir tomato sauce into diced ham until well mixed. Add black pepper to taste. Layer mozzarella and provolone slices over the dough circles, leaving about ½ inch around the edges bare. Spoon ham and sauce onto one side of the dough circles, dividing the ham equally over the turnovers. Carefully lift the dough from the side without ham and lay it over the ham filling. Press the edges of the dough together to form a sealed turnover.

3. Prepare a gas or charcoal grill so the cooking surface is medium-hot. Brush the grill rack with vegetable oil. Slide the turnovers onto the grill rack over the hot coals or heating element. Close the lid immediately and grill for 3 to 4 minutes or until dough is cooked on the bottom and grill marks appear. Carefully flip the turnover over and cook the other side for 5 to 7 minutes. Remove from the grill and cool slightly before serving.

One Good Turn

Pizza turnovers, when well crafted, are actually easier to handle than pizzas. The toppings are all encased in crust and less likely to slide around and fall off. But it's important to remember that until the turnover begins to bake, the dough is still fragile. Don't overstuff your turnovers, and try to keep the dough at an even thickness so there are no weak spots.

Grilled Spinach and Ricotta Turnovers

This is a simple vegetarian recipe. If you'd like something more complex, add finely chopped pepperoni or cooked, crumbled Italian sausage to the mix.

❊　❊　❊

Makes two 12-inch-long turnovers

¹/₂ recipe Pizza Crust for the Grill dough (page 35)
Cornmeal and flour for dusting
Vegetable oil
1 cup Slow-Simmered Tomato Sauce (page 40)
2 cups steamed spinach, squeezed dry and chopped
¹/₄ cup minced green onion
1 egg, beaten
2 pounds ricotta cheese
Black pepper and salt to taste
¹/₄ teaspoon dried oregano
2 cups shredded mozzarella cheese

1. On a lightly floured board or on parchment, roll out two 12-inch dough circles. Place each circle of dough on a metal pizza peel or rimless baking sheet generously sprinkled with flour and cornmeal.

2. In a large bowl, stir tomato sauce into chopped spinach and green onion until well mixed. Stir in beaten egg, then fold in ricotta cheese. Add black pepper and salt to taste and stir in oregano. Fold mozzarella into the mixture. Spoon filling mixture onto one side of the dough circles, leaving dough edges bare. Divide mixture evenly. Carefully lift the dough from the uncovered side and lay it over the filling. Press the edges of the dough together to form a sealed turnover.

3. Prepare a gas or charcoal grill so the cooking surface is medium-hot. Brush the grill rack with vegetable oil. Slide the turnovers onto the grill rack over the hot coals or heating element. Close the lid immediately and grill for 3 to 4 minutes or until dough is cooked on the bottom and grill marks appear. Carefully flip the turnover over and cook the other side for 5 to 7 minutes. Remove from the grill and cool slightly before serving.

Spears from 2 cored, peeled
fresh pineapples
¹/₂ recipe Pizza Crust for the
Grill dough (page 35)
Cornmeal and flour for
dusting
Vegetable oil
3 tablespoons olive oil
1 cup Slow-Simmered Tomato
Sauce (page 40)
¹/₂ pound sliced mozzarella
cheese
¹/₂ pound sliced provolone
cheese
2 cups finely diced Canadian
bacon
1 small red bell pepper, cored
and diced
2 cups shredded mild
Cheddar cheese

Grilled Pineapple Pizza

Sweet-and-savory pizzas make excellent summertime fare.

✳ ✳ ✳

1. Using a well-oiled or nonstick vegetable basket, grill the pineapple spears over medium heat until exteriors are lightly browned and the fruit is heated through and fragrant. Remove from the grill and set aside. When cooled enough to handle, cut the fruit into bite-sized pieces.

2. On a lightly floured board or on parchment, roll out two 12-inch dough circles. Place one circle of dough on a metal pizza peel or rimless baking sheet generously sprinkled with flour and cornmeal.

3. Check gas or charcoal grill settings. One area should be hot, while another side or corner is medium-hot. Brush the grill rack liberally with vegetable oil. Slide the pizza onto the grill rack over the hot coals or heating element. Close the lid immediately and grill for 2 to 3 minutes or until pizza dough is cooked on the bottom and grill marks appear. Remove dough to peel or baking sheet, turning the grilled side up.

4. Brush the grilled pizza side with half the olive oil, then quickly spread half the tomato sauce over the grilled crust. Cover the sauce with half the slices of mozzarella and half the slices of provolone. Top with half the diced pineapple, half the Canadian bacon, and half the red bell pepper. Sprinkle with 1 cup of Cheddar cheese.

5. Carefully slide the pizza back onto the grill, placing it over the medium-hot area. Close grill cover and cook 3 minutes. Check to make sure crust isn't browning too quickly. If it is, move some coals to the opposite side or lower gas grill thermostat. Continue to cook for another 4 to 5 minutes or until browned and bubbly. Remove from heat, cool slightly, and serve. Repeat process with second pizza.

Smoky Fruit Pizza

Serve this not-too-sweet pizza with wedges of Camembert, Port Salut, Gouda, and Cheddar cheese for a unique cheese-course dish.

Makes two 12-inch pizzas

$^1/_2$ recipe Pizza Crust for the Grill dough (page 35)
Cornmeal and flour for dusting
Vegetable oil
3 tablespoons melted butter
1 cup apricot preserves, warmed
2 cups sliced fresh peaches
1 cup sliced fresh plumbs
1 cup pitted fresh cherries
1 cup fresh blueberries
4 tablespoons brown sugar

✳ ✳ ✳

1. On a lightly floured board or on parchment, roll out two 12-inch dough circles. Place one circle of dough on a metal pizza peel or rimless baking sheet generously sprinkled with flour and cornmeal.

2. Prepare a gas or charcoal grill so that one area is hot while another side or corner is medium-hot. Brush the grill rack with vegetable oil. Slide the pizza onto the grill rack over the hot coals or heating element. Close the lid immediately and grill for 2 to 3 minutes or until pizza dough is cooked on the bottom and grill marks appear. Remove dough to peel or baking sheet, turning the grilled side up.

3. Brush the grilled pizza side with half the butter, then quickly spread half the apricot jam over the top. Cover the sauce with half the slices of peaches and plums, half the cherries, and half the blueberries. Sprinkle the fruit with 2 tablespoons brown sugar. Carefully slide the pizza back onto the grill, placing it over the medium-hot area. Close grill cover and cook 3 minutes. Check to make sure crust isn't browning too quickly. If it is, move some coals to the opposite side of the grill or lower gas grill thermostat to reduce heat. Continue to cook for another 4 to 5 minutes or until crust is browned and fruit is softened. Remove from heat, cool slightly, and serve. Repeat cooking process with second pizza.

Calzones and Pizza Turnovers

Makes three 8-inch
calzones

½ recipe Classic Crust dough
    (page 16) or Whole-
    Wheat Crust dough
    (page 22)
3 tablespoons olive oil
2 cups chopped cooked
    broccoli
1 small onion, minced
2 cups duck sausage, thinly
    sliced
3 cups shredded mozzarella
    cheese
1 cup bleu cheese, crumbled
Salt and black pepper to taste
3 tablespoons cornmeal

Broccoli and Duck Sausage Calzones

*Duck sausage gives this calzone a rich, distinctive flavor. If you
prefer, you can always substitute a smoked chicken or pork sausage.*

*   *   *

1. Separate dough into three pieces. Place segments on a
   heavily floured work surface and roll each one into an 8-
   inch circle. Brush each circle with 1 tablespoon of olive oil.

2. Combine chopped broccoli and minced onion. Spread one-
   third of the mixture onto half of each dough circle, leaving
   one inch of the edges bare. Distribute ⅔ cup duck sausage
   over the broccoli on each calzone, followed by 1 cup mozzarella cheese and ⅓ cup bleu cheese. Season with salt and
   black pepper to taste.

3. Fold dough over the filling to form a crescent. Press dough
   edges together, brushing edges with a little water if necessary. Sprinkle cornmeal over a baking sheet or pizza tiles
   and place calzones on the cornmeal. Cover with a damp
   towel and let stand 1 hour.

4. With a sharp knife, cut two or three slits in the tops of the
   calzones. Bake at 375° for 20 to 25 minutes. Remove from
   oven and let stand a few minutes before serving.

Just Ducky

*Duck sausage and shredded duck breast can be combined
with diced apples and shredded red cabbage, or diced
apples and dried cranberries, to make a savory-sweet filling
for calzones or turnovers. Buy duck sausage at specialty
meat markets or from online purveyors.*

Porcini and Chicken Calzones

Fresh porcini mushrooms—sometimes called cèpes—can be found in the produce section of many large supermarkets. Other mushrooms can be substituted, or use rehydrated dried porcinis.

✳   ✳   ✳

Makes three 8-inch calzones

¹/₂ recipe Classic Crust dough (page 16) or Whole-Wheat Crust dough (page 22)
¹/₃ cup Garlic and Oil Sauce (page 44)
3 cups shredded cooked chicken
3 green onions, minced
1 cup chopped porcini mushrooms
3 cups ricotta cheese
1 cup shredded mozzarella cheese
Salt and black pepper to taste
3 tablespoons cornmeal

1. Separate dough into three pieces. Place segments on a heavily floured work surface and roll each one into an 8-inch circle. Brush each circle with Garlic and Oil Sauce.

2. Combine shredded chicken, green onion, and mushrooms. Spread 1 cup of the ricotta onto half of each dough circle, leaving one inch around the edges bare. Distribute one-third of the chicken mixture over the ricotta, followed by ⅓ cup mozzarella cheese. Season with salt and black pepper to taste.

3. Fold dough over the filling to form a crescent. Press dough edges together, brushing edges with a little water if necessary. Sprinkle cornmeal over a baking sheet or pizza tiles and place calzones on the cornmeal. Cover with a damp towel and let stand 1 hour.

4. With a sharp knife, cut two or three slits in the tops of the calzones. Bake at 375° for 20 to 25 minutes. Remove from oven and let stand a few minutes before serving.

³/₄ cup olive oil
¹/₂ cup minced green onion
5 cloves garlic, minced
¹/₂ cup minced parsley
3 pounds fresh spinach, well-rinsed and chopped
Salt and pepper to taste
¹/₂ teaspoon dried oregano
4 eggs, lightly beaten
2 cups ricotta cheese
2 cups crumbled feta cheese
1 cup shredded Parmesan cheese
24 sheets phyllo dough

Phyllo and Spinach Wedges

Keep phyllo sheets covered with a damp towel to keep the delicate layers from drying out.

❉   ❉   ❉

1. In a large, heavy saucepan, heat 3 tablespoons olive oil over medium-high heat. Add green onion, garlic, and parsley. Sauté for 3 minutes, stirring constantly. Add spinach to the saucepan and cook just until wilted, about 2 minutes. Stir in salt, pepper, and oregano. Place mixture in a large strainer to drain and let cool.

2. In a large bowl, combine eggs, ricotta, feta, and Parmesan cheese. Fold in drained spinach mixture.

3. Brush a 12" deep-sided pizza or quiche pan with olive oil. Place a layer of phyllo dough in the pan, overlapping the sheets and allowing the corners to rise up the sides. Brush phyllo layer with olive oil and place another layer in the pan. Brush that layer with olive oil. Repeat until you've used 12 sheets of phyllo. Spoon spinach and cheese mixture over the phyllo layers and fold overhanging edges over the filling. Brush filling lightly with olive oil, then begin layering remaining 12 sheets of phyllo over the top. Brush each sheet liberally with olive oil. With a butter knife, push overhanging phyllo sheets into the sides of the pan.

4. Bake at 350° for 35 to 40 minutes or until top is golden brown. Remove from oven and let stand for a few minutes. Cut into 8 wedges and serve warm.

Pepperoni Roll

This is a favorite Italian snack along the Eastern Seaboard.

✳ ✳ ✳

1. On a floured surface, roll dough into a 9 × 16-inch rectangle. Brush liberally with olive oil, then cover dough with pepperoni slices. Sprinkle mozzarella and Parmesan over the top, then sprinkle with black pepper.

2. Starting from a long side of the dough, lift the edge and begin rolling the dough tightly, jelly-roll fashion, being careful to encase the filling with each turn.

3. Sprinkle a baking sheet with cornmeal and place the roll on the sheet. Cover and let stand 1 hour. Bake at 375° for 20 to 25 minutes or until nicely browned. Let stand a few minutes, then slice crosswise and serve.

Makes one 16-inch roll

$1/2$ recipe Classic Crust dough (page 16)
2 tablespoons olive oil
2 cups sliced pepperoni
2 cups shredded mozzarella cheese
1 cup shredded Parmesan cheese
Black pepper to taste
2 tablespoons cornmeal

Hot Pastrami Stromboli

This is a great snack to serve at parties.

✳ ✳ ✳

1. On a floured surface, roll dough into a 9 × 16-inch rectangle. Brush liberally with olive oil, then cover dough with pastrami slices. Sprinkle mozzarella and Parmesan over the top, then sprinkle with black pepper.

2. Starting from a long side of the dough, lift the edge and begin rolling the dough tightly, jelly-roll fashion, being careful to encase the filling with each turn.

3. Sprinkle a baking sheet with cornmeal and place the roll on the sheet. Cover and let stand 1 hour. Bake at 375° for 20 to 25 minutes or until nicely browned. Let stand a few minutes, then slice crosswise and serve with mustard or pizza sauce for dipping.

Makes one 16-inch roll

$1/2$ recipe Classic Crust dough (page 16)
2 tablespoons olive oil
$1/2$ pound sliced pastrami
2 cups shredded mozzarella cheese
1 cup shredded provolone cheese
Black pepper to taste
2 tablespoons cornmeal
Hot mustard or pizza sauce for dipping (optional)

½ recipe Classic Crust dough
(page 16) or Whole-
Wheat Crust dough
(page 22)
3 tablespoons olive oil
3 cups prepared bread or
cornbread stuffing
1 pint small oysters, lightly
sautéed
1 jalapeño pepper, minced
2 green onions, minced
1 rib celery, minced
3 cups shredded Gruyère
cheese
Salt and black pepper to taste
3 tablespoons cornmeal

Oyster Stuffing Turnovers

*Use your own stuffing recipe or a commercially packaged brand
to make this dish. It's a great way to recycle leftover stuffing.*

✳   ✳   ✳

1. Separate dough into three pieces. Place segments on a
   heavily floured work surface and roll each one into an 8-
   inch circle. Brush each circle with 1 tablespoon of olive oil.

2. Toss prepared stuffing with oysters in the sauté pan. Add
   jalapeño, green onions, and celery and mix well. Spread
   one-third of the mixture onto half of each dough circle,
   leaving one inch around the edges bare. Distribute 1 cup
   Gruyère cheese over each mound of stuffing. Season with
   salt and black pepper to taste.

3. Fold dough over the filling to form a crescent. Press dough
   edges together, brushing edges with a little water if necessary. Sprinkle cornmeal over a baking sheet or pizza tiles
   and place calzones on the cornmeal. Cover with a damp
   towel and let stand 1 hour.

4. With a sharp knife, cut two or three slits in the tops of the
   turnovers. Bake at 375° for 20 to 25 minutes. Remove from
   oven and let stand a few minutes before serving.

Stuffing Safety
*Do not add cold stuffing to hot oysters. Both the oysters and
the stuffing should be either hot or cold when combined in
order to retard the growth of bacteria. If your turnovers will
be standing longer than 1 hour, cover the baking sheet and
place them in the refrigerator.*

Zucchini and Tomato Turnovers

Drain tomatoes for a few minutes and blot excess moisture from zucchini before combining ingredients in this recipe.

* * *

1. Separate dough into three pieces. Place segments on a heavily floured work surface and roll each one into an 8-inch circle. Spread one-third of the sauce over each circle.

2. Combine ricotta, basil, garlic, zucchini, and tomatoes. Spread one-third of the mixture onto half of each dough circle, leaving one inch around the edges bare. Distribute 1 cup Asiago cheese over filling on each turnover. Season with salt and black pepper to taste.

3. Fold dough over the filling to form a crescent. Press dough edges together, brushing edges with a little water if necessary. Sprinkle cornmeal over a baking sheet or pizza tiles and place calzones on the cornmeal. Cover with a damp towel and let stand 1 hour.

4. With a sharp knife, cut two or three slits in the tops of the calzones. Bake at 375° for 20 to 25 minutes. Remove from oven and let stand a few minutes before serving.

Makes three 8-inch turnovers

½ recipe Classic Crust dough (page 16) or Whole-Wheat Crust dough (page 22)
½ cup Slow-Simmered Tomato Sauce (page 40) or Speed-Scratch Tomato Sauce (page 40)
3 cups ricotta cheese
¼ cup minced fresh basil
2 cloves garlic, minced
2 cups shredded zucchini
1⅓ cups diced tomatoes
3 cups shredded Asiago cheese
Salt and black pepper to taste
3 tablespoons cornmeal

½ recipe Classic Crust dough
(page 16) or Whole-
Wheat Crust dough
(page 22)
3 tablespoons olive oil
3 cups chopped cooked
lobster meat
3 cups yellow corn kernels
3 cups cooked potatoes, diced
small
1 small onion, minced
1 tablespoon minced fresh
parsley
1 tablespoon minced fresh
tarragon
¼ cup heavy cream
2 cups shredded Cheddar
cheese
Salt and black pepper to taste
3 tablespoons cornmeal

Lobster, Corn, and Potato Calzones

*Overcooked lobster, while flavorful, tends to be chewy and tough.
To guard against this problem, chop lobster meat very finely
before adding to the recipe.*

❋　　❋　　❋

1. Separate dough into three pieces. Place segments on a heavily floured work surface and roll each one into an 8-inch circle. Brush each circle with 1 tablespoon of olive oil.

2. Combine chopped lobster, corn, potatoes, minced onion, parsley, and tarragon. Moisten with heavy cream and mix well. Spread one-third of the mixture onto half of each dough circle, leaving one inch around the edges bare. Distribute one-third of the Cheddar cheese over lobster mixture on each calzone. Season with salt and black pepper to taste.

3. Fold dough over the filling to form a crescent. Press dough edges together, brushing edges with a little water if necessary. Sprinkle cornmeal over a baking sheet or pizza tiles and place calzones on the cornmeal. Cover with a damp towel and let stand 1 hour.

4. With a sharp knife, cut two or three slits in the tops of the calzones. Bake at 375° for 20 to 25 minutes. Remove from oven and let stand a few minutes before serving.

Muffaletta Turnovers

Olive salad is a mixture of different types of olives, plus pimiento, celery, onions, and other ingredients. Buy it ready-made or make a batch to your liking.

❄   ❄   ❄

1. Separate dough into three pieces. Place segments on a heavily floured work surface and roll each one into an 8-inch circle. Spread one-third of the sauce over each circle.

2. Combine olive salad, peppers, ham, salami, mortadella, and provolone. Spoon one-third of the mixture onto half of each dough circle, leaving edges bare. Season with black pepper to taste.

3. Fold dough over the filling to form a crescent. Press dough edges together, brushing edges with a little water if necessary. Sprinkle cornmeal over a baking sheet or pizza tiles and place turnovers on the cornmeal. Cover with a damp towel and let stand 1 hour.

4. With a sharp knife, cut two or three slits in the tops of the turnovers. Bake at 375° for 20 to 25 minutes. Remove from oven and let stand a few minutes before serving.

What Makes a Muffaletta?

Central Grocery in the French Quarter of New Orleans is the home of the original Muffaletta sandwich, and it's still made at the grocery deli counter and wrapped in white paper. The sandwich, which has Sicilian roots, is made by splitting a large round loaf of crusty Italian bread and filling it with many layers of cured meats and cheeses. The crowning glory is a layer of olive salad that seeps into the bread and flavors the entire sandwich.

Makes three 8-inch turnovers

½ recipe Classic Crust dough (page 16) or Whole-Wheat Crust dough (page 22)
½ cup Garlic and Oil Sauce (page 44)
1⅓ cups olive salad, drained
½ cup chopped roasted red peppers
1 cup diced ham
1 cup diced salami
1 cup diced mortadella
3 cups diced provolone cheese
Black pepper to taste
3 tablespoons cornmeal

$^1/_2$ recipe Classic Crust dough (page 16) or Whole-Wheat Crust dough (page 22)
$^1/_2$ cup Garlic and Oil Sauce (page 44)
1 cup sliced green olives
1 cup chopped kalamata olives
1 teaspoon dried oregano
2 cups diced feta cheese
3 cups grape tomatoes, halved
1 cup shredded mozzarella cheese
$^1/_2$ cup toasted pine nuts
Black pepper to taste
3 tablespoons cornmeal

Feta, Olive, and Tomato Calzones

The feta cheese and olives will probably make this dish salty enough without adding extra salt.

✳   ✳   ✳

1. Separate dough into three pieces. Place segments on a heavily floured work surface and roll each one into an 8-inch circle. Spread one-third of the sauce over each circle.

2. Combine olives, oregano, feta cheese, and tomatoes. Spoon one-third of the mixture onto half of each dough circle, leaving one inch around the edges bare. Sprinkle fillings with one-third of the pine nuts and one-third of the mozzarella cheese. Season with black pepper to taste.

3. Fold dough over the filling to form a crescent. Press dough edges together, brushing edges with a little water if necessary. Sprinkle cornmeal over a baking sheet or pizza tiles and place calzones on the cornmeal. Cover with a damp towel and let stand 1 hour.

4. With a sharp knife, cut two or three slits in the tops of the calzones. Bake at 375° for 20 to 25 minutes. Remove from oven and let stand a few minutes before serving.

Shrimp and Tasso Calzones

Tasso is a spicy, smoke-cured meat made from beef, ham, or even turkey. It's a favorite seasoning ingredient among South Louisiana cooks.

1. Separate dough into three pieces. Place segments on a heavily floured work surface and roll each one into an 8-inch circle. Spread one-third of the sauce over each circle.

2. Spoon 1 cup of ricotta onto half of each dough circle, leaving one inch around the edges bare. Combine parsley, garlic, green onions, bell pepper, tasso, shrimp, and Tabasco. Spread one-third of the mixture over the ricotta on each dough circle. Distribute Colby cheese over filling on each calzone. Season with salt and black pepper to taste.

3. Fold dough over the filling to form a crescent. Press dough edges together, brushing edges with a little water if necessary. Sprinkle cornmeal over a baking sheet or pizza tiles and place calzones on the cornmeal. Cover with a damp towel and let stand 1 hour.

4. With a sharp knife, cut two or three slits in the tops of the calzones. Bake at 375° for 20 to 25 minutes. Remove from oven and let stand a few minutes before serving.

Everybody Loves Shrimp
Americans eat more than four pounds of shrimp per person every year, thanks in part to an abundance of less-expensive farm-raised shrimp flooding the market. Like all seafoods, shrimp contain a large percentage of water. In stews and soups, that liquid adds flavor to the dish. But to keep savory pies, tarts, and pizzas from getting soggy, lightly cook shrimp before using in recipes.

Makes three 8-inch calzones

½ recipe Classic Crust dough (page 16) or Whole-Wheat Crust dough (page 22)
½ cup Slow-Simmered Tomato Sauce (page 40) or Speed-Scratch Tomato Sauce (page 40)
3 cups ricotta cheese
¼ cup minced fresh parsley
2 cloves garlic, minced
2 green onions, minced
1 small green bell pepper, cored and diced
1 cup diced tasso
2 cups cooked, diced shrimp
Dash Tabasco
1 cup shredded Colby cheese
Salt and black pepper to taste
3 tablespoons cornmeal

Crawfish Turnovers

Makes three 8-inch turnovers

$^1/_2$ cup butter
$^1/_4$ cup minced fresh parsley
2 cloves garlic, minced
2 green onions, minced
1 small onion, minced
1 small green bell pepper, cored and diced
1 pound peeled crawfish tails
$^1/_2$ cup water
Dash Tabasco
2 cups cooked white rice
Salt and black pepper to taste
$^1/_2$ recipe Classic Crust dough (page 16) or Whole-Wheat Crust dough (page 22)
3 tablespoons cornmeal

Peeled shrimp can be substituted for crawfish in this recipe. Since raw shrimp holds more water than crawfish tails, reduce the water in the recipe to $^1/_4$ cup.

❋   ❋   ❋

1. In a heavy saucepan over high heat, combine butter, parsley, garlic, green onions, onion, and bell pepper. Cook, stirring constantly, for 3 minutes. Add crawfish tails and ½ cup of water. Reduce heat and cook, stirring often, for 10 minutes. Add Tabasco, rice, salt, and black pepper to taste. Mix to blend and remove from heat. Allow to cool.

2. Separate dough into three pieces. Place segments on a heavily floured work surface and roll each one into an 8-inch circle. Spoon crawfish mixture onto half of each circle, leaving one inch around the edges bare.

3. Fold dough over the filling to form a crescent. Press dough edges together, brushing edges with a little water if necessary. Sprinkle cornmeal over a baking sheet or pizza tiles and place turnovers on the cornmeal. Cover with a damp towel and let stand 45 minutes.

4. With a sharp knife, cut two or three slits in the tops of the turnovers. Bake at 375° for 20 to 25 minutes. Remove from oven and let stand a few minutes before serving.

Thai Peanut Chicken Turnovers

Makes three 8-inch turnovers

For a richer sauce, coconut milk can be substituted for the chicken broth.

* * *

1. In a food processor, combine chicken broth, peanut butter, soy sauce, honey or maple syrup, garlic, and red pepper flakes. In a bowl, toss spinach and chicken in sauce until well blended. Add salt and pepper to taste and stir in peanuts.

2. Separate dough into three pieces. Place segments on a heavily floured work surface and roll each one into an 8-inch circle. Spoon chicken mixture onto half of each circle, leaving one inch around the edges bare.

3. Fold dough over the filling to form a crescent. Press dough edges together, brushing edges with a little water if necessary. Sprinkle cornmeal over a baking sheet or pizza tiles and place turnovers on the cornmeal. Cover with a damp towel and let stand 45 minutes.

4. With a sharp knife, cut two or three slits in the tops of the turnovers. Bake at 375° for 20 to 25 minutes. Remove from oven and let stand a few minutes before serving.

$1/3$ cup chicken broth
$1/2$ cup smooth peanut butter
2 tablespoons soy sauce
1 tablespoon honey or maple syrup
2 cloves garlic, minced
1 teaspoon red pepper flakes
1 cup cooked spinach, drained and finely chopped
3 cups shredded cooked chicken
Salt and black pepper to taste
1 cup chopped peanuts
$1/2$ recipe Classic Crust dough (page 16) or Whole-Wheat Crust dough (page 22)
3 tablespoons cornmeal

½ recipe No-Yeast Crust
    dough (page 27)
½ cup Barbecue Sauce
    (page 45)
3 cups browned ground beef
    or shredded cooked beef
¼ cup minced fresh parsley
2 cloves garlic, minced
2 green onions, minced
1 jalapeño pepper, minced
½ teaspoon cumin
Salt and black pepper to taste
Vegetable oil for frying

Natchitoches Meat Pies

These little meat pies are a favorite nosh among families along the Texas–Louisiana border. They're often served on Christmas Eve.

❊   ❊   ❊

1. With floured hands, divide dough into six portions. Roll each portion into a 4-inch circle. In a bowl, combine Barbecue Sauce, beef, parsley, garlic, green onions, jalapeño pepper, cumin, salt, and pepper. Mix well.

2. Spoon a little beef mixture onto half of each dough circle, leaving a half-inch around the edges bare. Fold bare dough over the filling, forming a crescent shape. Moisten dough with water and crimp edges together to seal the pockets.

3. Pour cooking oil to a depth of 2 inches into a deep skillet or Dutch oven. Turn heat to medium-high. When oil is hot, cook meat pies two at a time for 6 to 8 minutes or until golden on both sides. (Turn carefully at least once during cooking.)

4. Remove pies from oil and drain on paper towels. Cool for several minutes before serving.

Curried Lamb Turnovers

If you're not a fan of lamb, this dish can be made with finely diced beef or shredded chicken or turkey.

* * *

1. With floured hands, divide dough into six portions. Roll each portion into a 4-inch circle. In a bowl, combine tomato sauce, lamb, parsley, mint, garlic, green onions, jalapeño pepper, cumin, curry powder, salt, and pepper. Mix well.

2. Spoon a little lamb mixture onto half of each dough circle, leaving one-half inch around the edges bare. Fold bare dough over the filling, forming a crescent shape. Moisten dough with water and crimp edges together to seal the pockets.

3. Place turnovers on a baking sheet lined with nonstick foil. Brush tops liberally with melted butter and make a small slit in the top of each turnover. Bake turnovers at 350° for 20 to 25 minutes or until crusts are nicely browned. Let stand a few minutes before serving.

A Dish or a Spice?

Although most Westerners think of curry as anything laced with curry powder, most Indians and Asians think of curry as a type of stew. Far Eastern curries are seasoned with pastes of galangal root, kafir lime leaves, lemongrass, peppers, and other ingredients, while Indian curries tend to start with dried spices roasted in a hot skillet. Curry powder is merely the packaging of some common spices used to make Indian curry, and different blends can vary greatly in freshness and flavor.

$^1/_2$ recipe No-Yeast Crust dough (page 27)
1 cup Speed-Scratch Tomato Sauce (page 40)
3 cups finely diced roast lamb
$^1/_4$ cup minced fresh parsley
$^1/_4$ cup minced fresh mint
2 cloves garlic, minced
2 green onions, minced
1 jalapeño pepper, minced
$^1/_2$ teaspoon cumin
$^1/_2$ teaspoon hot curry powder
Salt and black pepper to taste
3 tablespoons melted butter

½ recipe Cornmeal Crust
    dough (page 25)
½ cup Picante Sauce
    (page 48)
3 cups cooked shredded beef
    brisket
1½ cups drained black beans
1 (15-ounce) can chile-
    seasoned tomato sauce
¼ cup minced fresh cilantro
2 cloves garlic, minced
2 green onions, minced
1 jalapeño pepper, minced
½ teaspoon cumin
Salt and black pepper to taste
2 cups shredded Monterey
    jack cheese
2 cups shredded Cheddar
    cheese
3 tablespoons cornmeal

Chile-Beef Calzones

*Your favorite leftover chili can substitute for
the chile-bean mixture in this dish.*

✳   ✳   ✳

1. Separate dough into three pieces. Place segments on a heavily floured work surface and roll each one into an 8-inch circle. Spread one-third of the Picante Sauce over each circle.

2. In a large bowl, combine beef, beans, chile sauce, cilantro, garlic, green onions, jalapeño pepper, cumin, salt, and pepper. Spoon one-third of the mixture over half of each dough circle, leaving one inch around the edges bare. Distribute cheeses over the filling on each calzone.

3. Fold dough over the filling to form a crescent. Press dough edges together, brushing edges with a little water if necessary. Sprinkle cornmeal over a baking sheet or pizza tiles and place calzones on the cornmeal. Cover with a damp towel and let stand 1 hour.

4. With a sharp knife, cut two or three slits in the tops of the calzones. Bake at 375° for 20 to 25 minutes. Remove from oven and let stand a few minutes before serving.

Three-Sausage Calzones

*Fresh Italian sausage gives these calzones a hint of sweetness
and fennel flavoring, while the andouille and kielbasa
offer spicy and smoky tastes.*

Makes three 8-inch
calzones

*¹/₂ recipe Classic Crust dough
(page 16) or Whole-
Wheat Crust dough
(page 22)
1 cup Speed-Scratch Tomato
Sauce (page 40)
3 cups ricotta cheese
2 cups bulk Italian sausage,
browned and drained
1 cup diced andouille sausage
1 cup diced kielbasa sausage
1¹/₂ cups shredded mozzarella
cheese
Salt and black pepper to taste
3 tablespoons cornmeal*

✳   ✳   ✳

1. Separate dough into three pieces. Place segments on a heavily
   floured work surface and roll each one into an 8-inch circle. Brush
   each circle with Speed-Scratch Tomato Sauce.

2. Spread 1 cup of the ricotta onto half of each dough circle, leaving
   one inch around the edges bare. Combine the three sausages in a
   bowl. Distribute one-third of the sausage mixture over the ricotta
   on each calzone, followed by one-third of the mozzarella cheese.
   Season with salt and black pepper to taste.

3. Fold dough over the filling to form a crescent. Press dough edges
   together, brushing edges with a little water if necessary. Sprinkle
   cornmeal over a baking sheet or pizza tiles and place calzones on
   the cornmeal. Cover with a damp towel and let stand 1 hour.

4. With a sharp knife, cut two or three slits in the tops of the calzones. Bake at 375° for 20 to 25 minutes. Remove from oven and
   let stand a few minutes before serving.

Served Fresh, Smoked, or Cured

*Europeans brought sausage to the New World in the fifteenth
century. Making smoked or salted and cured sausage—rich with
bacteria-retarding fats—was a way of preserving meats of all
varieties. Most farm families had their own recipes for sausage,
and sausage vendors did a brisk business selling to ships going
out to sea. Fresh sausage, which was seasoned but not yet dried
or smoked, was a delicacy and one of the treats of the sausage
kitchen.*

1/2 recipe Classic Crust dough
    (page 16) or Whole-
    Wheat Crust dough
    (page 22)
2 cups Slow-Simmered
    Tomato Sauce (page 40)
3 cups shredded mozzarella
    cheese
2 cups diced pepperoni
1 cup bulk sausage, browned
    and drained
2 cups sliced mushrooms
1 green bell pepper, cored
    and diced
1 1/2 cups shredded Parmesan
    cheese
Salt and black pepper to taste
3 tablespoons cornmeal

Classic Pizza Turnovers

*This turnover mimics a pizza sandwich. Fill it with your
favorite pizza toppings and enjoy!*

❋   ❋   ❋

1. Separate dough into three pieces. Place segments on a
    heavily floured work surface and roll each one into an
    8-inch circle. Brush each circle with one-third of the tomato
    sauce, leaving one inch around the edges bare.

2. Spread 1 cup of the mozzarella over the sauce on each
    dough circle. (You will have cheese over the entire circle.)
    Combine the pepperoni and sausage in a bowl. Distribute
    one-third of the meat mixture over half of each dough circle,
    leaving edges bare. Follow that with one-third of the mush-
    rooms and peppers and one-third of the Parmesan cheese.
    Season with salt and black pepper to taste.

3. Fold dough over the filling to form a crescent. Press dough
    edges together, brushing edges with a little water if neces-
    sary. Sprinkle cornmeal over a baking sheet or pizza tiles
    and place turnovers on the cornmeal. Cover with a damp
    towel and let stand 1 hour.

4. With a sharp knife, cut two slits in the tops of the turnovers.
    Bake at 375° for 20 to 25 minutes. Remove from oven and let
    stand a few minutes before serving.

Savory Pumpkin Calzones

Caribbean and Mexican cooks often include pumpkin as a filling for savory tamales and turnovers, as well as an ingredient in spicy soups.

✳   ✳   ✳

1. Separate dough into three pieces. Place segments on a heavily floured work surface and roll each one into an 8-inch circle. Brush each circle with Cheesy Cream Sauce.

2. Spread 1 cup of the ricotta onto half of each dough circle, leaving one inch around the edges bare. Combine the pumpkin with the cinnamon, cumin, ginger, cayenne, salt, and pepper in a bowl. Distribute one-third of the pumpkin mixture over the ricotta on each calzone.

3. Fold dough over the filling to form a crescent. Press dough edges together, brushing edges with a little water if necessary. Brush tops of calzones with melted butter and sprinkle pumpkin seeds over each. Sprinkle cornmeal over a baking sheet or pizza tiles and place calzones on the cornmeal. Cover with a damp towel and let stand 1 hour.

4. With a sharp knife, cut two or three slits in the tops of the calzones. Bake at 375° for 20 to 25 minutes. Remove from oven and let stand a few minutes before serving.

Makes three 8-inch calzones

---

¹/₂ recipe Classic Crust dough (page 16) or Whole-Wheat Crust dough (page 22)
1 cup Cheesy Cream Sauce (page 40)
3 cups ricotta cheese
2 cups drained pumpkin purée or canned pumpkin
1 teaspoon cinnamon
¹/₂ teaspoon cumin
¹/₄ teaspoon ginger
¹/₄ teaspoon cayenne
Salt and black pepper to taste
2 tablespoons melted butter
3 tablespoons shelled pumpkin seeds
3 tablespoons cornmeal

Makes three 8-inch
calzones

¹/₂ recipe Classic Crust dough
    (page 16) or Whole-
    Wheat Crust dough
    (page 22)
5 tablespoons melted butter
4 cups diced fresh pears
3 tablespoons flour
3 tablespoons brown sugar
¹/₂ teaspoon cinnamon
2 cups diced Port Salut cheese,
    rind removed
3 tablespoons sliced almonds
3 tablespoons cornmeal

Pear and Port Salut Calzones

*Port Salut is a delicate, semisoft cheese originally made by
Trappist monks in Brittany. Its creamy flavor makes it a favorite
for fruit-and-cheese-course platters.*

❋   ❋   ❋

1. Separate dough into three pieces. Place segments on a
    heavily floured work surface and roll each one into an
    8-inch circle. Brush each circle with 1 tablespoon melted
    butter.

2. Combine the pears with the flour, sugar, and cinnamon.
    Distribute one-third of the pear mixture over half of each
    dough circle. Top the pear mixture on each calzone with
    one-third of the diced Port Salut.

3. Fold dough over the filling to form a crescent. Press dough
    edges together, brushing edges with a little water if neces-
    sary. Brush tops of calzones with remaining melted butter
    and sprinkle sliced almonds over each. Sprinkle cornmeal
    over a baking sheet or pizza tiles and place calzones on the
    cornmeal. Cover with a damp towel and let stand 1 hour.

4. With a sharp knife, cut two or three slits in the tops of the
    calzones. Bake at 375° for 20 to 25 minutes. Remove from
    oven and let stand a few minutes before serving.

Apple Walnut Calzones

This not-too-sweet fruit calzone makes a great offering on a brunch buffet table or at tea time. To make a sweeter offering, drizzle warm caramel sauce over the calzone after baking.

Makes three 8-inch calzones

$\frac{1}{2}$ recipe Classic Crust dough (page 16) or Whole-Wheat Crust dough (page 22)
5 tablespoons melted butter
3 cups ricotta cheese
$\frac{1}{3}$ cup sugar
1 teaspoon vanilla
3 cups peeled, diced Granny Smith or Rome apples
3 tablespoons flour
1 teaspoon cinnamon
3 tablespoons brown sugar
1 cup walnut halves
1 cup chopped walnuts
3 tablespoons cornmeal

※　※　※

1. Separate dough into three pieces. Place segments on a heavily floured work surface and roll each one into an 8-inch circle. Brush each circle with 1 tablespoon melted butter.

2. Combine the ricotta with sugar and vanilla. Spread 1 cup of the ricotta onto half of each dough circle, leaving one inch around the edges bare. Combine the apples with the flour, cinnamon, brown sugar, and walnut halves in a bowl. Distribute one-third of the apple mixture over the ricotta on each calzone.

3. Fold dough over the filling to form a crescent. Press dough edges together, brushing edges with a little water if necessary. Brush tops of calzones with melted butter and sprinkle chopped walnuts over each. Sprinkle cornmeal over a baking sheet or pizza tiles and place calzones on the cornmeal. Cover with a damp towel and let stand 1 hour.

4. With a sharp knife, cut two or three slits in the tops of the calzones. Bake at 375° for 20 to 25 minutes. Remove from oven and let stand a few minutes before serving.

Apple Varieties

Dozens of varieties of apples grow in the U.S., although the apple itself is not a native fruit. Food historians believe apples originated in the mountains of present-day Kazakstan more than 10,000 years ago. Modern varieties include those bred for sweetness, for color, for size, and for cookability. The best apples for cooking and baking are varieties that have tart, crisp flesh that can hold its texture and flavor when heated. Think Rome, Gala, Winesap, Granny Smith, and Northern Spy, among others.

Makes 6 turnovers

*½ recipe No-Yeast Crust
   dough (page 27)*
*3 tablespoons peach
   preserves, melted*
1 tablespoon butter, melted
*2 cups peeled, chopped
   peaches*
¼ cup sugar
2 teaspoons cornstarch
Vegetable oil for frying
Confectioners' sugar

Fried Peach Turnovers

*Sweet summer peaches are best in these pies, but you can also
use thawed frozen peaches or reconstituted dried peaches.*

✳   ✳   ✳

1. With floured hands, divide dough into six portions. Roll each portion into a 4-inch circle. Brush dough with melted preserves. In a bowl, combine butter, peaches, sugar, and cornstarch. Mix well.

2. Spoon a little peach mixture onto half of each dough circle, leaving one-half inch around the edges bare. Fold bare dough over the filling, forming a crescent shape. Moisten dough with water and crimp edges together to seal the pockets.

3. Pour cooking oil to a depth of 2 inches into a deep skillet or Dutch oven. Turn heat to medium-high. When oil is hot, cook peach pies two at a time for 6 to 8 minutes or until golden on both sides. (Turn carefully at least once during cooking.)

4. Remove pies from oil and drain on paper towels. Dust with confectioners' sugar. Cool for several minutes before serving.

CHAPTER 13
Pizzas to Make with Kids

Makes two 12-inch pizzas

2 (12-inch) thin-style pizza
    crusts, ready to top
2 cups pizza sauce or thick
    pasta sauce
4 cups shredded mozzarella
    cheese
1 cup shredded Cheddar
    cheese
1 cup cubed Cheddar cheese

Smiley-Face Pizzas

*Help children create their own pizzas with fewer spills by pouring
pizza sauce into two plastic squeeze bottles. Put cheese in
bowls big enough for little hands.*

❋　❋　❋

1. Place pizza crusts on a table covered with waxed paper.
    Squeeze 1 cup of sauce onto each pizza. Use the back of a
    spoon to spread the sauce.

2. Sprinkle half the mozzarella onto each pizza, covering the
    center completely. Take a small open-sided metal biscuit
    cutter and place it in the middle of the top left quarter of
    one of the pies. Drop a small handful of Cheddar cheese
    into the circle. Carefully remove the biscuit cutter and place
    it opposite the Cheddar "eye" on the right top quarter of the
    pizza. Fill that with Cheddar, then repeat the process on the
    other pizza.

3. Use a spoon handle to draw a broad smile across the bot-
    tom half of each pizza. Place Cheddar cubes along each
    smile. Place pizzas on perforated pizza pans. Bake each
    pizza at 400° for 12 minutes. Let stand until cool enough to
    handle. Bring to the table whole, then slice and serve.

Cooking with Kids

*Children love to help in the kitchen, even if their participation
isn't always exactly helpful. Set aside extra time and plan
cooking projects with their height and dexterity in mind.
Keep plenty of paper towels and wet wipes around so spills
don't have to be a big deal. Aprons are also a good idea;
kids love to wear them, and they will help prevent stains on
clothes.*

Make-Your-Own Pizzas

Don't splurge on super-size or flaky-pastry biscuits for this recipe. Garden-variety refrigerator biscuits work best. This recipe makes a perfect slumber party activity.

✻ ✻ ✻

1. Tear ten large sheets of waxed paper and place one biscuit on each. Using rolling pins or smooth-sided unbreakable glasses, have children roll out biscuit into a flat, round pizza crust.

2. Have sauce in two or three squirt bottles. Place cheese and meats in separate bowls and green pepper on a plate. Pass sauce bottles around until each child has topped a biscuit crust. Allow children to add cheese and other toppings as they desire.

3. Place pizzas on cookie sheets lined with nonstick foil. Use colored wood toothpicks to help keep track of which pizza belongs to whom. Bake one or two sheets at a time in a 400° oven for 8 to 10 minutes until pizza crust is browned and cheese is melted.

4. When all pizzas have been baked and are slightly cooled, serve on colorful paper plates.

Makes 10 personal pizzas

1 can of 10 biscuits
2 cups pizza or pasta sauce
2 cups shredded mozzarella cheese
2 cups shredded Cheddar cheese
1 cup pepperoni slices
1 cup diced ham
2 cups ground beef
1 green bell pepper, cut in strips

Makes one 9 × 13-inch
pizza

1 can refrigerated pizza crust
    dough
1½ cups mild salsa
3 cups refried beans, warmed
    to soften
2 cups taco-seasoned
    shredded or ground
    chicken
4 cups shredded Mexican
    cheese blend

Mexican Pizza

*This kid-friendly pizza is easily assembled from ingredients that
you might have on hand. Leftover roast chicken can
be simmered in taco seasoning.*

✳   ✳   ✳

1. Lightly grease a baking sheet. Unroll pizza crust and stretch
   to cover the pan. Spoon salsa over the crust and allow children to spread with a spoon or sauce brush. Spoon warm
   refried beans over the sauce in several spots and lightly
   press with the back of a spoon to spread.

2. Top the beans with chicken, then add the cheese in handfuls over the pizza. Bake at 400° for 12 to 15 minutes or until
   crust is browned and cheese melted. Let stand for 10 minutes before cutting and serving.

Makes eight 4-inch pizzas

1 pound frozen bread dough,
    thawed
2 cups pizza sauce or pasta
    sauce
2 cups grated blanched
    carrots
4 cups shredded mozzarella
    cheese

Cutout Pizzas

Kids will love personalizing their pizzas by choosing shapes.

✳   ✳   ✳

1. Place dough in a warm place, covered, until doubled in
   bulk. Punch down and place on a lightly floured surface.
   Roll out as thinly as possible. Hand children large cookie
   cutters—geometric shapes work best—and let them cut out
   a shaped crust.

2. Place crusts on cookie sheets lined with nonstick foil. Allow
   children to add sauce from plastic squirt bottles, then top
   pizzas with carrots and cheese.

3. Bake at 400° for 12 to 15 minutes or until pizzas are browned
   and bubbly. Remove from the oven and let stand 10 minutes
   before serving.

Pinwheel Pizzas

Any toppings, finely chopped, can be used to make these easy pizza rolls. Try chopped broccoli, chopped niçoise olives, and Gorgonzola cheese to serve these to adults.

✳   ✳   ✳

1. Unroll pizza dough on a waxed-paper-covered surface. Spread— or have children spread—pizza or pasta sauce over the dough. Sprinkle pepperoni and cheese over the sauce.

2. Lift crust from one of the long sides and roll tightly into a log with toppings encased. At this point, an adult with a sharp knife should slice the log into eight pinwheel rolls.

3. Place rolls on a baking sheet lined with nonstick foil and bake at 350° for 12 to 15 minutes until rolls are nicely browned. Let stand several minutes before serving.

Makes 8 pinwheels

1 can refrigerated pizza dough
1½ cups pizza sauce or pasta sauce
1½ cups finely chopped pepperoni
3 cups shredded mozzarella cheese

American Cheese Pizza

Think of this pizza as cheese toast, that childhood favorite, with a little sauce. If your child likes fresh tomatoes, tomato slices can be substituted for the sauce.

✳   ✳   ✳

1. Place pizza crusts on perforated pizza pans. Spread 1 cup sauce over each crust. Place 12 cheese slices, overlapping and placed diagonally, over each crust.

2. Bake each pizza at 400° for 10 to 12 minutes or until cheese is melted and lightly browned. Let stand several minutes before serving.

Makes two 12-inch pizzas

2 (12-inch) ready-to-top pizza crusts
2 cups pizza sauce or pasta sauce
24 slices American cheese

Hot Dog Pizza

Makes two 12-inch pizzas

2 (12-inch) ready-to-top pizza crusts
4 cups prepared mild chili
1 pound frankfurters, cooked and sliced
4 cups shredded mild Cheddar cheese

Have chopped onions, relish, and mustard on hand as garnish for kids who like their hot dogs "all the way."

❊ ❊ ❊

1. Place pizza crusts on perforated pizza pans. Have kids spoon chili onto the crusts and spread with the back of a spoon. The frankfurter slices go over the chili, evenly divided, on each pizza. Children can place the cheese in handfuls over the chili and hot dog bits.
2. Bake pizzas at 400° for 10 to 12 minutes. Let stand a few minutes before serving with preferred hot dog garnishes.

Double Pepperoni Pizza

Makes two 12-inch pizzas

2 (12-inch) ready-to-top pizza crusts
2 cups pizza sauce or pasta sauce
2 cups finely chopped pepperoni
4 cups shredded mozzarella cheese
2 cups pepperoni slices

Even children who shy away from sausages and other meats will often embrace pepperoni—as long as it comes on top of a pizza.

❊ ❊ ❊

1. Place crusts on perforated pizza pans. Have children spread 1 cup of pizza sauce over each crust, followed by 1 cup of chopped pepperoni on each. Drop cheese by handfuls over each pizza, then top cheese with pepperoni slices.
2. Bake pizzas at 400° for 10 to 12 minutes or until browned and bubbly. Let stand 10 minutes before serving.

Cracker Pizzas

Just a dab of pizza sauce will do it on these little snacks. Too much sauce will make crackers soggy instead of crisp.

Makes 12 cracker snacks

12 large wheat crackers
1/2 cup pizza sauce
3 square slices American and
   mozzarella cheese
3 slices Canadian bacon,
   quartered

✳   ✳   ✳

1. Place crackers on a baking sheet lined with nonstick foil. Dot each cracker with a dab of pizza sauce. Have children divide the cheese slices into four quarters and place one-quarter on each cracker. Place one-quarter slice Canadian bacon on each cracker pizza.

2. Bake at 400° for 5 minutes or just long enough to melt the cheese. Remove from oven and cool briefly before serving.

Pizza Burgers

Serve these burgers open-faced. For more adventurous kids, garnishes might include sliced olives, mushrooms, onions, and peppers.

Makes 6 pizza burgers

3 hamburger buns
1 cup pizza sauce
6 cooked hamburger patties
2 cups shredded mozzarella
   cheese
1 cup cooked, crumbled
   bacon

✳   ✳   ✳

1. Split hamburger buns and toast lightly. Place bun halves cut-side up on a baking sheet lined with nonstick foil. Help kids spread a little pizza sauce over each half, then top with a burger patty, cheese, and bacon bits.

2. Place burger pizzas in a 400° oven for 5 minutes or until cheese is melted. Let stand a few minutes, then serve with a side of fries or fruit.

2 (12-inch) ready-to-top
   pizza crusts
2 cups barbecue sauce or
   1 cup honey-mustard
   sauce
2 cups shredded Colby cheese
2 cups shredded mozzarella
   cheese
32 breaded chicken nuggets,
   cooked

Chicken Nugget Pizza

*Use chicken nuggets from your favorite fast-food restaurant
or use frozen nuggets fried in hot oil or baked until browned.
The pizza doesn't cook long enough to thaw and
brown nuggets straight from the freezer.*

✳   ✳   ✳

1. Place pizza crusts on perforated pizza pans. Allow children
   to spread each with half the barbecue sauce or honey mustard sauce. Sprinkle 1 cup Colby cheese and 1 cup mozzarella cheese over each pizza.

2. Have children count out 16 chicken nuggets and arrange
   them evenly over the first pizza, then arrange the remaining
   nuggets over the second pizza. Bake each pizza at 400° for
   10 to 12 minutes.

Nuggets Everywhere

*Bits of crispy fried protein appeal to most kids. Chicken
nuggets are a favorite, but you could substitute catfish
nuggets, breaded cheese sticks, or even vegetarian nuggets
made from soy protein. If you think nuggets sound too fatty,
keep in mind that baking nuggets results in less fat content
than frying.*

Two-Crust Pizza

Think of this as a pizza sandwich. Supervising adults should cut the pie into four to six slices with a sharp knife.

✴ ✴ ✴

Makes one 9 × 9-inch pizza

1 can refrigerated pizza dough
1 tablespoon vegetable oil
1 cup pizza sauce
8 slices ham
4 slices turkey breast
4 slices mozzarella cheese
4 slices American cheese

1. On a lightly floured surface, unroll pizza crust and stretch into a 9 × 18-inch rectangle. Cut the crust in half, making two 9 × 9-inch squares. Brush squares lightly with oil and place on a baking sheet lined with nonstick foil. Bake at 400° for 10 minutes or until crust is lightly browned.

2. Brush the crusts with pizza sauce, then layer ham, turkey, and cheeses over one crust. Cover the top with the remaining crust and return to oven for 5 minutes or until cheese has melted. Let stand briefly, then slice and serve.

Pizza Pockets

Rolled-out biscuits can become quick pizza turnover crusts for kids' snacks. Just layer toppings over half a flattened, uncooked biscuit. Fold the other half over the toppings and pinch to seal. Bake at 350° for 12 to 14 minutes or until turnover has browned.

Pizza Quesadilla

Makes three 10-inch pizzas

6 (10-inch) flour tortillas
1 cup pizza sauce
1¹⁄₂ cups shredded chicken, chopped ham, or sliced leftover meatballs
3 cups shredded Italian cheese blend
1 tablespoon melted butter

This recipe can be prepared in the microwave for a real quick-fix treat. For a more authentic grilled flavor, sear the tortillas in a lightly buttered skillet.

1. Lay three tortillas on a baking sheet lined with nonstick foil. Help children brush each with one-third of the pizza sauce, followed by ½ cup of the chicken, ham, or meatballs and 1 cup of shredded cheese.

2. Place remaining tortillas on top of the quesadilla pizzas and brush tops with melted butter. Bake at 350° for 10 minutes or until cheese has melted and tortillas are lightly browned. Cut into wedges and serve.

Fruit Pizza Turnovers

Makes two 9-inch turnovers

1 roll refrigerated pizza dough
2 cups ricotta cheese
¹⁄₂ cup sugar
2 teaspoons vanilla
1 large can apple or cherry pie filling
Confectioners' sugar

For a thicker crust, try this recipe with frozen bread dough.

1. Unroll pizza dough on a work surface and stretch to a 9 × 18-inch rectangle. Slice rectangle in half and turn halves to form two 9-inch diamonds.

2. Whisk together ricotta cheese, sugar, and vanilla. Spoon cheese mixture onto the bottom half of the diagonals, leaving a half inch at the edges bare. Spoon fruit pie filling over the sweetened ricotta. Turn top half of dough over the filling and pinch around the edges to seal.

3. Place turnovers on a baking sheet lined with nonstick foil. Bake at 350° for 12 to 14 minutes or until crust is lightly browned. Remove from oven and sprinkle turnovers with confectioners' sugar. Let stand to cool slightly before serving.

Breakfast Pizza

*If your young diners like mushrooms or green peppers, they can
be added to the skillet before the eggs.*

✳ ✳ ✳

Makes six 6-inch pizzas

———————————

1 can 6 large, flaky buttermilk-
   style biscuits
1 cup thick pasta sauce
2 cups shredded Cheddar–
   Monterey jack cheese
   blend
2 tablespoons vegetable oil
12 eggs
$1/3$ cup milk
Salt and pepper to taste
$2/3$ cup crumbled cooked
   bacon

1. On a clean work surface, flatten biscuits a little using a roller
   or a plastic glass. Press each biscuit round into a lightly oiled
   or nonstick 6" tart pan. Brush bottom with a small amount of
   pasta sauce. Divide 1 cup of shredded cheese over the six pizzas.
   Place in a 350° oven and bake 8 to 10 minutes or until crust has
   browned and cheese is bubbly. Remove from the oven.

2. While pizza crusts are baking, add vegetable oil to a large skillet
   and place on medium-high heat. Break eggs into a large bowl
   and whisk together with milk, salt, and pepper. Add eggs to the
   skillet. As eggs begin to set, use a spatula to stir and turn the mixture, keeping eggs moist and fluffy. As soon as no liquid remains,
   remove eggs from heat.

3. Divide scrambled eggs over the six tart pans. Evenly distribute
   remaining cup of cheese over the eggs, then sprinkle the top of
   each breakfast pizza with crumbled bacon. Let pizzas stand until
   cheese melts over hot eggs. Cool slightly, then serve.

2 slices American cheese
4 cups prepared macaroni
    and cheese
1 cup pizza or pasta sauce
2 cups mozzarella cheese
1 cup chopped ham or sliced
    pepperoni

Mac-and-Cheese Pizza

*Macaroni and cheese always gets a thumbs-up from kids.
Serve this pie to your child's play-date friends.*

✳   ✳   ✳

1. Break up American cheese and stir into hot macaroni and cheese. Stir until added cheese has melted. Pour macaroni and cheese into a lightly buttered deep-dish pie plate. Allow to cool until mixture thickens and molds to the pie pan.

2. Pour pizza sauce over mac and cheese and spread with the back of a spoon. Allow children to sprinkle mozzarella over the top, followed by chopped ham or pepperoni.

3. Bake at 350° for 10 to 12 minutes or until cheese has melted and browned slightly. Let stand a few minutes, then serve in wedges.

Makes one 12-inch pie

6 cups cooked spaghetti
4 eggs
$1/3$ cup milk
Salt and pepper to taste
$1/2$ teaspoon mixed Italian
    seasoning
$1^1/_2$ cups pizza or pasta sauce
2 cups mozzarella cheese
1 cup sliced pepperoni

Spaghetti Pie

*This dish is a great, fun way to get kids to eat leftover spaghetti.
The pasta frittata crust also appeals to adults and, with a side
salad, makes a great midweek supper.*

✳   ✳   ✳

1. Place cooked spaghetti evenly over the bottom of a buttered deep pizza pan or 12" quiche pan. Whip together eggs, milk, salt, pepper, and Italian seasoning.

2. Bake at 350° until set, about 20 minutes. Remove from oven and pour sauce evenly over the top. Sprinkle with mozzarella cheese and distribute pepperoni over the top. Return to the oven for 5 minutes, just long enough for cheese to melt. Let stand briefly, then cut in wedges to serve.

Pizza Toast

This little twist on cheese toast can be embellished with the addition of leftover ground beef, chopped ham, or shredded chicken.

❄   ❄   ❄

1. Place toasted bread slices on a baking sheet lined with nonstick foil. Help children brush sauce over each and sprinkle with Parmesan cheese. Lay mozzarella slices over the top.

2. Bake at 350° for 8 to 10 minutes or until the bread is crisp and the cheese melted and bubbly. Let cool briefly before serving.

Makes 6 toast pizzas

6 slices white or wheat bread, toasted
²/₃ cup pizza or thick pasta sauce
3 tablespoons shredded Parmesan cheese
6 slices mozzarella cheese

Cookie Pizza Dessert

Refrigerated cookie dough of any flavor can form the basis for a quick, unique dessert crust that kids will love.

❄   ❄   ❄

1. Press each package of sugar cookie dough into a 12" pizza pan, evenly covering the bottom of the pan in a thin layer. Lightly score the dough into six or eight wedges. Bake each cookie crust at 375° for 10 minutes or until just done. Remove from oven and allow to cool completely.

2. Spread 1 pint of softened strawberry ice cream over each cookie crust, then top each with 2 cups of white chocolate curls. Sprinkle with M&Ms. Cut and serve. Store leftovers in the freezer.

Makes two 12-inch pizzas

2 rolls of refrigerated sugar cookie dough
1 quart strawberry ice cream, slightly softened
4 cups white chocolate curls
1 cup miniature M&Ms

1 pound frozen bread dough,
    thawed
$^1/_2$ cup butter, melted
$^2/_3$ cup brown sugar, packed
$^2/_3$ cup white sugar
$^1/_3$ cup cinnamon
1 cup raisins (optional)
3 cups confectioners' sugar
$^1/_4$ cup heavy cream

Cinnamon Pizza

*Think of this as an open-faced cinnamon roll. Other toppings,
such as chocolate or butterscotch chips, coconut,
jelly beans, and nuts, can be added.*

✳   ✳   ✳

1. Place thawed bread dough in a bowl in a warm spot. Cover and let rise until doubled in size, about 1 hour. Remove to a floured surface and divide in half. Roll each half into a 12-inch round and place in a lightly greased pizza pan.

2. Brush melted butter liberally over each crust. In a bowl, combine sugars and cinnamon. Allow children to spoon cinnamon sugar over crust until well covered. Add raisins if desired.

3. Bake pizzas at 400° for 15 to 18 minutes or until puffy and browned. Let stand for a few minutes. Whisk together confectioners' sugar and cream until smooth. Pour into a squeeze bottle and allow children to squeeze crosshatches of glaze over the pizzas. Serve in wedges.

A Little Dough

Frozen bread dough makes great homemade sweet rolls. If a "pizza" format isn't important, follow the above recipe and tightly roll topped dough into a log instead of leaving open-faced. Slice the log into rolls and let stand a few minutes to rise. Then bake until browned. Drizzle with confectioners' sugar glaze or brush with melted jam.

CHAPTER 14
Celebrate: Pizza Parties

$^1/_2$ recipe Classic Crust dough
   (page 16) or Whole-
   Wheat Crust dough
   (page 22)
3 tablespoons olive oil
1 cup Cheesy Cream Sauce
   (page 44)
1$^1/_2$ cup lump crabmeat
$^1/_4$ cup minced parsley
1 cup Pesto Sauce (page 43)
12 large boiled shrimp, peeled
$^1/_4$ cup minced basil

Pizza Canapés I and II

*These canapés offer a pleasant alternative to cheese on crackers.
If you're not a fan of seafood, diced ham and chunks
of grilled chicken can be substituted.*

✳ ✳ ✳

1. Divide dough in half, then break each half into twelve pieces. With fingers, flatten each bit into a tiny pizza crust. Line two baking sheets with nonstick foil. Place 12 dough circles on each baking sheet. Brush tops lightly with olive oil and bake at 350° for 10 minutes or until lightly browned.

2. Allow crusts to cool. Spread twelve with Cheesy Cream Sauce and top each of those with lump crabmeat. Sprinkle parsley on top and place six on each of two serving platters.

3. Spread remaining crusts with Pesto Sauce. Place a shrimp in the center of each and sprinkle with minced basil. Place six on each serving platter and serve.

Generous Offerings
When hosting a party, try not to load all the food onto one table, forcing everyone to crowd around. Instead, encourage good party flow and mingling by creating several small islands of food—a tray here, a tray there. And never put the bar next to the main buffet.

Red, White, and Green Pizza Feast

This veggie pizza trio makes a great offering for Columbus Day,
St. Joseph's Day, or any other Italian-inspired celebration.

✻　✻　✻

1. Roll or press pizza dough into three 14-inch circles, slightly thicker at the edges than in the center. If using pizza pans, sprinkle the bottom with cornmeal or coat with olive oil and place dough in pan. If using a pizza stone, sprinkle with cornmeal and place stone in oven. Preheat oven to 400°.

2. Spread 1 cup sauce in the center of each pizza, leaving edges bare. Combine cheeses and divide over the pizzas.

3. Arrange red pepper strips in a spoke pattern around one pizza, overlapping strips as necessary. Arrange potato slices in a circular pattern covering another pizza. Spread blanched broccoli over the last pizza. Salt and pepper both pizzas to taste.

4. If using a hot stone or tiles, use a well-floured pizza peel to carefully lift one pizza from preparation surface and place on stone. If using pizza pans, place first pizza in the center of the oven. Bake for 15 to 20 minutes or until the crust is lightly browned and cheese is melted.

5. Remove pizza from oven carefully (use peel if baking with a stone). Set aside to rest briefly before slicing. Repeat baking process with remaining pies.

Makes three 14-inch pizzas

$^1/_2$ recipe Classic Crust dough (page 16) or Bread Machine Crust dough (page 17)
2 tablespoons cornmeal or 1 tablespoon olive oil
3 cups Slow-Simmered Tomato Sauce (page 40)
$1^1/_2$ cups shredded provolone cheese
$1^1/_2$ cups shredded white Cheddar cheese
3 cups shredded mozzarella cheese
2 cups roasted red pepper strips
2 cups thinly sliced boiled potatoes
2 cups chopped blanched broccoli
Salt and pepper to taste

Makes four 6-inch calzones

1/2 recipe Classic Crust dough
    (page 16) or Whole-
    Wheat Crust dough
    (page 22)
1 cup Mustard Cream Sauce
    (page 51)
2 cups shredded red cabbage
1 small onion, minced
4 whole cooked bratwurst
4 cups shredded Cheddar
    cheese
Salt and black pepper to taste

Octoberfest Brats Calzones

*Serve these calzones to your favorite couch coaches during
football season. Don't forget a selection of ales.*

✳   ✳   ✳

1. Separate dough into four pieces. Place segments on a heavily floured work surface and roll each one into a 6-inch circle. Brush each circle with Mustard Cream Sauce.

2. Combine shredded cabbage and minced onion. Spread one-fourth of the mixture onto half of each dough circle, leaving a half-inch around the edges bare. Place one bratwurst on each calzone, followed by 1 cup Cheddar cheese. Season with salt and black pepper to taste.

3. Fold dough over the filling to form a crescent. Press dough edges together, brushing edges with a little water if necessary. Place calzones on a baking sheet lined with nonstick foil. Cover with a damp towel and let stand 30 minutes.

4. With a sharp knife, cut two or three slits in the tops of the calzones. Bake at 375° for 20 minutes. Remove from oven and let stand a few minutes before serving.

Brat Basics

Bratwurst aficionados like to parboil the fresh sausages in beer or ale, then finish the cooking process over hot coals. If you don't have time to fire up the grill, just sear your brats on preheated, ridged grill pan.

Thin-Crust Tapenade Pizza

Serve this rich pizza in slender wedges as a cocktail snack. Balance the briny olive paste with a bowl of sweet grapes or melons.

* * *

1. Roll or press pizza dough into two very thin 12-inch circles, slightly thicker at the edges than in the center. If using pizza pans, sprinkle the bottom with cornmeal or coat with oil and place dough in pan. If using a pizza stone, sprinkle with cornmeal and place rolled dough directly on stone.

2. Spread 1½ cups tapenade evenly over each pizza. Sprinkle cheeses over the tapenade.

3. Place one pizza in the oven at 425°. Bake 10 to 12 minutes or until crust is browned and cheese is melted. Repeat with remaining pizza. Let pizzas rest briefly, then slice with a sharp knife.

Makes two 12-inch pizzas

½ recipe California Thin Crust dough (page 21)
2 tablespoons cornmeal or 1 tablespoon oil
3 cups olive tapenade
1½ cups shredded Gruyère cheese
1½ cups shredded Emmentaler cheese

Crab and Ricotta Appetizer Pizzas

Tarragon, basil, lemon thyme, and parsley make a nice mix for the fresh herb topping on these mini pizzas.

* * *

1. Divide dough in half, then break each half into twelve pieces. With fingers, flatten each bit into a tiny pizza crust. Line two baking sheets with nonstick foil. Place twelve dough circles on each baking sheet. Brush tops lightly with olive oil and bake at 350° for 8 minutes.

2. Spread crusts with a small amount of tomato sauce and add a dollop of ricotta cheese. Divide crab legs over pizzas, then top with cheese and minced herbs. Return to oven 3 to 5 minutes or until mozzarella melts. Place six on each serving platter and serve.

Makes 24 mini-pizzas

½ recipe Classic Crust dough (page 16) or Whole-Wheat Crust dough (page 22)
3 tablespoons olive oil
1 cup Slow-Simmered Tomato Sauce (page 40)
2 cups ricotta cheese
2 cups peeled, sliced crab legs
2 cups mozzarella cheese
⅓ cup fresh herbs

Makes four 6-inch calzones

½ recipe Classic Crust dough
   (page 16) or Whole-
   Wheat Crust dough
   (page 22)
1 cup Sauce Piquant
   (page 49)
2 cups ricotta cheese
2 cups chopped cooked
   lobster
½ cup diced cooked pancetta
3 green onions, minced
1 cup shredded Asiago cheese
Salt and black pepper to taste

Bacon and Lobster Calzones

*Pancetta is Italian bacon that's cured and seasoned,
but not smoked. It has a delicate, sweet flavor.
Substitute crisp-cooked bacon if you prefer.*

✳   ✳   ✳

1. Separate dough into four pieces. Place segments on a heavily floured work surface and roll each one into a 6-inch circle. Brush each circle with Sauce Piquant.

2. Spread ½ cup of the ricotta onto half of each dough circle, leaving a half-inch around the edges bare. Distribute one-fourth of the lobster over the ricotta on each circle, followed by one-fourth of the pancetta. Sprinkle with minced green onion. Season with salt and black pepper to taste.

3. Fold dough over the filling to form a crescent. Press dough edges together, brushing edges with a little water if necessary. Place calzones on a baking sheet lined with nonstick foil. Cover with a damp towel and let stand 30 minutes.

4. With a sharp knife, cut two or three slits in the tops of the calzones. Bake at 375° for 20 minutes. Remove from oven and let stand a few minutes before serving.

Luscious Lobster
Fat-clawed, sweet Maine lobsters are the gold standard of crustaceans. However, for many recipes that call for chopped or sliced lobster, less expensive spiny or rock lobsters will do the trick. Spiny lobsters actually are a different species of creature than Maine lobsters and they have no claws. But the meat is edible and tasty. Most grow in warm waters around the Caribbean and Australasia.

Scrabble Night Pizza Casserole

Think of this as lasagna on a crust. If you want to pile on a few more toppings, consider chopped spinach or diced pepperoni.

❋ ❋ ❋

1. On a floured board, roll pizza dough into a rectangle. Coat a deep, oblong baking dish with olive oil and sprinkle with cornmeal. Press dough into the pan, spreading it to the corners.

2. Spread tomato sauce over the top of the dough. In a bowl, combine beef, sausage, onion, and bell pepper. Layer over the sauce. Dot ricotta cheese over the pizza by the teaspoonful. Grind black pepper over sauce to taste.

3. Combine Parmesan and mozzarella cheeses. Spread evenly over the top of the pizza. Preheat oven to 400°. Bake 20 to 25 minutes or until top is browned and bubbly. Serve with forks and plenty of napkins.

$^1/_2$ recipe Sicilian Crust dough (page 18)
2 tablespoons olive oil
2 tablespoons cornmeal
2 cups Slow-Simmered Tomato Sauce (page 40)
2 cups cooked ground beef
1 cup cooked bulk Italian sausage
1 onion, minced
1 small green bell pepper, cored and diced
1 cup ricotta cheese
Salt and black pepper to taste
1 cup shredded Parmesan cheese
2 cups shredded mozzarella cheese

Hot Shrimp Cocktail Pizza

Horseradish sauce gives this pizza an unexpected kick.

❋ ❋ ❋

1. Roll or press pizza dough into two very thin 12-inch circles, slightly thicker at the edges than in the center. If using pizza pans, sprinkle the bottom with cornmeal or coat with oil and place dough in pan. If using a pizza stone, sprinkle with cornmeal and place rolled dough directly on stone.

2. Combine Speed-Scratch and Horseradish sauces. Spread 1 cup sauce evenly over each pizza. Sprinkle cheeses over the sauce and arrange shrimp evenly on top. Top with fresh basil.

3. Place one pizza in the oven at 425°. Bake 10 to 12 minutes or until crust is browned and cheese is melted. Repeat with remaining pizza. Let pizzas rest briefly, then slice with a sharp knife.

Makes two 12-inch pizzas

$^1/_2$ recipe California Thin Crust dough (page 21)
2 tablespoons cornmeal or 1 tablespoon oil
1 cup Speed-Scratch Tomato Sauce (page 40)
1 cup Horseradish Sauce (page 45)
1$^1/_2$ cups shredded mozzarella cheese
1$^1/_2$ cups shredded Monterey jack cheese
3 dozen large shrimp, cooked and peeled
$^1/_4$ cup minced fresh basil or oregano

1 pound frozen bread dough,
    thawed
1 cup Speed-Scratch Tomato
    Sauce (page 40)
2 cups ricotta cheese
18 small meatballs
$1/3$ cup parsley, minced
1 cup shredded Parmesan
    cheese
1 cup shredded mozzarella
    cheese
Salt and black pepper to taste

Meatballs-in-Blankets
Pizza Turnovers

*Serve this when you need a quick, fun dish for company. Use your
favorite brand of frozen meatballs and pizza sauce from
a jar if you're really pressed for time.*

❋   ❋   ❋

1. Allow dough to rise until doubled in bulk. Punch down.
   Separate dough into four pieces. Place segments on a heavily floured work surface and roll each one into a 6-inch
   circle. Brush each circle with tomato sauce.

2. Spread ½ cup of the ricotta onto half of each dough circle,
   leaving edges bare. Distribute one-fourth of the lobster over
   the ricotta on each circle, followed by one-fourth of the
   pancetta. Sprinkle with minced green onion. Season with
   salt and black pepper to taste.

3. Fold dough over the filling to form a crescent. Press dough
   edges together, brushing edges with a little water if necessary. Place calzones on a baking sheet lined with nonstick
   foil. Cover with a damp towel and let stand 30 minutes.

4. With a sharp knife, cut two or three slits in the tops of the
   turnovers. Bake at 375° for 20 minutes. Remove from oven
   and let stand a few minutes before serving.

Fourth of July Three-Pizza Party

America is the home of the meat-lover's pizza and the heartland of the barbecue tradition. So, for Independence Day, celebrate with these barbecue-based meat pies.

✳   ✳   ✳

Makes three 14-Inch pizzas

1/2 recipe Classic Crust dough (page 16) or Bread Machine Crust dough (page 17)
2 tablespoons cornmeal or 1 tablespoon olive oil
3 cups Barbecue Sauce (page 45)
1 1/2 cups shredded provolone cheese
1 1/2 cups shredded white Cheddar cheese
3 cups shredded mozzarella cheese
2 cups shredded beef brisket
2 cups diced grilled chicken
2 cups sliced grilled andouille sausage
Salt and pepper to taste

1. Roll or press pizza dough into three 14-inch circles, slightly thicker at the edges than in the center. If using pizza pans, sprinkle the bottom with cornmeal or coat with olive oil and place dough in pan. If using a pizza stone, sprinkle with cornmeal and place stone in oven. Preheat oven to 400°.

2. Spread 1 cup sauce in the center of each pizza, leaving one inch around the edges bare. Combine cheeses and divide over the pizzas.

3. Distribute shredded beef brisket over one pizza. Spread diced grilled chicken over the next pizza. Arrange sausage slices in a circular pattern covering the last pizza. Add salt and pepper to taste.

4. If using a hot stone or tiles, use a well-floured pizza peel to carefully lift one pizza from preparation surface and place on stone. If using pizza pans, place first pizza in the center of the oven. Bake for 15 to 20 minutes or until the crust is lightly browned and cheese is melted.

5. Remove pizza from oven carefully (use peel if baking with a stone). Set aside to rest briefly before slicing. Repeat baking process with remaining pies.

3 cups cornmeal
1 cup flour
2 teaspoons salt
2 teaspoons baking powder
1 teaspoon baking soda
2 cups milk
3 eggs
$1/4$ cup melted butter
1 jalapeño pepper, minced
1 cup Picante Sauce (page 48)
3 cups taco-seasoned beef
3 cups Mexican shredded
　　cheese blend
Sour cream
Sliced black olives

Cinco de Mayo Cornbread Pizza

This fun cornbread makes a great contribution to the office potluck. Or serve it to your bridge club.

✳　　✳　　✳

1. In a large bowl, combine cornmeal, flour, salt, baking powder, and baking soda. Stir with a whisk to break up any lumps. In a separate bowl, whisk together milk, eggs, and butter. Pour into cornmeal mixture and whisk until smooth. Stir in jalapeño pepper.

2. Pour batter into a well-oiled 9 × 16-inch baking dish. Bake at 400° for 30 minutes. Remove from oven and spread picante sauce over the top, followed by taco-seasoned beef and Mexican cheese blend. Return pan to the oven and bake 10 minutes or until cheese is melted and browned.

3. Remove from oven and let stand 10 minutes. Cut with a spatula and serve in squares with sour cream and olives.

Mardi Gras Pizza Turnovers

Think of this as jambalaya in a crust. Serve ice-cold beer and sweetened iced tea with these turnovers.

✳   ✳   ✳

Makes four 6-inch turnovers

1. In a heavy saucepan over high heat, combine butter, parsley, garlic, green onions, onion, and bell pepper. Cook, stirring constantly, for 3 minutes. Add tomato sauce, shrimp, sausage, and ½ cup of water. Bring to a boil. Reduce heat and cook, stirring often, for 10 minutes. Add Tabasco, rice, and salt and black pepper to taste. Mix to blend, and remove from heat. Allow to cool.

2. Separate dough into four pieces. Place segments on a heavily floured work surface and roll each one into a 6-inch circle. Spoon rice mixture onto half of each circle, leaving one-half inch around the edges bare.

3. Fold dough over the filling to form a crescent. Press dough edges together, brushing edges with a little water if necessary. Sprinkle cornmeal over a baking sheet or pizza tiles and place calzones on the cornmeal. Cover with a damp towel and let stand 30 minutes.

4. With a sharp knife, cut two or three slits in the tops of the turnovers. Bake at 375° for 20 minutes. Remove from oven and let stand a few minutes before serving.

Here Comes the King

The appropriate dessert for a Mardi Gras party is King Cake. These ring-shaped yeast-risen cakes made of sweet roll dough usually have a profusion of purple-, green-, and gold-dyed frosting and a tiny plastic baby doll stuck inside. According to custom, whoever gets "the baby" is the king or queen of the party and is obligated to give the next King Cake party.

¼ cup butter
¼ cup minced fresh parsley
2 cloves garlic, minced
2 green onions, minced
1 small onion, minced
1 small green bell pepper, cored and diced
1 cup tomato sauce
½ pound peeled small shrimp
½ pound chopped andouille sausage
½ cup water
Dash Tabasco
2 cups cooked white rice
Salt and black pepper to taste
½ recipe Classic Crust dough (page 16) or Whole-Wheat Crust dough (page 22)
3 tablespoons cornmeal

Makes 24 canapés

¹/₂ recipe Classic Crust dough
  (page 16) or Whole-
  Wheat Crust dough
  (page 22)
3 tablespoons olive oil
1 cup crème fraiche
1¹/₂ cups red caviar
1¹/₂ cups black caviar
1 cup chopped boiled eggs

*Makes one 9 x 16-inch
pizza*

¹/₂ recipe Sicilian Crust dough
  (page 18)
2 tablespoons olive oil
2 tablespoons cornmeal
2 cups Mustard Cream Sauce
  (page 51)
2 cups shredded cooked
  corned beef
2 cups diced cooked potatoes
1 onion, minced
2 cups shredded Cheddar
  cheese
Salt and black pepper to taste
1 cup shredded Parmesan
  cheese
8 poached eggs

Yin and Yang Party Pizzas

*Lumpfish caviar isn't as expensive as the real thing. If you prefer, make
the yin-yang design with herb pesto and sun-dried tomato pesto.*

✳   ✳   ✳

1. Divide dough in half, then break each half into twelve pieces.
   With fingers, flatten each bit into a tiny pizza crust. Line two
   baking sheets with nonstick foil. Place twelve dough circles
   on each baking sheet. Brush tops lightly with olive oil and
   bake at 350° for 10 minutes or until lightly browned.

2. Allow crusts to cool. Spread lightly with crème fraiche.
   Carefully spoon red caviar on the pizzas, making a comma
   shape, with the top fatter than the bottom. Using the black
   caviar, fill in the other side of the pizzas, making the comma
   in reverse for a classic yin and yang pattern. Serve with
   chopped egg on the side.

St. Patrick's Day Brunch Pizza

Poach eggs lightly in an egg-poaching insert over a water bath.

✳   ✳   ✳

1. On a floured board, roll dough into a rectangle. Coat a deep,
   9 × 16-inch baking dish with olive oil and sprinkle with cornmeal. Press dough into the pan, including the corners.

2. Spread Mustard Cream sauce over the top of the dough. In
   a bowl, combine corned beef, potatoes, and onions. Layer
   over the sauce. Sprinkle with Cheddar cheese and sprinkle
   with salt and pepper to taste.

3. Preheat oven to 400°. Bake 20 to 25 minutes or until top is
   browned and bubbly. Remove from oven and carefully slip
   poached eggs, in two rows of four, on top of the pizza. Sprinkle with Parmesan. Let stand 10 minutes before serving.

Cheese Mini-Pizzas for Cocktails

Your guests will go crazy for these tasty minis

* * *

1. Divide dough in half, then break each half into twelve pieces. Flatten each bit into a tiny pizza crust. Line two baking sheets with nonstick foil. Place twelve dough circles on each sheet. Brush tops lightly with olive oil and bake at 350° for 5 minutes.

2. Spread crusts with a small amount of tomato sauce. Combine shredded cheeses. Divide cheese over pizzas, then sprinkle with salt and pepper to taste.

3. Return pizzas to oven and bake for 6 to 8 minutes. Remove from oven and set aside briefly to cool before serving.

Makes 24 pizzas

¹/₂ recipe Classic Crust dough (page 16) or Whole-Wheat Crust dough (page 22)
3 tablespoons olive oil
1 cup Slow-Simmered Tomato Sauce (page 40)
2 cups shredded mozzarella cheese
1 cup shredded Asiago cheese
1 cup shredded Gouda cheese
1 cup shredded Gruyère cheese
Salt and pepper to taste

Day-After Turkey and Stuffing Turnovers

This is a great way to make use of Thanksgiving leftovers.

* * *

1. Separate dough into four pieces. Place segments on a heavily floured work surface and roll each one into a 6-inch circle. Brush each circle with cranberry sauce, leaving the edges bare.

2. Spread ½ cup of the stuffing onto half of each dough circle. Top that with ½ cup shredded turkey. Sprinkle minced parsley and cheese over each. Season with salt and pepper.

3. Fold dough over the filling to form a crescent. Press dough edges together, brushing edges with a little water if necessary. Place turnovers on a baking sheet lined with nonstick foil. Cover with a damp towel and let stand 30 minutes.

4. With a sharp knife, cut two or three slits in the tops of the turnovers. Bake at 375° for 20 minutes. Remove from oven and let stand a few minutes before serving.

Makes four 6-inch turnovers

¹/₂ recipe Classic Crust dough (page 16) or Whole-Wheat Crust dough (page 22)
1 cup cranberry sauce
2 cups stuffing
2 cups shredded cooked turkey
¹/₃ cup parsley, minced
1 cup shredded Colby cheese
Salt and black pepper to taste

1/2 recipe Classic Crust dough
  (page 16) or Bread
  Machine Crust dough
  (page 17)
2 tablespoons cornmeal or
  1 tablespoon olive oil
2 tablespoons extra virgin
  olive oil
2 cloves garlic, minced
4 ripe plum tomatoes, sliced
3 cups diced fresh mozzarella
  cheese
1/2 cup fresh basil ribbons

Open House Pizza Margherita

*Diced fresh mozzarella—available in brine-soaked balls
at some supermarkets and delis—turns into creamy
pools on this classic pizza.*

* * *

1. Roll or press pizza dough into two 12-inch circles, slightly
   thicker at the edges than in the center. If using pizza pans,
   sprinkle the bottom with cornmeal or coat with olive oil
   and place dough in pan. If using a pizza stone, sprinkle with
   cornmeal and place stone in oven. Preheat oven to 400°.

2. Brush 1 tablespoon extra virgin olive oil over each pizza,
   leaving edges bare. Sprinkle minced garlic evenly over the
   oil.

3. Distribute sliced tomatoes evenly over each pizza crust, followed by diced mozzarella and basil ribbons.

4. If using a hot stone or tiles, use a well-floured pizza peel to
   carefully lift one pizza from preparation surface and place
   on stone. If using pizza pans, place first pizza in the center
   of the oven. Bake for 15 to 20 minutes or until the crust is
   lightly browned and cheese is melted.

5. Remove pizza from oven carefully (use peel if baking with
   a stone). Set aside to rest briefly before slicing. Repeat baking process with second pie. Let stand briefly before cutting
   with a sharp knife or pizza wheel.

An Homage from the Oven

*Legend has it that Neapolitan baker Raffaele Esposito
created this pizza in 1889 as a tribute to Queen Margherita
of Italy. The red, white, and green ingredients represent the
colors of the Italian flag. Modern variations include
Margherita Bianca, which is made without the tomatoes.*

Christmas Stocking Sweet Turnovers

*These turnovers hide a bit of chocolate treasure. Serve them
Christmas Eve before tucking in to await Santa.*

❄   ❄   ❄

Makes 6 turnovers

$^1/_2$ recipe No-Yeast Crust
   dough (page 27)
6 tablespoons strawberry
   preserves, melted
2 cups mascarpone cheese
$^1/_4$ cup confectioners' sugar
1 teaspoon vanilla
6 miniature chocolate bars
Vegetable oil for frying
Turbinado sugar

1. With floured hands, divide dough into six portions. Roll each portion into a 4-inch circle. Brush dough with melted preserves. In a bowl, combine mascarpone cheese, confectioners' sugar, and vanilla. Mix well.

2. Spoon ⅓ cup mascarpone mixture onto half of each dough circle, leaving one-half inch around the edges bare. Place one chocolate in the center of each turnover. Fold bare dough over the filling, forming a crescent shape. Moisten dough with water and crimp edges together to seal the pockets.

3. Pour cooking oil to a depth of 2 inches into a deep skillet or Dutch oven. Turn heat to medium-high. When oil is hot, cook turnovers two at a time for 6 to 8 minutes or until golden on both sides. (Turn carefully at least once during cooking.)

4. Remove pies from oil and drain on paper towels. Sprinkle liberally with turbinado sugar. Cool for several minutes before serving.

Makes 6 turnovers

½ recipe No-Yeast Crust
  dough (page 27)
6 tablespoons apricot
  preserves, melted
12 ounces cream cheese
2 tablespoons sour cream
1 cup confectioners' sugar
1 teaspoon vanilla
1 cup chopped dried apricots
Vegetable oil for frying
Turbinado sugar

Nights of Lights Fried Cream Cheese Turnovers

Invite friends over to light the Hanukkah menorah, sing songs, and enjoy a supper of veggie pizza followed by these sweet treats.

❋   ❋   ❋

1. With floured hands, divide dough into six portions. Roll each portion into a 4-inch circle. Brush dough with melted preserves. In a bowl, combine cream cheese, sour cream, confectioners' sugar, and vanilla. Mix well.

2. Spoon one-sixth of the cream cheese mixture onto half of each dough circle, leaving one-half inch around the edges bare. Sprinkle chopped apricots in the center of each turnover. Fold bare dough over the filling, forming a crescent shape. Moisten dough with water and crimp edges together to seal the pockets.

3. Pour cooking oil to a depth of 2 inches into a deep skillet or Dutch oven. Turn heat to medium-high. When oil is hot, cook turnovers two at a time for 6 to 8 minutes or until golden on both sides. (Turn carefully at least once during cooking.)

4. Remove pies from oil and drain on paper towels. Sprinkle liberally with turbinado sugar. Cool for several minutes before serving.

Oil for Days

Hanukkah commemorates a miraculous time during which the consecrated oil in the Temple should have only lasted one day. However, the lamp was lit and the oil lasted eight days. In deference to that history, many Jewish people enjoy foods fried in oil during Hanukkah. Latkes and jelly donuts are favorites. Fried sweet turnovers could become a new tradition.

CHAPTER 15

For the Health-Conscious Pizza Lover

½ recipe Multigrain Crust
    dough (page 24)
2 tablespoons cornmeal or
    1 tablespoon olive oil
1½ cups Slow-Simmered
    Tomato Sauce (page 40)
3 cups shredded part-skim
    mozzarella cheese
1 cup shredded sharp
    Cheddar cheese
1 cup diced yellow squash
1 cup diced plum tomatoes
1 cup chopped blanched
    broccoli
2 cups sliced mushrooms
1 small onion, sliced
1 small green bell pepper,
    cored and diced
¼ cup minced fresh basil

Multigrain Veggie Pizza

*A small amount of sharp Cheddar cheese gives extra flavor
to this healthful veggie entrée.*

❋   ❋   ❋

1. Roll or press pizza dough into two 12-inch circles, slightly thicker at the edges than in the center. If using pizza pans, sprinkle the bottom with cornmeal or coat with olive oil and place dough in pan. If using a pizza stone, sprinkle with cornmeal and place stone in oven. Preheat oven to 400°.

2. Spread ¾ cup sauce in the center of each pizza, leaving one inch around the edges bare. Combine mozzarella and Cheddar cheeses and divide evenly over each pizza.

3. Layer squash, tomatoes, broccoli, mushrooms, onion, and bell pepper over the cheese. Sprinkle with fresh basil.

4. If using a hot stone or tiles, use a well-floured pizza peel to carefully lift one pizza from preparation surface and place on stone. If using pizza pans, place first pizza in the center of the oven. Bake for 15 to 20 minutes or until the crust is lightly browned and cheese is melted.

5. Remove pizza from oven carefully (use peel if baking with a stone). Set aside to rest briefly before slicing. Repeat baking process with second pie.

Mad for Mushrooms

Mushrooms are Nature's sponges. Thinly sliced raw mushrooms will soften when baked on pizzas, releasing a tiny bit of flavorful broth as they cook. If you prefer, you can sauté mushrooms—and flavor them with oil, garlic, herbs, and wine—before adding them to your pizza.

Multigrain Spinach and Artichoke Pizza

To give this pizza an extra kick, mix a bit of Tabasco sauce into the Garlic and Oil Sauce before spreading on the crusts.

1. Roll or press pizza dough into two 12-inch circles, slightly thicker at the edges than in the center. If using pizza pans, sprinkle the bottom with cornmeal or coat with olive oil and place dough in pan. If using a pizza stone, sprinkle with cornmeal and place stone in oven. Preheat oven to 400°.

2. Spread ¼ cup sauce over each pizza, leaving one inch around the edges bare. Place spinach in a sieve and press out as much moisture as possible. Chop spinach and divide over the pizzas. Distribute 1 cup of artichoke hearts over the spinach on each pizza, followed by half the green onions and half the parsley.

3. Dot the pizzas with bits of cream cheese. Combine Parmesan and mozzarella cheeses and divide over the two pizzas. Season with salt and pepper to taste.

4. If using a hot stone or tiles, use a well-floured pizza peel to carefully lift one pizza from preparation surface and place on stone. If using pizza pans, place first pizza in the center of the oven. Bake for 15 to 20 minutes or until the crust is lightly browned and cheese is melted.

5. Remove pizza from oven carefully (use peel if baking with a stone). Set aside to rest briefly before slicing. Repeat baking process with second pie.

Makes two 12-inch pizzas

½ recipe Multigrain Crust dough (page 24)
2 tablespoons cornmeal or 1 tablespoon olive oil
½ cup Garlic and Oil Sauce (page 44)
3 pounds spinach, cooked and drained
2 cups diced artichoke hearts, freshly cooked or canned
3 green onions, minced
¼ cup minced parsley
8 ounces reduced-fat cream cheese
2 cups shredded Parmesan cheese
1 cup shredded mozzarella cheese
Salt and black pepper to taste

Multigrain Thin-Crust Cheese Pizza

Makes two 12-inch pizzas

$^1/_2$ recipe California Thin Crust
   dough (page 21)
   (see Note)
2 tablespoons cornmeal or
   1 tablespoon olive oil
1$^1/_2$ cups Slow-Simmered
   Tomato Sauce (page 40)
   or Speed-Scratch Tomato
   Sauce (page 40)
2 cups shredded part-skim
   mozzarella cheese
$^1/_2$ cup shredded provolone
   cheese
$^1/_2$ cup shredded Asiago
   cheese
$^1/_2$ cup shredded Parmesan
   cheese
$^1/_2$ cup shredded Romano
   cheese

Note: When preparing your California Thin Crust dough, substitute 2 cups of multigrain flour for 2 cups of the high-protein flour in the recipe.

* * *

1. Roll or press pizza dough into two 12-inch circles, slightly thicker at the edges than in the center. If using pizza pans, sprinkle the bottom with cornmeal or coat with olive oil and place dough in pan. If using a pizza stone, sprinkle with cornmeal and place stone in oven. Preheat oven to 400°.

2. Spread ¾ cup sauce in the center of each pizza, leaving one inch around the edges bare.

3. In a large bowl, combine all the cheeses and toss gently to mix. Sprinkle half of the cheese blend over the sauce on each pizza, leaving edges bare.

4. If using a hot stone or tiles, use a well-floured pizza peel to carefully lift one pizza from preparation surface and place on stone. If using pizza pans, place first pizza in the center of the oven. Bake for 15 to 20 minutes or until the crust is lightly browned and cheese is melted.

5. Remove pizza from oven carefully (use peel if baking with a stone). Set aside to rest briefly before slicing. Repeat baking process with second pie.

A Little or a Little More
If you're trying to moderate your dairy fat intake, you have two choices: use a small amount of full-fat cheese or choose reduced-fat cheese and get to eat a bit more. Some cheeses, like part-skim mozzarella and part-skim ricotta, are naturally low in fat and taste just fine. Others taste rubbery and bland. Consider your preferences and your goals and make your own choice.

Salmon Pizza Turnovers

Any flaky fish can be used in this recipe, although salmon gives the end product a nice flavor and color.

❋ ❋ ❋

Makes three 8-inch turnovers

---

¹/₂ recipe Whole-Wheat Crust dough (page 22)
3 tablespoons olive oil
2 cups part-skim ricotta cheese
3 cups flaked cooked salmon
3 green onions, minced
1 cup chopped mushrooms
¹/₄ cup chopped fresh dill
1 cup shredded part-skim mozzarella cheese
Salt and black pepper to taste
3 tablespoons cornmeal

1. Separate dough into three pieces. Place segments on a heavily floured work surface and roll each one into an 8-inch circle. Brush each circle with olive oil.

2. Spread one-third of the ricotta onto half of each dough circle, leaving one inch around the edges bare. Combine the salmon, green onions, mushrooms, and dill. Distribute one-third of the salmon mixture over the ricotta on each circle, followed by ⅓ cup mozzarella cheese. Season with salt and black pepper to taste.

3. Fold dough over the filling to form a crescent. Press dough edges together, brushing edges with a little water if necessary. Sprinkle cornmeal over a baking sheet or pizza tiles and place turnovers on the cornmeal. Cover with a damp towel and let stand 1 hour.

4. With a sharp knife, cut two or three slits in the tops of the turnovers. Bake at 375° for 20 to 25 minutes. Remove from oven and let stand a few minutes before serving.

Salmon Savvy

Wild Alaskan salmon costs a little more than the farmed variety, but it contains more of the Omega-3 fatty acids so prized for health benefits. Frozen wild salmon fillets and patties are available at large discount stores and are less expensive than fresh fillets.

_____

1/2 recipe Whole-Wheat Crust
    dough (page 22)
3 tablespoons olive oil
2 cups part-skim ricotta
    cheese
1 pound chopped wild
    mushrooms
3 green onions, minced
3 cloves minced garlic
1/4 cup chopped fresh basil
1 cup shredded part-skim
    mozzarella cheese
Salt and black pepper to taste
3 tablespoons cornmeal

Wild Mushroom Pizza Turnovers

Buy mixed mushrooms or make your own blend of chanterelles, straw mushrooms, oyster mushrooms, shiitakes, and Portobellos.

✳   ✳   ✳

1. Separate dough into three pieces. Place segments on a heavily floured work surface and roll each one into an 8-inch circle. Brush each circle with olive oil.

2. Spread one-third of the ricotta onto half of each dough circle, leaving one inch around the edges bare. Combine the mushrooms, green onions, garlic, and basil. Distribute one-third of the mushroom mixture over the ricotta on each circle, followed by 1/3 cup mozzarella cheese. Season with salt and black pepper to taste.

3. Fold dough over the filling to form a crescent. Press dough edges together, brushing edges with a little water if necessary. Sprinkle cornmeal over a baking sheet or pizza tiles and place turnovers on the cornmeal. Cover with a damp towel and let stand 1 hour.

4. With a sharp knife, cut two or three slits in the tops of the turnovers. Bake at 375° for 20 to 25 minutes. Remove from oven and let stand a few minutes before serving.

Olive Pizza Tarts

Serve these intensely flavored little pies with a lightly dressed salad of mixed greens, ripe tomatoes, and toasted nuts.

1. Divide dough into eight portions. Press each portion into a lightly greased tart pan, spreading the dough evenly up the sides of the pans.

2. Spread ¼ cup ricotta cheese over the bottom of each tart, and top with ¼ cup tapenade, followed by ¼ cup Gorgonzola cheese.

3. Bake tarts in a 350° oven for 10 to 15 minutes or until dough is browned and olive mixture is hot and fragrant. Remove from oven and let stand 10 minutes before serving.

Homemade Tapenade

Olive tapenade can be purchased at many supermarkets. To make your own, place pitted olives in a food processor with an anchovy or a bit of anchovy paste and a few capers. Add a spritz of lemon juice and a drizzle of olive oil and pulse until the mixture is finely ground.

Makes eight 4-inch tarts

¹/₂ recipe Whole-Wheat Crust dough (page 22)
2 cups part-skim ricotta cheese
2 cups mixed olive tapenade
2 cups Gorgonzola cheese

Makes two 12-inch pizzas

½ recipe Whole-Wheat Crust
   dough (page 22)
2 tablespoons cornmeal or
   1 tablespoon olive oil
2 cups Slow-Simmered
   Tomato Sauce (page 40)
2 cups shredded part-skim
   mozzarella cheese
2 cups shredded Asiago
   cheese
1 teaspoon mixed Italian
   seasoning
3 cups cooked ground turkey
2 cups thinly sliced fennel
   bulb
1 small red bell pepper, cored
   and cut into strips
1 sweet onion, trimmed and
   cut into strips
Salt and black pepper to taste

Ground Turkey and Fennel Pizza

Whole-wheat crust and fragrant fennel give this pizza a rustic flavor. For variety, bulk turkey sausage can be used in place of ground turkey.

✳   ✳   ✳

1. Roll or press pizza dough into two 12-inch circles, slightly thicker at the edges than in the center. If using pizza pans, sprinkle the bottom with cornmeal or coat with olive oil and place dough in pan. If using a pizza stone, sprinkle with cornmeal and place stone in oven. Preheat oven to 400°.

2. Spread half the sauce over each pizza, leaving one inch around the edges bare. Combine cheeses and sprinkle over the sauce.

3. Mix Italian seasoning with the ground turkey. Distribute 1½ cups evenly over each pizza. Top each pizza with half the fennel, half the bell pepper, and half the onion. Sprinkle with salt and black pepper to taste.

4. If baking on a hot stone or tiles, use a well-floured pizza peel to carefully lift one pizza from preparation surface and place on stone. If using pizza pans, place first pizza in the center of the oven. Bake for 15 to 20 minutes or until the crust is lightly browned and toppings are bubbly.

5. Remove pizza from oven carefully (use peel if baking with a stone). Set aside to rest briefly before slicing. Repeat baking process with second pie.

Shredded Turkey and Black Bean Pizza

*This recipe offers a great way to make leftover turkey feel like
something other than leftovers.*

1. Roll or press pizza dough into two 12-inch circles, slightly thicker at the edges than in the center. If using pizza pans, sprinkle the bottom with cornmeal or coat with olive oil and place dough in pan. If using a pizza stone, sprinkle with cornmeal and place stone in oven. Preheat oven to 400°.

2. Spread 1 cup picante sauce over each pizza crust, leaving one inch around the edges bare. Combine cheeses and divide evenly over each pizza.

3. In a bowl, combine shredded turkey, black beans, cumin, and hot pepper flakes. Toss to mix well. Spread half over the cheese on each pizza. Sprinkle bell pepper, onion, and diced tomatoes over the pizzas, followed by the cilantro.

4. If baking on a hot stone or tiles, use a well-floured pizza peel to carefully lift one pizza from preparation surface and place on stone. If using pizza pans, place first pizza in the center of the oven. Bake for 15 to 20 minutes or until the crust is lightly browned and toppings are bubbly.

5. Remove pizza from oven carefully (use peel if baking with a stone). Set aside to rest briefly before slicing. Repeat baking process with second pie.

Tricks with Turkey
Three ounces of skinless roasted turkey breast has only 115 calories and less than a gram of fat. What's more, the firm texture makes sliced or pounded turkey breast a good substitute for veal, pork medallions, or duck in a variety of recipes. Season the turkey with spice rubs and low-fat, high-flavor sauces for maximum impact.

Makes two 12-inch pizzas

¹/₂ recipe Honey-Wheat Crust
   dough (page 23)
2 tablespoons cornmeal or
   1 tablespoon olive oil
2 cups Picante Sauce
   (page 48)
1 cup shredded reduced-fat
   Cheddar cheese
1 cup shredded reduced-fat
   Monterey Jack cheese
2 cups shredded part-skim
   mozzarella cheese
4 cups cooked, shredded
   turkey breast
1¹/₂ cups cooked black beans,
   drained and rinsed
1 teaspoon cumin
¹/₂ teaspoon hot pepper flakes
1 small green bell pepper,
   diced
1 sweet onion, finely diced
1 cup diced tomatoes
¹/₄ cup minced cilantro

2 large Vidalia onions, sliced
2 tablespoons peanut oil
1 clove garlic, minced
1 teaspoon curry powder
Pinch cayenne
1 tablespoon orange juice
1 1/2 cups finely diced chicken
    breast
1/2 recipe Whole-Wheat Crust
    dough (page 22)
2 tablespoons cornmeal or
    2 tablespoons olive oil
1 cup Slow-Simmered Tomato
    Sauce (page 40)
1 cup plain yogurt (optional)
Freshly ground black pepper
    to taste

Curried Chicken and Onion Pizza

*Serve this cheese-free pizza to friends who eschew
dairy products, or just for a change of pace.*

✳   ✳   ✳

1. In a large skillet or Dutch oven, combine onions, peanut oil, and garlic. Cook over medium heat, stirring often, until onions turn a rich brown. Stir in curry powder, cayenne, and orange juice. Simmer for 1 minute, then add chicken and mix well.

2. Roll dough into two 12-inch circles, slightly thicker at the edges than in the center. If using pizza pans, sprinkle the bottom with cornmeal or coat with olive oil and place dough in pan. If using a pizza stone, sprinkle with cornmeal and place stone in oven. Preheat oven to 400°.

3. Spread a thin layer of pizza sauce over each crust, leaving one inch around the edges bare. Divide the curry-spiced chicken mixture over the sauce on each pizza.

4. Bake pizzas, one at a time if necessary, at 400° in the center of the oven for 15 minutes or until browned. Remove and let stand for 5 minutes, then slice and serve.

Portobello Mushroom Pizza with Turkey Sausage

A meaty Portobello mushroom cap forms the crust for this flavorful pizza. Just what your low-carb diet ordered.

✳ ✳ ✳

1. Rinse mushroom caps and pat dry. Place oil in a heavy skillet over medium-high heat. Add garlic. Quickly sear mushroom caps top-down in the skillet. Place caps, underside up, on a baking sheet lined with nonstick foil.

2. Brush Portobello caps with Pesto Sauce. Place ½ cup sausage over each mushroom cap, then top with Parmesan cheese and shredded mozzarella. Season with black pepper.

3. Bake mushrooms at 350° for 10 to 12 minutes or until cheese is melted and bubbly. Remove from oven and let stand briefly before serving.

Makes six mushroom-cap pizzas

6 large Portobello mushroom caps
2 tablespoons olive oil
1 garlic clove, minced
½ cup Pesto Sauce (page 43)
3 cups bulk turkey sausage, browned and drained
1 cup shredded Parmesan cheese
1½ cups shredded part-skim mozzarella cheese
Black pepper to taste

Makes two 12-inch pizzas

---

¹/₂ recipe Whole-Wheat Crust
    dough (page 22)
2 tablespoons olive oil
2 large zucchini, thinly sliced
3 yellow squash, thinly sliced
2 leek bulbs, cleaned and
    sliced
1 egg
2 egg whites
¹/₄ cup skim milk
¹/₂ teaspoon Italian seasoning
    blend
Salt and pepper to taste
2 cups shredded part-skim
    mozzarella cheese
4 cups Chunky Tomato Sauce
    (page 41)
2 cups shredded Parmesan
    cheese

Deep-Dish Summer Squash Pizza Tart

Eggs hold the squash layer together in this deep-dish pie. Serve it to your book club with a glass of crisp Sauvignon Blanc.

❋   ❋   ❋

1. Roll out two circles of pizza dough. Spread olive oil in two 12" deep-dish pizza or pie pans. Press dough circles into pans and prick bottoms a few times with a fork.

2. Layer the zucchini, yellow squash, and leeks over the bottom of each pan. Whisk together egg, egg whites, milk, Italian seasoning, salt, and pepper. Pour over the squash in the two pans. Place pans in a 375° oven and bake 10 minutes.

3. Remove pizzas from the oven. Sprinkle 1 cup mozzarella over the squash layer in each pan. Ladle 2 cups of tomato sauce into each pan, followed by 1 cup of Parmesan. Return pans to oven and bake at 375° for 10 to 15 minutes or until crust is browned and cheese is melted and bubbly. Remove from oven and let stand briefly before serving.

Veggies on the Grill
Even if you're not ready to practice your grilled pizza technique, you can get that smoky flavor by grilling oil-coated vegetables in a grill basket. Just grill a few extra cups of vegetables next time you barbecue, then refrigerate them for pizza the next day.

Three-Pepper Pizza

If you're a fan of roasted peppers in tomato sauce, feel free to substitute Speed-Scratch Tomato Sauce for the Garlic and Oil Sauce.

✳   ✳   ✳

Makes two 12-inch pizzas

¹/₂ recipe Multigrain Crust
      dough (page 24)
2 tablespoons cornmeal or
      1 tablespoon olive oil
¹/₂ cup Garlic and Oil Sauce
      (page 44)
2 cups part-skim ricotta
      cheese
2 cups shredded part-skim
      mozzarella cheese
1 cup roasted red bell pepper
      strips
1 cup roasted green bell
      pepper strips
¹/₂ cup finely chopped hot
      cherry peppers
¹/₄ cup minced parsley
Salt and black pepper to taste

1. Roll or press pizza dough into two 12-inch circles, slightly thicker at the edges than in the center. If using pizza pans, sprinkle the bottom with cornmeal or coat with olive oil and place dough in pan. If using a pizza stone, sprinkle with cornmeal and place stone in oven. Preheat oven to 400°.

2. Spread ¼ cup sauce over each pizza, leaving one inch around the edges bare. Spread 1 cup ricotta over each crust, followed by 1 cup mozzarella.

3. Layer the roasted bell pepper strips over each pizza and sprinkle the hot cherry peppers over each, followed by the minced parsley. Season with salt and pepper to taste.

4. If using a hot stone or tiles, use a well-floured pizza peel to carefully lift one pizza from preparation surface and place on stone. If using pizza pans, place first pizza in the center of the oven. Bake for 15 to 20 minutes or until the crust is lightly browned and cheese is melted.

5. Remove pizza from oven carefully (use peel if baking with a stone). Set aside to rest briefly before slicing. Repeat baking process with second pie.

Makes two 10-inch stacks

10 (10-inch) soft wheat
    tortillas
2 cups shredded reduced-fat
    Monterey jack cheese
2 cups taco-seasoned
    shredded chicken
2 cups refried beans
1 cup chunky salsa
2 cups shredded reduced-fat
    Cheddar cheese
Reduced-fat sour cream

Layered Whole-Wheat Tortilla Pizza

*Veggie-flavored tortillas are only whole-wheat
if they say so on the package.*

✳   ✳   ✳

1. Cover a large baking sheet with nonstick foil. Place two tortillas side by side on the sheet. Sprinkle 1 cup of Monterey jack cheese over each, and top that with another tortilla. Top that tortilla with a cup of shredded chicken, followed by another tortilla. Spread refried beans over the two tortilla stacks, then layer on another tortilla. Spread that tortilla with chunky salsa. Top each stack with a final tortilla and a cup of Cheddar cheese.

2. Bake tortilla pizzas at 350° for 12 minutes or until shredded cheese is melted and lightly brown. Serve with sour cream.

Makes two 12-inch pizzas

¹/₂ recipe Whole-Wheat Crust
    dough (page 22)
2 tablespoons cornmeal or
    1 tablespoon oil
1¹/₂ cups Speed-Scratch
    Tomato Sauce (page 40)
4 cups part-skim ricotta
    cheese
1 cup shredded part-skim
    mozzarella cheese
¹/₂ cup shredded Parmesan
    cheese
4 plum tomatoes, thinly sliced
¹/₄ cup fresh basil ribbons
Salt and pepper to taste

Whole-Wheat Ricotta Pizza

Cheese lovers will really enjoy this pizza.

✳   ✳   ✳

1. Roll or press pizza dough into two 12-inch circles, slightly thicker at the edges than in the center. If using pizza pans, sprinkle the bottom with cornmeal or coat with oil and place dough in pan. If using a pizza stone, sprinkle with cornmeal and place rolled dough directly on stone.

2. Spread ¾ cup sauce evenly over each pizza, leaving one inch around the edges bare. Spoon 2 cups ricotta onto each pizza and spread with the back of a spoon. Top ricotta with mozzarella and Parmesan. Arrange tomato slices over each pie and sprinkle with basil ribbons, salt, and pepper.

3. Bake pizzas separately at 400° for 15 to 18 minutes.

Whole-Wheat Bruschetta Pizza

If you don't have hearts of palm on hand, chopped olives, capers, or diced canned artichoke hearts can substitute.

❋   ❋   ❋

1. With a bread knife, slice loaf in half horizontally, then cut pieces in half vertically to create four 6-inch bread crusts. Place bread, soft side up, on a baking sheet covered with nonstick foil. Brush olive oil over the top of each loaf. Place in a 350° oven for 5 to 10 minutes to toast loaves slightly.

2. In a large bowl, combine garlic, basil, tomatoes, hearts of palm, pine nuts, salt, and pepper. Mix well. Remove bread from oven and divide mixture evenly over each loaf. Sprinkle ¼ cup crumbled Farmer cheese and ½ cup of the mozzarella cheese over each loaf.

3. Return pizzas to oven and bake 10 minutes. Let stand briefly before serving.

Eat a Tree

Heart of palm is literally the tender core of a palm tree. A whole palm tree—usually a sabal palm—must be harvested to produce a 1-inch-diameter heart. To preserve trees, hearts of palm production is tightly controlled in the U.S. Although some gourmet markets and mail order sources offer crispy fresh hearts of palm, mostly the product is available canned.

Makes four 6-inch-long pizzas

1 (12-inch) loaf whole-wheat French bread
$^1/_3$ cup olive oil
2 teaspoons minced garlic
$^1/_4$ cup minced fresh basil
2 cups diced plum tomatoes
1 cup sliced hearts of palm
$^1/_2$ cup toasted pine nuts
Salt and black pepper to taste
1 cup crumbled Farmer cheese
2 cups shredded low-fat mozzarella cheese

Makes two 12-inch pizzas

½ recipe Oatmeal Crust
    dough (page 26)
2 tablespoons cornmeal or
    1 tablespoon olive oil
2 cups Slow-Simmered
    Tomato Sauce (page 40)
8 eggs
2 cups finely diced ham
2 cups shredded part-skim
    mozzarella cheese
1 cup shredded Asiago cheese
Salt and black pepper to taste

Oat Crust Breakfast Pizza

*Break eggs into a biscuit cutter that's lightly pressed into the pizza.
That will help hold each egg in place on the pizza.*

✳ ✳ ✳

1. Roll or press pizza dough into two 12-inch circles, slightly thicker at the edges than in the center. Sprinkle the bottom of two pizza pans with cornmeal or coat with olive oil and place dough in pan. Preheat oven to 400°.

2. Spread half the sauce over each pizza, leaving one inch around the edges bare. Carefully break eggs, one at a time, into a cup. Place four raw eggs on each pizza, one per quarter. Sprinkle 1 cup diced ham over the crust of each pizza, being careful not to disturb the eggs.

3. Combine mozzarella and Asiago cheeses and lightly spread over the pizzas. Season with salt and pepper.

4. Place first pizza in the center of the oven. Bake for 15 to 20 minutes or until the crust is lightly browned and the eggs are set. Remove pizza from oven carefully (use peel if baking with a stone). Set aside to rest briefly before slicing. Repeat baking process with second pie.

Mini-Bagel Treats

*Think of these as quick hors d'oeuvres for the dieting crowd, or as
a light lunch when a substantial dinner has been planned.*

✳   ✳   ✳

1. Toast bagel halves in a toaster or in the oven. Place toasted halves on a baking sheet lined with nonstick foil. Spread each with pasta sauce and 1 slice of Canadian bacon. Sprinkle cheese over each bagel.

2. Bake at 350° for 10 minutes or until cheese is melted and lightly browned. Remove from oven and let stand briefly before serving.

Makes 12 snack pizzas

6 mini whole-grain bagels
1 cup thick pasta sauce
12 slices Canadian bacon
2 cups shredded part-skim
    mozzarella cheese

Quiche-Crust Pizza

*Don't confuse evaporated milk with condensed milk.
Condensed milk is sweetened, evaporated isn't.*

✳   ✳   ✳

1. Place eggs, egg whites, evaporated milk, green onion, parsley, salt, and pepper in a blender. Blend until parsley and green onion are puréed and eggs are frothy. Pour into a lightly greased 12" deep pizza or quiche pan. Sprinkle with Cheddar cheese.

2. Bake crustless quiche at 350° for 15 minutes. Remove from oven and top with tomatoes, ham, oregano, and mozzarella cheese. Return to oven for 10 minutes or until cheese has melted. Let stand 10 minutes before cutting into wedges.

Makes one 12-inch pizza

8 eggs
4 egg whites
1 cup evaporated skimmed
    milk
1 green onion
¼ cup chopped parsley
Salt and pepper to taste
1 cup shredded sharp
    Cheddar cheese
2 cups grape tomatoes,
    halved
1 cup diced ham
½ teaspoon dried oregano
2 cups shredded part-skim
    mozzarella cheese

4 egg whites
$^1/_2$ teaspoon cream of tartar
Pinch salt
1 teaspoon almond extract
1 cup Splenda artificial
    sweetener
1 cup no-sugar-added
    almond butter
$^1/_3$ cup skim milk
1 cup blueberry fruit spread,
    warmed
1 cup fresh blueberries
4 ounces dark chocolate curls

Almond Blueberry Dessert Pizza

*Use 65-percent cocoa-content chocolate for the curls.
Make them by chilling the chocolate bar, then scraping
across the sides with a vegetable peeler.*

❊   ❊   ❊

1. In a large bowl, place egg whites, cream of tartar, salt, and almond extract. Beat with a mixer on high speed until foamy. Slowly add Splenda and continue beating until glossy peaks form. Spread egg white mixture over the bottom of a 12" pizza pan lined with nonstick foil or parchment. Bake at 300° for 1 hour, then turn the oven off but leave the pan in the oven for another hour. Remove crust to a clean, dry rack and let cool completely.

2. Place crust on a large platter. Mix almond butter and milk until smooth and pourable. Very carefully spread almond butter over the meringue crust. Drizzle warm blueberry fruit spread over the almond butter and lightly spread with the back of spoon. Sprinkle fresh blueberries on top and cover with chocolate curls. Use a sharp knife to cut in wedges to serve.

About Artificial Sweeteners

The U.S. Food and Drug Administration reviews the safety of all food additives in the U.S., including artificial sweeteners. At present, there are several sweeteners generally considered safe for human consumption, including aspartame, acesulfame potassium, Sucralose, and Neotame. The sweeteners are many hundreds of times sweeter than sugar, which means that tiny amounts—nutritionally insignificant— are all that's needed to sweeten foods. Some products, such as Sucralose (Splenda), hold their sweetness during cooking, while others (aspartame, for instance) cannot withstand high temperatures.

artisan cheese

Cheeses made in small batches at creameries using milk from their own herds or from nearby farms. Like wines, these cheeses have flavors unique to their region and their makers.

blanch

To lightly cook ingredients by dropping in boiling water for a very short period. After blanching, ingredients are often plunged in cold water to stop the cooking process.

bread flour

A high-gluten flour that yields superior results when used in yeasted breads and crusts.

California style

When used in reference to pizza, usually means a very thin-crust pizza topped with unusual or expensive toppings.

calzone

A pizza crust folded over to encase toppings and create a half-moon-shaped turnover. Some variations on the calzone include stromboli, panzarotti, and "pizza turnover."

caramelize

To heat so that the sugars in foods oxidize on the surface, or "caramelize," resulting in a browned appearance and slightly sweet flavor. When caramelizing fruits and vegetables, care must be taken to stir often so that surfaces brown without scorching.

Chicago style

When used in reference to pizza, refers to a deep-dish pizza made in a high-sided pan. The crust is very rich and ingredients are layered inside.

crème fraiche

A smooth cultured cream with a tart, tangy flavor. Similar to sour cream, it can be made by adding acid to heavy cream and allowing the mixture to stand for several hours.

dice

To cut into small to medium cubes or squares.

dough hook

An attachment for a stand mixer. A dough hook can be used to stir and knead doughs and heavy batters, instead of hand-kneading.

ganache

A mixture of heavy cream and melted chocolate. The proportion of chocolate to cream depends on how the ganache will be used in a recipe.

knead

The process of turning and working dough to develop elasticity and pliability.

mozzarella

The best-known pizza cheese, authentically made from the milk of the water buffalo. Fresh mozzarella is delivered in its own liquid to maintain moisture, while aged can be sold in a variety of shapes. The best mozzarella is dense, rich, and delicate—not at all rubbery.

Neapolitan

Literally, the term means "from Naples." As it relates to pizza, it usually refers to a thin- to medium-crust pie topped lightly with sauce and cheese.

pie

Any dish that includes a crust topped with sweet or savory ingredients. In some circles, pizza is called tomato pie or pizza pie.

pizza peel

A large wooden paddle used to lift pizza to and from a hot oven. A peel is especially useful when baking pizza directly on stones, a brick oven floor, or a grill.

pizza stone

A hard, heat-safe surface for baking pizzas. Pizza stones can be made from actual polished stones or from man-made materials. They mimic the action of a brick or stone oven and allow home cooks to create crisp-crusted breads or pizzas.

pizza tiles

Pizza tiles serve the same purpose, and are usually made from the same materials, as a pizza stone. The smaller tiles can be inserted into a baking sheet, making it easy to remove a pizza from the oven without using a peel.

poach

To cook in slow-simmering water until just done. This cooking method is often used for poultry, eggs, salmon, and vegetables.

Sicilian

Pertaining to pizza, usually refers to a very thick-crusted pizza topped with sauce, meats, vegetables, and cheeses—in that order. However, Sicily's indigenous pizza is a very simple, thick bread topped with oil, herbs, and anchovies.

Resources

Books

American Pie: My Search for the Perfect Pizza, by Peter Reinhart

In this unique book, the author traces the origins and history of pizza from Italy to the United States, and also shares tips, secrets, and recipes he developed throughout his experience as a baker and culinary instructor.

Chez Panisse Pasta, Pizza & Calzone, by Alice Waters

First published in 1982, this book is still a classic. Read the recipes for inspiration, then either follow them as is or adapt them to your own tastes. Borrow a sauce here, a technique there. The spirit of the book is in its embrace of fresh flavors and seasonal ingredients.

Everybody Loves Pizza: The Deep Dish on America's Favorite Food, by Penny Pollack and Jeff Ruby

The authors began their research by asking anyone and everyone to name their favorite pizzeria. After sifting through an avalanche of mail—and cataloging hundreds of recommendations—they penned a book that covers the vast scope of pizza styles and variations, and gives delicious insights into a dish that is both cultural phenomenon and culinary staple.

Pizza: A Slice of Heaven, by Ed Levine

Part history lesson, part travelogue, part memoir, this homage to pizza in America is a great read. Levine includes essays by such great food writers as Ruth Reichl, Calvin Trillin, Mario Batali, and Jeffrey Steingarten in his attempt to quantify and qualify our passion for all types of pizza.

Your Brick Oven: Building It and Baking in It, by Russell Jeavons

Australian restaurateur Russell Jeavons is well known for the crisp, oven-fired pizzas he serves at his casual-chic wine-country restaurant. After hearing more than one patron pine for a backyard brick oven of his or her own, Jeavons came up with this step-by-step primer on building the best oven for making breads and pizzas. It's a big project, but one with great rewards for the home chef.

Web Sites

About Italian Cuisine

Kyle Phillips, the About.com Guide to Italian Cuisine, runs this site, which includes tips, recipes, product recommendations, and other great resources for everything you ever wanted to know about Italian food—including pizza! Check out pizza recipes such as

Pizza al Prosciutto, Pizza ai Quattro Formaggi, and many more.

✍ *http://italianfood.about.com*

Cooking.com

Pizza pans, stones, inserts, and tools from a variety of manufacturers and vendors can be ordered from this online retailer.

✍ *www.cooking.com*

Cooking for Engineers

If the "why" of cooking is as important to you as the "how," you'll love this site. It's packed with great recipes, right-brain-friendly directions, no-nonsense product reviews, plus input from an active Web community. The section on pizza is excellent.

✍ *www.cookingforengineers.com*

Pizzatherapy.com

Albert Grande's Web site is dedicated to the notion that making and eating great pizza is a soul-satisfying process that can foster great communication and great fun. Although the schtick is pizza as therapy, the site is packed full of pizzamaking tips, recipes, facts, and feedback. It's a virtual must-tour for pizza lovers.

✍ *www.pizzatherapy.com*

Pizza Ovens

EarthStone Wood-Fired Ovens
6717 San Fernando Road
Glendale, California 91201
✍ *www.earthstoneovens.com*

Forno Bravo
399 Business Park Court
Windsor, California 95492
✍ *www.fornobravo.com*

Mugnaini Imports, Inc.
11 Hangar Way
Watsonville, California 95076
✍ *www.mugnaini.com*

Ovencrafters
5600 Marshall-Petaluma Road
Petaluma, California 94952
✍ *www.ovencrafters.net*

Tuscany Fire
99-107 Shelton Avenue
New Haven, Connecticut 06511
✍ *www.tuscanyfire.com*

Wood Stone Home
1801 West Bakerview Road
Bellingham, Washington 98226
✍ *www.woodstonehome.com*

Index

THE EVERYTHING SERIES!

BUSINESS & PERSONAL FINANCE

Everything® Accounting Book
Everything® Budgeting Book
Everything® Business Planning Book
Everything® Coaching and Mentoring Book
Everything® Fundraising Book
Everything® Get Out of Debt Book
Everything® Grant Writing Book
Everything® Guide to Personal Finance for Single Mothers
Everything® Home-Based Business Book, 2nd Ed.
Everything® Homebuying Book, 2nd Ed.
Everything® Homeselling Book, 2nd Ed.
Everything® Improve Your Credit Book
Everything® Investing Book, 2nd Ed.
Everything® Landlording Book
Everything® Leadership Book
Everything® Managing People Book, 2nd Ed.
Everything® Negotiating Book
Everything® Online Auctions Book
Everything® Online Business Book
Everything® Personal Finance Book
Everything® Personal Finance in Your 20s and 30s Book
Everything® Project Management Book
Everything® Real Estate Investing Book
Everything® Retirement Planning Book
Everything® Robert's Rules Book, $7.95
Everything® Selling Book
Everything® Start Your Own Business Book, 2nd Ed.
Everything® Wills & Estate Planning Book

COOKING

Everything® Barbecue Cookbook
Everything® Bartender's Book, $9.95
Everything® Cheese Book
Everything® Chinese Cookbook
Everything® Classic Recipes Book
Everything® Cocktail Parties and Drinks Book
Everything® College Cookbook
Everything® Cooking for Baby and Toddler Book
Everything® Cooking for Two Cookbook
Everything® Diabetes Cookbook
Everything® Easy Gourmet Cookbook
Everything® Fondue Cookbook
Everything® Fondue Party Book
Everything® Gluten-Free Cookbook
Everything® Glycemic Index Cookbook
Everything® Grilling Cookbook

Everything® Healthy Meals in Minutes Cookbook
Everything® Holiday Cookbook
Everything® Indian Cookbook
Everything® Italian Cookbook
Everything® Low-Carb Cookbook
Everything® Low-Fat High-Flavor Cookbook
Everything® Low-Salt Cookbook
Everything® Meals for a Month Cookbook
Everything® Mediterranean Cookbook
Everything® Mexican Cookbook
Everything® No Trans Fat Cookbook
Everything® One-Pot Cookbook
Everything® Pizza Cookbook
Everything® Quick and Easy 30-Minute, 5-Ingredient Cookbook
Everything® Quick Meals Cookbook
Everything® Slow Cooker Cookbook
Everything® Slow Cooking for a Crowd Cookbook
Everything® Soup Cookbook
Everything® Stir-Fry Cookbook
Everything® Tex-Mex Cookbook
Everything® Thai Cookbook
Everything® Vegetarian Cookbook
Everything® Wild Game Cookbook
Everything® Wine Book, 2nd Ed.

GAMES

Everything® 15-Minute Sudoku Book, $9.95
Everything® 30-Minute Sudoku Book, $9.95
Everything® Blackjack Strategy Book
Everything® Brain Strain Book, $9.95
Everything® Bridge Book
Everything® Card Games Book
Everything® Card Tricks Book, $9.95
Everything® Casino Gambling Book, 2nd Ed.
Everything® Chess Basics Book
Everything® Craps Strategy Book
Everything® Crossword and Puzzle Book
Everything® Crossword Challenge Book
Everything® Crosswords for the Beach Book, $9.95
Everything® Cryptograms Book, $9.95
Everything® Easy Crosswords Book
Everything® Easy Kakuro Book, $9.95
Everything® Easy Large Print Crosswords Book
Everything® Games Book, 2nd Ed.
Everything® Giant Sudoku Book, $9.95
Everything® Kakuro Challenge Book, $9.95
Everything® Large-Print Crossword Challenge Book

Everything® Large-Print Crosswords Book
Everything® Lateral Thinking Puzzles Book, $9.95
Everything® Mazes Book
Everything® Movie Crosswords Book, $9.95
Everything® Online Poker Book, $12.95
Everything® Pencil Puzzles Book, $9.95
Everything® Poker Strategy Book
Everything® Pool & Billiards Book
Everything® Sports Crosswords Book, $9.95
Everything® Test Your IQ Book, $9.95
Everything® Texas Hold 'Em Book, $9.95
Everything® Travel Crosswords Book, $9.95
Everything® Word Games Challenge Book
Everything® Word Scramble Book
Everything® Word Search Book

HEALTH

Everything® Alzheimer's Book
Everything® Diabetes Book
Everything® Health Guide to Adult Bipolar Disorder
Everything® Health Guide to Controlling Anxiety
Everything® Health Guide to Fibromyalgia
Everything® Health Guide to Postpartum Care
Everything® Health Guide to Thyroid Disease
Everything® Hypnosis Book
Everything® Low Cholesterol Book
Everything® Massage Book
Everything® Menopause Book
Everything® Nutrition Book
Everything® Reflexology Book
Everything® Stress Management Book

HISTORY

Everything® American Government Book
Everything® American History Book, 2nd Ed.
Everything® Civil War Book
Everything® Freemasons Book
Everything® Irish History & Heritage Book
Everything® Middle East Book

HOBBIES

Everything® Candlemaking Book
Everything® Cartooning Book
Everything® Coin Collecting Book
Everything® Drawing Book
Everything® Family Tree Book, 2nd Ed.
Everything® Knitting Book
Everything® Knots Book
Everything® Photography Book

Everything® Quilting Book
Everything® Scrapbooking Book
Everything® Sewing Book
Everything® Soapmaking Book, 2nd Ed.
Everything® Woodworking Book

HOME IMPROVEMENT

Everything® Feng Shui Book
Everything® Feng Shui Decluttering Book, $9.95
Everything® Fix-It Book
Everything® Home Decorating Book
Everything® Home Storage Solutions Book
Everything® Homebuilding Book
Everything® Organize Your Home Book

KIDS' BOOKS

All titles are $7.95
Everything® Kids' Animal Puzzle & Activity Book
Everything® Kids' Baseball Book, 4th Ed.
Everything® Kids' Bible Trivia Book
Everything® Kids' Bugs Book
Everything® Kids' Cars and Trucks Puzzle
& Activity Book
Everything® Kids' Christmas Puzzle
& Activity Book
Everything® Kids' Cookbook
Everything® Kids' Crazy Puzzles Book
Everything® Kids' Dinosaurs Book
Everything® Kids' First Spanish Puzzle and
Activity Book
Everything® Kids' Gross Cookbook
Everything® Kids' Gross Hidden Pictures Book
Everything® Kids' Gross Jokes Book
Everything® Kids' Gross Mazes Book
Everything® Kids' Gross Puzzle and
Activity Book
Everything® Kids' Halloween Puzzle
& Activity Book
Everything® Kids' Hidden Pictures Book
Everything® Kids' Horses Book
Everything® Kids' Joke Book
Everything® Kids' Knock Knock Book
Everything® Kids' Learning Spanish Book
Everything® Kids' Math Puzzles Book
Everything® Kids' Mazes Book
Everything® Kids' Money Book
Everything® Kids' Nature Book
Everything® Kids' Pirates Puzzle and Activity Book
Everything® Kids' Presidents Book
Everything® Kids' Princess Puzzle and Activity Book
Everything® Kids' Puzzle Book
Everything® Kids' Riddles & Brain Teasers Book
Everything® Kids' Science Experiments Book
Everything® Kids' Sharks Book
Everything® Kids' Soccer Book
Everything® Kids' States Book
Everything® Kids' Travel Activity Book

KIDS' STORY BOOKS

Everything® Fairy Tales Book

LANGUAGE

Everything® Conversational Japanese Book with
CD, $19.95
Everything® French Grammar Book
Everything® French Phrase Book, $9.95
Everything® French Verb Book, $9.95
Everything® German Practice Book with CD,
$19.95
Everything® Inglés Book
**Everything® Intermediate Spanish Book with
CD, $19.95**
**Everything® Learning Brazilian Portuguese
Book with CD, $19.95**
Everything® Learning French Book
Everything® Learning German Book
Everything® Learning Italian Book
Everything® Learning Latin Book
**Everything® Learning Spanish Book with
CD, 2nd Edition, $19.95**
Everything® Russian Practice Book with CD, $19.95
Everything® Sign Language Book
Everything® Spanish Grammar Book
Everything® Spanish Phrase Book, $9.95
Everything® Spanish Practice Book
with CD, $19.95
Everything® Spanish Verb Book, $9.95
Everything® Speaking Mandarin Chinese Book
with CD, $19.95

MUSIC

Everything® Drums Book with CD, $19.95
**Everything® Guitar Book with CD, 2nd
Edition, $19.95**
Everything® Guitar Chords Book with CD, $19.95
Everything® Home Recording Book
Everything® Music Theory Book with CD, $19.95
Everything® Reading Music Book with CD, $19.95
Everything™ Rock & Blues Guitar Book
with CD, $19.95
**Everything® Rock and Blues Piano Book
with CD, $19.95**
Everything® Songwriting Book

NEW AGE

Everything® Astrology Book, 2nd Ed.
Everything® Birthday Personology Book
Everything® Dreams Book, 2nd Ed.
Everything® Love Signs Book, $9.95
Everything® Numerology Book
Everything® Paganism Book
Everything® Palmistry Book
Everything® Psychic Book
Everything® Reiki Book

Everything® Sex Signs Book, $9.95
Everything® Tarot Book, 2nd Ed.
Everything® Toltec Wisdom Book
Everything® Wicca and Witchcraft Book

PARENTING

Everything® Baby Names Book, 2nd Ed.
Everything® Baby Shower Book
Everything® Baby's First Year Book
Everything® Birthing Book
Everything® Breastfeeding Book
Everything® Father-to-Be Book
Everything® Father's First Year Book
Everything® Get Ready for Baby Book
Everything® Get Your Baby to Sleep Book, $9.95
Everything® Getting Pregnant Book
Everything® Guide to Raising a One-Year-Old
Everything® Guide to Raising a Two-Year-Old
Everything® Homeschooling Book
Everything® Mother's First Year Book
**Everything® Parent's Guide to Childhood
Illnesses**
Everything® Parent's Guide to Children
and Divorce
Everything® Parent's Guide to Children
with ADD/ADHD
Everything® Parent's Guide to Children
with Asperger's Syndrome
Everything® Parent's Guide to Children
with Autism
Everything® Parent's Guide to Children with
Bipolar Disorder
**Everything® Parent's Guide to Children with
Depression**
Everything® Parent's Guide to Children
with Dyslexia
**Everything® Parent's Guide to Children with
Juvenile Diabetes**
Everything® Parent's Guide to Positive Discipline
Everything® Parent's Guide to Raising a
Successful Child
Everything® Parent's Guide to Raising Boys
Everything® Parent's Guide to Raising Girls
Everything® Parent's Guide to Raising Siblings
Everything® Parent's Guide to Sensory
Integration Disorder
Everything® Parent's Guide to Tantrums
Everything® Parent's Guide to the Strong-Willed
Child
Everything® Parenting a Teenager Book
Everything® Potty Training Book, $9.95
Everything® Pregnancy Book, 3rd Ed.
Everything® Pregnancy Fitness Book
Everything® Pregnancy Nutrition Book
Everything® Pregnancy Organizer, 2nd Ed., $16.95
Everything® Toddler Activities Book
Everything® Toddler Book

Everything® Tween Book
Everything® Twins, Triplets, and More Book

PETS

Everything® Aquarium Book
Everything® Boxer Book
Everything® Cat Book, 2nd Ed.
Everything® Chihuahua Book
Everything® Dachshund Book
Everything® Dog Book
Everything® Dog Health Book
Everything® Dog Obedience Book
Everything® Dog Owner's Organizer, $16.95
Everything® Dog Training and Tricks Book
Everything® German Shepherd Book
Everything® Golden Retriever Book
Everything® Horse Book
Everything® Horse Care Book
Everything® Horseback Riding Book
Everything® Labrador Retriever Book
Everything® Poodle Book
Everything® Pug Book
Everything® Puppy Book
Everything® Rottweiler Book
Everything® Small Dogs Book
Everything® Tropical Fish Book
Everything® Yorkshire Terrier Book

REFERENCE

Everything® American Presidents Book
Everything® Blogging Book
Everything® Build Your Vocabulary Book
Everything® Car Care Book
Everything® Classical Mythology Book
Everything® Da Vinci Book
Everything® Divorce Book
Everything® Einstein Book
Everything® Enneagram Book
Everything® Etiquette Book, 2nd Ed.
Everything® Inventions and Patents Book
Everything® Mafia Book
Everything® Philosophy Book
Everything® Pirates Book
Everything® Psychology Book

RELIGION

Everything® Angels Book
Everything® Bible Book
Everything® Buddhism Book
Everything® Catholicism Book
Everything® Christianity Book
Everything® Gnostic Gospels Book
Everything® History of the Bible Book
Everything® Jesus Book

Everything® Jewish History & Heritage Book
Everything® Judaism Book
Everything® Kabbalah Book
Everything® Koran Book
Everything® Mary Book
Everything® Mary Magdalene Book
Everything® Prayer Book
Everything® Saints Book, 2nd Ed.
Everything® Torah Book
Everything® Understanding Islam Book
Everything® World's Religions Book
Everything® Zen Book

SCHOOL & CAREERS

Everything® Alternative Careers Book
Everything® Career Tests Book
Everything® College Major Test Book
Everything® College Survival Book, 2nd Ed.
Everything® Cover Letter Book, 2nd Ed.
Everything® Filmmaking Book
Everything® Get-a-Job Book, 2nd Ed.
Everything® Guide to Being a Paralegal
Everything® Guide to Being a Personal Trainer
Everything® Guide to Being a Real Estate Agent
Everything® Guide to Being a Sales Rep
Everything® Guide to Careers in Health Care
Everything® Guide to Careers in Law Enforcement
Everything® Guide to Government Jobs
Everything® Guide to Starting and Running a Restaurant
Everything® Job Interview Book
Everything® New Nurse Book
Everything® New Teacher Book
Everything® Paying for College Book
Everything® Practice Interview Book
Everything® Resume Book, 2nd Ed.
Everything® Study Book

SELF-HELP

Everything® Dating Book, 2nd Ed.
Everything® Great Sex Book
Everything® Self-Esteem Book
Everything® Tantric Sex Book

SPORTS & FITNESS

Everything® Easy Fitness Book
Everything® Running Book
Everything® Weight Training Book

TRAVEL

Everything® Family Guide to Cruise Vacations
Everything® Family Guide to Hawaii
Everything® Family Guide to Las Vegas, 2nd Ed.
Everything® Family Guide to Mexico
Everything® Family Guide to New York City, 2nd Ed.
Everything® Family Guide to RV Travel & Campgrounds
Everything® Family Guide to the Caribbean
Everything® Family Guide to the Walt Disney World Resort®, Universal Studios®, and Greater Orlando, 4th Ed.
Everything® Family Guide to Timeshares
Everything® Family Guide to Washington D.C., 2nd Ed.

WEDDINGS

Everything® Bachelorette Party Book, $9.95
Everything® Bridesmaid Book, $9.95
Everything® Destination Wedding Book
Everything® Elopement Book, $9.95
Everything® Father of the Bride Book, $9.95
Everything® Groom Book, $9.95
Everything® Mother of the Bride Book, $9.95
Everything® Outdoor Wedding Book
Everything® Wedding Book, 3rd Ed.
Everything® Wedding Checklist, $9.95
Everything® Wedding Etiquette Book, $9.95
Everything® Wedding Organizer, 2nd Ed., $16.95
Everything® Wedding Shower Book, $9.95
Everything® Wedding Vows Book, $9.95
Everything® Wedding Workout Book
Everything® Weddings on a Budget Book, $9.95

WRITING

Everything® Creative Writing Book
Everything® Get Published Book, 2nd Ed.
Everything® Grammar and Style Book
Everything® Guide to Magazine Writing
Everything® Guide to Writing a Book Proposal
Everything® Guide to Writing a Novel
Everything® Guide to Writing Children's Books
Everything® Guide to Writing Copy
Everything® Guide to Writing Research Papers
Everything® Screenwriting Book
Everything® Writing Poetry Book
Everything® Writing Well Book

Available wherever books are sold! To order, call 800-258-0929, or visit us at *www.everything.com*.
Everything® and everything.com® are registered trademarks of F+W Publications, Inc.
Bolded titles are new additions to the series.
All Everything® books are priced at $12.95 or $14.95, unless otherwise stated. Prices subject to change without notice.